A Church's Broken Heart

Mason-Dixon Methodism

Russell E. Richey

NEW ROOM
B O O K S

A Church's Broken Heart: Mason-Dixon Methodism

The General Board of Higher Education and Ministry leads and serves The United Methodist Church in the recruitment, preparation, nurture, education, and support of Christian leaders—lay and clergy—for the work of making disciples of Jesus Christ for the transformation of the world. Its vision is that a new generation of Christian leaders will commit boldly to Jesus Christ and be characterized by intellectual excellence, moral integrity, spiritual courage, and holiness of heart and life. The General Board of Higher Education and Ministry of The United Methodist Church serves as an advocate for the intellectual life of the church. The Board's mission embodies the Wesleyan tradition of commitment to the education of laypersons and ordained persons by providing access to higher education for all persons.

The name *New Room Books* comes from the New Room, a historic building in Bristol, England, and the place of John Wesley's study. Built in 1739, it is the oldest Methodist chapel in the world.

A Church's Broken Heart: Mason-Dixon Methodism

HIGHER EDUCATION & MINISTRY
General Board of Higher Education and Ministry
THE UNITED METHODIST CHURCH

New Room Books Editorial Board

Contents

CHAPTER 2 | 23
Outreach

CHAPTER 3 | 67
Formation
Methodism's Churching Its Members

CHAPTER 4 | 113
Connection
From Ground-Up, Conference-Out, Connectionally Resourced to Churching from the Center-Down

Conclusion | 147

A Long Personal Postscript | 165
Race and the Renewal of the Church

Appendix | 179

Preface

This preface is being drafted in early June 2020. Hourly newscasts report demonstrations across the world parading outrage at the killing of George Floyd. The last of the several funeral services is occurring as I write. "Black Lives Matter" placards, cries, appeals, graffiti, and chalked sidewalks situate Floyd's death within the long, sordid history of racial violence against blacks, police misconduct, the COVID-19 crisis, and consequent mounting US deaths. As I revise this preface, further police killings have occurred, many more have come to light, and nationally televised coverage brings the traumas into homes. Each crisis reinforces the somber mood. Other societies across the globe, also wracked by racial prejudice, add their local misdeeds to the world's accounting.

In the shadow of American racial discord, this book may well feel to some as though framed to take advantage of the turmoil. Actually, the research and argument found here have been in preparation for a decade. The overwhelming global reaction to Floyd's death and to the centuries of killing, maiming, and ill-treatment of blacks simply helps me to alert the reader to the book's overall focus. Successive chapters unfold the various ways in which nineteenth-century Methodism prospered greatly for whites but meagerly, if at all, for blacks. The culprits? Sunday schools, annual conferences, the publishing enterprise—Methodism's nineteenth-century strides forward. The book could well be retitled as its concerns do seem very timely:

"Mason-Dixon Methodism: Black Lives **Didn't** Matter in Ohio; **Mattered** for Field Hands and House Servants in Kentucky; but **Prospered** for Whites in Both States"

Such labeling would convey a major motif of the book.

Why the Book?

In treating nineteenth-century Methodism in the two states, this entirely historical enquiry should remind readers in the Wesleyan traditions of the imperative for us to come to terms with the several reinvigorated controversies demanding societal attention. "Black Lives Matter" has further enflamed what were diverse but ongoing controversies over the highly public statues erected for—and the states, cities and military bases named for—national and Confederate "big-men," southern military leaders, separatist causes, and racist commitments. The regular lynchings and several mass killings—Wilmington Insurrection of 1898, Tulsa Race Massacre of 1921, and other hysteria-driven large human butcherings—have finally become nationally newsworthy.

Crowds have knocked over and broken statues. Others sometimes have been hurried away by authorities for safekeeping. NASCAR judged that Confederate flags could no longer be flown. Similar outcries now come from state and national legislatures. Congressional leaders question, and even urge, the renaming of military bases.

Freshly and now globally, efforts abound to purge public space of monuments and jettison names of previously revered institutions, cities, and states. Might such renaming, in the long run, undercut the race-relations adjustments and societal reorientation sought? Might not future generations benefit from having some reminders of the sordid side of American greatness? Slavery smeared American shores from the earliest days of colonization, ranged north and south, was managed by Yankee as well as British and Spanish companies, tainted greats among Puritan and Middle colony religious leaders, and persisted in various locales in the north into the nineteenth century. Strike those names, along with the array of American presidents who held slaves: George Washington, Thomas Jefferson, James Madison, James Monroe, Andrew Jackson, Martin Van Buren, William Henry Harrison, John Tyler, James K. Polk, Zachary Taylor, Andrew Johnson, and Ulysses S. Grant? Rename the state of Washington or cities honoring Jefferson, Madison, and Jackson? Purge the physical landscape and textual recollection of significant individuals who by birth, circumstance, or locale have been embedded in slavery or segregation?

I am especially mindful of the taint because of personal, if historic, ties to two figures recently pilloried by Methodist historians.[1] The chat for the Historical Society of The United Methodist Church (hsumc-chat) centered on what to do with national and denominational individuals involved in slavery or racist antics. Among those named was Julian S. Carr, his crimes recently discovered: offensive racist off-script comments about a young girl uttered as he was commemorating a building at the University of North Carolina and his involvement with the Ku Klux Klan. The parading of those two misdeeds led to the renaming of school buildings at both the University of North Carolina, Chapel Hill (UNC CH) and Duke University, and objection to keeping his name on an important North Carolina town. His career, however, included quite a range of actions and expenditures on behalf of the region's black people. Although not participating in the arraignment of Carr, I had personal interests in the exchanges on hsumc-chat (almost all of them entered by other southerners and mostly friends or long-time acquaintants). My wife and I graduated from a junior high school named for Julian S. Carr, and we worship regularly in Trinity United Methodist Church where the huge men's bible class—held under the entire sanctuary—also bears his name.

Another personal interest? Robert E. Lee! In various locales, his statue has been knocked over or damaged. From a number of sites, the statue or depiction has been removed. One relocation took his likeness from the portico of Duke Chapel and away from the other "sacred" images. Some Black Lives Matter advocates question continuing to link his, and perhaps George Washington's, name with the university where Lee presided until his death. Here, too, I wince at the removal. Among his pallbearers was one representing the student body: my great-grandfather. Further, both our daughter and son-in-law played soccer, graduated from Washington and Lee University (W & L), and support it actively from their home in Colorado. After graduation and establishing herself with a Harvard degree in architecture, our daughter served on the W & L alumni/ae advisory committee.

Should Washington and Lee and Carrboro, North Carolina, be renamed? Should designations of institutions and other honoring of

---

1   Note the "I" in this preface. It occurs frequently throughout this study and especially in the postscript. The latter will explain why the personal tone and references. This enquiry has been, in some ways, a lifetime endeavor.

Southern leaders be expunged? I would keep the names, allow them to honor the men for what they did accomplish, and encourage communities to show the young and newcomers that progress on race, ethnicity, physical or mental disability, homosexuality, abortion, and other causes often comes slowly and with good folk zealously resisting the change.

Further, and to return to the nineteenth century and specifically to the 1850s, I want to show and to indicate to prospective readers that the northerners and southerners whose views or practices certainly warrant a racist label lived within an atmosphere where to breathe was to take in and depend upon race-laden oxygen. The Lees and Carrs operated within societies in which child-rearing, classroom banter, jokes, news coverage, political campaigns, business operations, farming, and indeed virtually everything radiated racism and effected black suppression through slavery or segregation. A racist *worldview*, to change the metaphor again, functioned sadly to orient and guide those who lived in the nineteenth century. The few southerners who saw the light—notably the Quakers—freed or sold any slaves they held and fled north. Similarly, Methodists in what today is termed the Delmarva Peninsula escaped the tyranny of slavery by freeing or selling their slaves and by migrating to Ohio. However, along with their clothes, many of them packed and transported negro-phobia and segregationist resolve. Such sentiments remained in the north until the eve of the Civil War, as will be shown in the chapters that follow.

Black Lives Matter seeks to reorient and guide those who live today out of that world, that society, that atmosphere. So, too, are my historical efforts here. It took the Civil War to alter Northern racist views. Sadly, those proved ephemeral, a story that lies beyond the scope of this book. Here I try to show that "Mason-Dixon Methodism: Black Lives ***Didn't*** Matter in Ohio, ***Mattered*** for Field Hands and House Servants in Kentucky, but ***Prospered*** for Whites in Both States."

Five Recurrent Motifs

A racist worldview, which guided or shaped signal nineteenth-century achievements by Kentucky and Ohio Methodists in most sectors of their lives, constitutes the first and overriding motif in this book.

A second motif (if there can be more than one) or emphasis of this study, is the effort to employ today's racial, social, economic, and political strains to explore their prefiguration, indeed formation, in nineteenth-century sectional conflict.

A third motif, implicit in the above, will be to move from pre-Civil War Ohio and Kentucky scenes and actions, to those "performed" more generally north and south sectionally, and to the play of those Mason-Dixon factors on the national stage.

A fourth, reversing the third above, will be to revisit the nineteenth-century racial and sectional politics and antics, especially those in Kentucky and Ohio, to reflect on the jurisdictional divisions in The United Methodist Church. Kentucky Methodists look to the Southeastern Jurisdiction and Ohio to the North Central Jurisdiction as the UMC struggles currently to deal with the global fight over homosexuality and the numerous plans to tear the denomination apart.

The reader will discover a fifth facet, speaking in the first person—also displayed above—a number of times in the regular chapters and explicitly in the autobiographical postscript (briefly described below). Those familiar with my other books and articles should find my "I" or "we" language strange, perhaps violating scholarly standards. Further, you will find that, in this study, I do try to reflect personally on sectional and racial differences that have shaped my life, and I judge that of my/our church(es) and nation.

Perhaps experienced as in some tension with that last autobiographical word is yet a further prefatory explication, namely that I limited research for this study to Methodism's publications. What the church reported officially, published for its leaders and people, and "voiced" via minutes or other denominational media is drawn upon and assessed here. Why? This book explores Methodism's divisions, specifically those that it wanted to be and needed to have on official records and, therefore, available.

Hence, throughout, the reader will encounter numerous—sometimes quite lengthy or extended—quotations and reproduced published materials. These documents are evidence for denominational doings and divisions. Such I have featured in this book as indeed the voice and voices of Methodism—historic, current, interactive, and personal. Readers, like me, inclined to skip or merely skim these citations, are urged to listen as Methodists then and now speak, as do I here. In quoting material or analysis thereof, I call attention at some places in the text to a specific motif that might be considered operative or suggestive or implied. When, as most frequently, one or more of the motifs might be at play, I leave to the reader to judge.

Postscript Was Introduction

Readers wishing to understand further why Russell Richey would write on this topic and center the book on nineteenth-century black-white relations might turn at this point to the postscript.[2] That section, as indicated elsewhere as well, I crafted to be the introduction. Although not touching on Lee or Carr, it tracks my personal experience with race relations improvement: from an infancy in a southern parsonage to teaching and writing on black history. The postscript shows, I hope, that a life committed to racial justice for three quarters of a century has, nevertheless, participated (though unwillingly) in problematic scenes or processes. After completing the intended introduction, I determined that some readers might presume the entire book to be autobiographical. So what was initially an introduction is repositioned now as postscript. My personal experience of southern and northern racism comes now at the rear of this history of Mason-Dixon Methodism.

The current introduction explains, and the table of contents maps, the book's chapters and topics. To determine where the reader might wish to go first, she or he might read the Table of Contents first. Welcome to nineteenth-century, Mason-Dixon Methodism!

Acknowledgments

Debts for this study I owe to quite a list, more than I can indicate or even recall. At the top would be my mother, father, and wife, whose roles I indicate and detail in the postscript.

A grant from the Louisville Institute, thanks to its director, Dr. Donald C. Richter, made the various trips for research possible. The money came for 2016–2017 as a "Project Grant for Researchers" for a project tentatively then entitled "Why Methodism's Broken Heart? Kentucky, Ohio, Tennessee and Indiana: 1816–1876" and to permit travel to seminary, college, and conference libraries in those states. Successive extensions permitted various research trips as I indicate below. Money for the project came as well

---

2   Again, note the "I" in this preface.

from two institutions at which I did much of the research and writing, Duke and Asbury.

Here I would acknowledge especially successive stipends from Professor Kenneth J. Collins, Professor of Historical Theology and Wesley Studies at Asbury Theological Seminary. At his invitation I have served as a member of the Board of Advisors of Asbury Theological Seminary's Wesleyan Studies Summer Seminar and as co-director in 2013, 2015, 2017, and 2019. The successive months of June in Kentucky permitted me to do much of the research on Kentucky and its nineteenth-century Methodist annual conference for this study. Dinners prepared for the group by his lovely wife and interaction with the younger scholars, often over other meals and in the group seminars, proved stimulating.

A similar debt I owe to directors of Duke Divinity School's Summer Wesley Seminar, Richard P. Heitzenrater and Randy L. Maddox, both William Kellen Quick Professors Emeriti of Church History and Wesley Studies. Here, too, I co-led the June seminars sustained by Duke's Center for Studies in the Wesleyan Tradition in 2009, 2011, 2014, and 2016. At both summer seminars, I tried out and received critical counsel on themes and arguments that now figure in this book.

The Divinity School's deans, Gregory Jones, Richard Hays, Elaine Heath, and Gregory Jones (again) permitted me an office, regular offering of tutorials focused on nineteenth-century Methodism, and use of the Divinity School's incredible library. Successive library staff and especially the directors, Roger Loyd, and our current head, Katie Benjamin, have accommodated my lavish book borrowing and permitted occasional and brief office use of non-circulating volumes.

Five research jaunts took me to Drew University, the Methodist Archives, and interaction with General Commission on Archives and History staff: with its general secretary, currently Alfred Day, and previously Robert Williams and Charles Yrigoyen, and with key archivist staff Mark Shenise and Dale Patterson. Two research trips took me to Kentucky Wesleyan, one to each of these UMC theological schools: Wesley, Garrett-Evangelical, and Candler. The latter, of course, was my home for a decade, and my research profited in various ways from Dean Jan Love's helpful provisioning (including a year's terminal leave).

Similar indirect but nevertheless important debts I owe to my *Methodist Review* colleague editors, Ted Campbell (Perkins) and Rex Matthews (Candler). Our efforts to take this 200-year Methodist journal onto an online-only plane took and continues to take almost daily investment of computer time. Jane Donovan, Book Review editor for *Methodist History*, steered books pertinent to this study my way. The editor of quite a number of my books, Kathy Armistead, belongs among those needing lavish thanks, as also my colleague writers for *The Methodist Experience in America*, Kenneth Rowe and Jean Miller Schmidt. Our collective scholarship informing that book underlies this foray into *Methodistica*. Reliance on other of my books is indicated in footnotes.

Further, relying on the interpretation AND the incredible and well-documented secondary sources cited there, I have kept such footnoting quite spare here. *A Church's Broken Heart: Mason-Dixon Methodism* draws on and liberally displays the denomination's nineteenth-century publications. So invoked, Ohio and Kentucky Methodists champion their own accomplishments and overlook or seek to obscure their segregation and slavery policy and practice.

Russell E. Richey
Initially drafted June 9, 2020, but subsequently amplified.

Methodism's Broken Heart

Mason-Dixon Methodism in Ohio and Kentucky

Q. 41. Are there any Directions to be given concerning the Negroes?

A. Let every Preacher, as often as possible, meet them in Class. And let the Assistant always appoint a proper White Person as their Leader. Let the Assistants also make a regular Return to the Conference, of the Number of Negroes in Society in their respective Circuits.

Q. 42. What Methods can we take to extirpate Slavery?

A. We are deeply conscious of the Impropriety of making new Terms of Communion for a religious Society already established, excepting on the most pressing Occasion: and such we esteem the Practice of holding our Fellow-Creatures in Slavery. We view it as contrary to the Golden Law of God on which hang all Law and the Prophets, and the unalienable Rights of Mankind, as well as every Principle of the Revolution, to hold in the deepest Debasement, in a more abject Slavery than is perhaps to be found in any Part of the World except America, so many Souls that are all capable of the Image of God.

We therefore think it our most bounden Duty, to take immediately some effectual Method to extirpate this Abomination from among us: And for that Purpose we add the following to the Rules of our Society: viz.

1. Every Member of our Society who has Slaves in his Possession, shall within twelve Months after Notice given to him. . . .

5. No Person holding Slaves shall, in future, be admitted into Society or to the Lord's Supper, till he previously complies with these Rules concerning Slavery.

N. B. These Rules are to affect the Members of our Society no further than as they are consistent with the Laws of the States in which they reside.

And respecting our Brethren in Virginia that are concerned, and after due Consideration of their peculiar Circumstances, we allow them two Years from the Notice given, to consider the Expedience of Compliance or Non-Compliance with these Rules.

Q. 43. What shall be done with those who buy or sell Slaves, or give them away?

A. They are immediately to be expelled: unless they buy them on purpose to free them.[1]

Methodism's Broken Heart? The 1784 Christmas Conference that birthed the new church, the Methodist Episcopal Church (MEC), baptized it immediately into (the above) remarkable and detailed anti-slavery commitments. Such heartfelt resolves to ending slavery had animated earlier conference gatherings. However, in the 1784 *Discipline*, the church also regularized white control and included a proviso that the South (Virginia) might demand further slavery concessions. The largely sectional divisions over slavery generated early and regular retreats from these 1784 pledges. Indeed, that happened, quickly and consistently, and led the MEC to drop the exacting 1784 strictures for ending slavery from what it soon labeled the *Discipline*. By 1808, the church's code-authorizing body, the General Conference (GC), had moved its slavery commitments to the end of the *Discipline*. The first of three resolutions declared "that we are as much as ever convinced of the great evil of slavery" and urged manumissions as laws and circumstances permitted. The second called for forfeiture of ministerial standing if preachers became slaveholders, again if emancipation conformed "to the laws of the state in which he resides." By the third, "The general conference authorizes each annual conference to form their own regulations, relative to buying and selling of slaves."[2]

Why Methodism's Broken Heart? Why its heart as life and work on either side of the Mason-Dixon line? After all, slaveholding and usage had

---

1   *Minutes of Several Conversations Between the Rev. Thomas Coke, LL. D., the Rev. Francis Asbury and others, at a Conference, Begun in Baltimore, in the State of Maryland, on Monday, the 27th of December, in the Year 1784. Composing a FORM of DISCIPLINE for the Ministers, preachers, and other Members of the Methodist Episcopal Church in America* (Philadelphia: Charles Cist, 1785), 15–17. For the full set of regulations, see the appendix.

2   *The Doctrines and Discipline of the Methodist Episcopal Church* (New York: John Wilson and Daniel Hitt for the Methodist Connection, 1808), 210–11.

been widespread across the colonies in the seventeenth and early eigh-teenth centuries. And slavery persisted up to the Civil War in states on the Mason side of the line and anti-slavery commitments on the Dixon side. Why then a reexamination of the middle decades of the nineteenth century? The short answer? Focusing on Methodist life in Kentucky and Ohio during the weeks and months leading up to the Civil War permits glimpses in the programmatically complex ways in which leaders and laity structured congregations and conferences. Orienting attention to Sunday schools, mission societies, colleges, and Sunday rhythms in proxi-mate areas of the North and South provides some sense of how race, slavery, language, ethnicity, gender, and ecclesial authority governed Methodism day-to-day. In many ways, religious communities on the two sides of the Ohio River lived with what appear to be similar rhythms and routines, sustained keepsake denominational practices, innovated with print and educational institutions, and honored traditional Wesleyan dic-tates. But Methodists there, like Americans generally, lived with everyday formal and informal—highly prejudicial and sometimes violent—race patterns, racial practices, and racial prejudices.

This study ranges widely over denominational life but notes, as appro-priate and needed, the powerful shaping effects of slavery and segrega-tion.[3] To track those racial dynamics within the important organizational transformations through which Methodism was going on the eve of the Civil War, the illustrations of and documentation for key initiatives come from the actual records of southern and northern Methodism. Although dependent on recent and classic treatments of those dynamics,[4] the

3   In various of my own and in collaborative efforts, I have addressed Methodism's struggles with race, most fully in Russell E. Richey, Kenneth E. Rowe, and Jean Miller Schmidt, *The Methodist Experience in America: A History* and *The Methodist Experience in America: A Sourcebook*, 2 vols. (Nashville: Abingdon Press, 2010, 2000). In the endnotes of the *History*, 565–670, we attend to scholarship on which this present endeavor depends and which I primarily update here.

4   For further treatment of the sectional conflict in the two states, see Luke E. Harlow, *Religion, Race, and the Making of Confederate Kentucky, 1830–1880* (New York: Cam-bridge University Press, 2014); Gary R. Matthews, *More American than Southern: Ken-tucky, Slavery, and the War for an American Ideology, 1828–1861* (Knoxville: University of Tennessee Press, 2014); Andrew R. L. Cayton, especially his *Ohio: The History of a People* (Columbus: Ohio State University Press, 2002); Adam I. P. Smith, *The Stormy Present: Conservatism and the Problem of Slavery in Modern Politics, 1846–1865* (Print publica-tion, 2017, North Carolina Scholarship Online, 2018); Molly Oshatz, *Slavery and Sin: The Fight against Slavery and the Rise of Liberal Protestantism* (Print publication 2011, Pub-lished to Oxford Scholarship Online, January 2012) for both treatment and coverage of pertinent literature; and a recent instance of the annual survey of the literature,

presentation of Methodist concerns, activities, divisions, and dis-ordering will exhibit and cite published materials from the 1840s and 1850s.

Note that what follows amplifies and explains the fivefold pattern of concerns or motifs, outlined in the preface, that govern the entirety of this book.

Why a Sectional Study and Why Attention to Racial Patterns?

Exposure to race relations in its intimate, direct, daily, and face-to-face expression *and* to the huge, systemic, ongoing, and national dimensions of racism has informed my life and career. Rehearsing that personal drama was drafted first, and constituted the lead into this introduction, but might have confused a reader as to the focus of this history and so is now located in the postscript at the end of this volume.

Why then this exploration of tensions in nineteenth-century Methodism? Why look afresh at the decades leading up to the Civil War? Why focus on Kentucky and Ohio Methodism? Why examine how slaveholders and Northern whites *and* their churches treated African Americans? Why expose Southern efforts to be pastoral across racial lines and Northern indifference to their black members? Why explore the institutions that Methodism created to care for its own: children, women and men, Native Americans, blacks and whites, the array of leaders and leadership positions? Why study Methodist life across, on each side, and on both sides of the Mason-Dixon line in the decade of national, sectional, and local dynamics that lead the nation into civil war?

Governing such a focus and shaping this study has been my own saga—as I will detail in the postscript—from being birthed, raised, and schooled in rigidly segregated North Carolina communities to being "educated" in/by America's struggles to overcome our racism in a Northern college, in Harlem field work during seminary, and in a long career teaching in seminaries committed to traveling the road toward fuller inclusion. I remain indebted, as well, to a former, indeed now deceased, Drew graduate student, Kenneth O. Brown. He took several of my courses, and I believe I guided his dissertation. Before or during his doctoral studies,

---

Thomas Thurston, "Slavery Annual Bibliographical Supplement (2018)," *Slavery & Abolition: A Journal of Slave and Post-Slave Issues*, 40, no. 4 (2019): 729–916.

he co-authored the *History of the Churches of Christ in Christian Union.*[5] This middle American, Methodist, Ohio-centered communion, once his, sustains itself today as a member of the Holiness-Pentecostal family. Largely forgotten or perhaps suppressed are the religious practices around which its founders had early proclaimed their cause, gathered adherents, and erected what would be denominational alignments. Not holiness banners as most now would imagine it! The real campaign Brown's study lays bare: Northern support for slavery, sympathy for the South, resistance to abolition, desire for cessation of civil war, and objection to or indifference toward the hostilities against the new Confederate nation. Christian Union began as a Methodist-led, Ohio-based movement of Northerners sympathizing with the South.[6]

Understanding this Copperhead church and sectional disquiet about the Civil War on the one hand or, on the other, revisiting the division of episcopal Methodism in 1844 over slavery, the national religious tensions in the 1850s and 1860s, missions to freed-persons post-war, and the long Methodist struggles over race and racism takes me over well-plowed terrain. What I propose keeps an eye on what yielded Copperhead-style Northern politics and comparably complex patterns in the upper South. A study examining such invites attention to the Midwest as an arena in which Methodism dramatized its racial struggles, setbacks, strategies, compromises, divisions, and traumas.[7]

Focusing on selected border states, I wish to keep in view the bigger Methodist story—that from John Wesley, Thomas Coke, and Francis Asbury to the present—as a people's struggle over:

---

5   Kenneth O. Brown and P. Lewis Brevard, *History of the Churches of Christ in Christian Union* (Circleville, OH: Circle Press, 1980). Brown authored a number of books on camp meetings. He also crafted *Holy Ground, Too: The Camp Meeting Family Tree* (Hazleton, PA: Published by Holiness Archives, 1997). It provides almost a hundred pages of camp meeting sites, indicating those that were ongoing at the time of his inventorying. It also lists close to one hundred and fifty pages of publications on the topic, pp. 98–234 and 2,263 entries. Titles also appear in the footnotes of his long, introductory essay and where he arrays them by topic and in some cases unpacks them.

6   For a study of a parallel movement in Indiana, though apparently less committed to the South, see Riley B. Case, *Faith and Fury: Eli Farmer on the Frontier, 1794–1881* (Indianapolis: Indiana Historical Society Press, 2018). For a firsthand account of the trauma in Kentucky, see Richard L. Troutman, *The Heavens Are Weeping: The Diaries of George Richard Browder, 1852–1886* (Grand Rapids: Zondervan, 1987).

7   On this drama in Ohio, see the works by Andrew R. L. Cayton, especially his *Ohio: The History of a People* (Columbus: Ohio State University Press, 2002), throughout, but especially chapter 4.

- their vocation to evangelize African Americans;
- their inability to incorporate black converts fully into community and leadership;
- the yawning of racism, racist practices, and Methodist ownership of slaves;
- their divisions over slavery and later segregation;
- and ongoing struggles in the recent past to live as a multiracial church.

Again, Methodism in Kentucky and Ohio will be the focus of this study. On these states and their conflicts over slavery, a number of very fine studies have focused recently.[8] The larger, national, sectional, and racial dynamics enter the narrative primarily as conferences, key leaders, local Methodist dynamics, and patterns of denominational programming experienced these traumas.[9] The statistics from 1844, gathered before the Methodist Episcopal Church broke apart over slavery, show the overall racial pattern. See figure 1 below:[10]

---

8   Bridget Ford, *Bonds of Union: Religion, Race, and Politics in a Civil War Borderland* (Chapel Hill: University of North Carolina Press, 2016); Mark R. Teasdale, *Methodist Evangelism, American Salvation: The Home Missions of the Methodist Episcopal Church, 1860–1920* (Eugene, OR: Pickwick Publications, 2014); Ginette Aley and J. L. Anderson, *Union Heartland: The Midwestern Home Front during the Civil War* (Carbondale: Southern Illinois University Press, 2013); Stanley Harrold, *Border War: Fighting over Slavery before the Civil War* (Chapel Hill: University of North Carolina Press, 2010); April E. Holm, *A Kingdom Divided: Evangelicals, Loyalty, and Sectionalism in the Civil War Era* (Baton Rouge: Louisiana State University Press, 2017); Nicole Etcheson, *The Emerging Midwest: Upland Southerners and the Political Culture of the Old Northwest, 1787–1861* (Bloomington & Indianapolis: Indiana University Press, 1996); and Matthew W. Hall, *Dividing the Union: Jesse Burgess Thomas and the Making of the Missouri Compromise* (Carbondale: Southern Illinois University Press, 2016). An earlier study, still useful for understanding German Methodism, is Mark Wyman, *Immigrants in the Valley: Irish, Germans, and Americans in the Upper Mississippi Country, 1830–1860* (Carbondale: Southern Illinois University Press, 1984, 2016).
9   For overviews of Methodism, nationally and by states; for summaries of the successive General Conferences; for biographies of major figures; and for bibliographies to date, see Nolan B. Harmon, ed., *Encyclopedia of World Methodism*, 2 vols. (Nashville: United Methodist Publishing House, 1974). Abbreviated hereafter as EWM. This resource is online: https://archive.org/details/encyclopediaofwo01harm.
10 *Minutes of the annual conferences of the Methodist Episcopal Church,* v. 3 (1839-45) (New York: Published by T. Mason and G. Lane for the Methodist Episcopal Church, [1840–1940], 603. HathiTrust Digital Library Rights Public Domain, Google-digitized. Permanent URL https://hdl.handle.net/2027/nyp.33433069134942. **NOTE**: Here and hereinafter items from the HathiTrust Digital Library, https://www.hathitrust.org/, are

GENERAL RECAPITULATION.

Page.	Conferences.	Whites.	Coloured.	Indians.	Total.	Tr. pr.	Sup'd.	Lo. pr.
479	Troy, (1844,)	29,698	124		29,822	175	10	142
182	Providence,	13,832			13,832	95	11	85
485	New-Hampshire.	21,977			21,977	161	22	116
488	Pittsburgh,	46,970	405		47,375	162	11	255
491	New-England,	16,031			16,031	113	12	69
494	Erie,	23,284	86		23,370	129	8	198
496	Black River,	18,248	35		18,283	107	11	168
499	Rock River,	15,998	23	130	16,151	104	9	205
501	Maine,	25,843			25,843	160	21	160
505	North Ohio,	30,252	40	5	30,297	128	1	253
507	Iowa,	5,391	12		5,403	37	1	60
509	Oneida,	29,676	84	80	29,840	171	24	201
512	Illinois,	28,658	71		28,729	94	10	425
514	Ohio,	70,240	523		70,763	215	17	472
518	Genesee,	34,062	74		34,136	186	24	273
522	Kentucky,	39,377	9,362		48,739	152	14	379
525	Indiana,	35,527	159		35,686	105	5	285
527	Missouri,	23,695	2,530		26,225	115	5	255
530	Michigan,	16,020	10	338	16,368	111	6	169
533	Holston, (last year,)	35,953	4,001	109	40,063	67	6	299
534	North Indiana,	27,296	47		27,343	101	4	220
537	Indian Mission,	85	133	2,992	3,210	28		27
538	Tennessee,	32,398	6,859		39,257	127	3	387
540	Virginia,	26,268	4,949		31,217	94	7	158
543	Arkansas,	7,706	1,775		9,481	46	2	99
544	Memphis,	23,342	4,843		28,185	92	7	275
547	North Carolina,	19,499	6,390		25,889	72	13	140
549	Mississippi,	13,257	7,799	115	21,171	108	6	237
551	South Carolina,	32,306	39,495		71,801	111	10	265
554	Eastern Texas,	2,743	424		3,167	28	1	39
555	Western Texas,	2,334	581		2,915	23	1	25
556	Georgia,	36,755	13,994		50,749	106	18	294
558	Florida,	4,163	2,653		6,816	32		58
560	Alabama,	26,514	13,537		40,051	106	2	394
563	Baltimore,	53,466	16,412		69,878	232	15	281
567	Philadelphia,	41,245	10,742		51,987	160	3	260
570	New-Jersey,	29,671	763		30,434	140	3	198
573	Troy, (1845,)	28,086	92		28,178	183	11	147
576	New-York,	47,530	380		47,910	259	25	270
581	Liberia Mission,		837		837	15		
	Total this year,	985,696	150,120	3,769	1,139,587	4,479	349	8,101
	last year,	1,021,818	145,409	4,129	1,171,356	4,282	339	8,067
	Decrease this year,	36,120	In. 4,711	De. 360	31,769	In. 197	10	14

Figure 1

Of necessity, this book will also mention some transformative, national racial developments. However, the controversial events of the 1840s and 1850s receive primary attention as their impact registered on regional, circuit, and personal religious life. The 1846 Wilmot Proviso,

routinely footnoted even when, as here, I own or Duke University owns, and I am using the hard copy. Some readers may lack access to the item, hence the addition to the note. HaithiTrust versions are accessed and used, often for correction purposes, according to its protocols and therefore with permission.

launch in 1848 of the Free Soil Party, the Compromise of 1850 and the Fugitive Slave Act, the 1854 undoing of the Missouri Compromise in the Kansas-Nebraska Act, Bleeding Kansas (1856), the Dred Scott Supreme Court decision, John Brown's 1859 raid, and Abraham Lincoln's election enter the picture as refracted through regional Methodist lenses. The postures, policies, and practices of Northern (MEC) and Southern (MECS) Methodism, as evidenced in Ohio and Kentucky, govern how the larger denominational, Protestant, regional, and national developments enter the narrative.[11] (Hereafter, the Southern church's name is frequently abbreviated as MECS and the Northern church's as MEC). Further, those familiar with the highly acrimonious, sometimes violent—political, legal, social, and religious—conflict in and between these two states will be surprised at how minimally engaged and muted Methodists were initially. In part, presentation here rests on the official documents of the two churches, Methodist Episcopal Church (MEC) and Methodist Episcopal Church, South (MECS) and of their respective conferences.[12]

The Pertinence Today and Post-2020?

We do not want for treatments of Methodism's two centuries of national and regional fights over race, slavery, and segregation. Nor do the current, now global, posturings—over race, sexual orientation, and nationality and whether the church can hang together—lack for attention. On the latter, I have made my own suggestion of how the United Methodists might survive.[13] Nor do we lack histories of individual

---

11 For extraordinarily helpful ordering of religious developments by year, denomination (MEC, MECS, MPC, UBC, EA, AMEC, AMEZC, and others, see Rex D. Matthews, *Timetables of History for Students of Methodism* (Nashville: Abingdon Press, 2007). In eight columns, Matthews charts by year key developments on a world, national, academic field, and Methodist (American and global) basis. For the AMEC, especially active in the period being studied here and engaged with the MEC, see Dennis C. Dickerson, *The African Methodist Episcopal Church: A History* (Cambridge: Cambridge University Press, 2020).

12 Note the abbreviations used here for the two churches: MEC and MECS.

13 See my "Today's Untied Methodism: Living with/into Its Two Centuries of Regular Division," in *Finding a Way Forward: Resources for Witness, Contextual Leadership and Unity: A Handbook for United Methodist Church Bishops on the work of the Commission on a Way Forward,* electronic publication (December 2017), 42–56, http://s3.amazonaws.com/Website_Properties/council-of-bishops/documents/COWF_Handbook_2017_REVISED3.pdf. See also "Today's Untied Methodism: Living with/into Its Two Centuries

conferences (regional, largely state-defined deployment entities) that give varying attention to denominational traumas. Nor have the several denominations with roots in Methodism's early, early struggles over race been ignored. Fine historical accounts attend to and focus upon the 1813-formed Union Church of Africans (variously named subsequently), the African Methodist Episcopal Church, the African Methodist Episcopal Zion Church, and the Christian Methodist Episcopal Church, and the several others, black and white, who championed African American or abolitionist causes.[14]

However and ironically, attention to specific Methodist denominations and to individual annual conferences obscures the way that racial dynamics have functioned across, above, and below inter- and intra-denominational lines. Further, it seems, the actors and scribes attending to religious life on local, conference, and regional levels have ignored, downplayed, or glossed over ongoing racial/racist patterns.

So, the way in which the largest Methodist denomination (and largely white one) ordered itself nationally in the 1939 reunion to accommodate racial prejudice greatly frustrates our ability to understand adequately how these racial dynamics functioned and continue to function. Racism-inspired structures outlived sectional tensions, civil war, Reconstruction, church divisions over race, Methodist efforts to put itself back together, and much of its internal politics today. Methodism "honored" its fractures over slavery and race when, in 1939, its Southern and Northern episcopal units came together (along with largely border-state Methodist Protestants). Unity came with a racist price. Methodism formalized racial divisions, indeed sanctified racism, by establishing a national structure, then termed a *jurisdiction*, into which it lodged all but a handful of its black congregations and preachers. The 1939 unification put white Methodists into five regional jurisdictions.

African Americans nationally constituted a Central Jurisdiction. Into the Southeastern and Southwestern jurisdictions went most of what had been the Methodist Episcopal Church, South. Conferences

---

of Regular Division" in *The Unity of the Church and Human Sexuality: Toward a Faithful United Methodist Witness* (Nashville: GBHEM, 2018), 311–46 [the two essays share a title, but the latter substantially revises and augments the first].

14 The most recent addition to the literature on these denominations is that of Dennis C. Dickerson, *The African Methodist Episcopal Church: A History* (Cambridge: Cambridge University Press, 2020).

of Civil War and segregation border states: Virginia and Tennessee went naturally into the Southeastern Jurisdiction and Missouri into South Central. Delaware, Maryland, West Virginia, Ohio, Indiana, and Illinois also perhaps naturally into the Northeastern. But Kentucky and Arkansas? They were located in the pro-segregation Southeastern and South Central but might have been in the more moderate Northeastern and North Central jurisdictions. Kentucky Methodists went into the Southeastern and Ohio Methodists into the North Central jurisdictions.

Clergy typically live out their lives in a single conference. They do elect or are elected to a once national, now global, General Conference. But they elect and deploy bishops within their jurisdiction. So, too, jurisdictions determine who will represent them on general church agencies and in other denomination-wide endeavors. And political fights, especially recently over homosexuality and abortion, break largely on jurisdictional lines.

Perhaps not surprisingly, United Methodists tell their overall story or relate conference stories describing the staging, actors, scenes, and action on or within their respective theaters. What is the effect of doing history honoring conference, jurisdictional, and general structures within which Methodist life is lived *and* its records kept?

What's Lost?

- the drama in the middle of the Methodist story;
- the drama enacted on Methodism's center stage;
- the drama to which it attracted the largest audience (membership);
- the drama boasting its most talented actors;
- the drama featuring scenes of Methodism both keeping and freeing slaves;
- the drama within which its blacks rose to (limited) leadership and within their respective folds;
- the drama that staged its fights for and against slavery;
- the drama at the heart of the Methodist story;
- the drama of being divided, indeed broken at its heart.

That's all that is lost. Just Methodism's central drama.

By confining our history within conference, jurisdictional, and national structures, we get a significantly blocked view of the stage, of key episodes of the action, and of the deeper meaning, larger dimensions, and fuller import of the great Methodist drama. This study endeavors to surmount that blockage by looking at nineteenth-century Methodism across the Mason-Dixon line.[15]

---

15 Recent American Methodism items especially influential in this study: Dee E. Andrews, *The Methodists and Revolutionary America, 1760–1800: The Shaping of an Evangelical Culture* (Princeton: Princeton University Press, 2000); Samuel Avery-Quinn, *Cities of Zion: The Holiness Movement and Methodist Camp Meeting Towns in America* (Lanham: Lexington Books, 2019); Riley B. Case, *Faith and Fury: Eli Farmer on the Frontier, 1794–1881* (Indianapolis: Indiana Historical Society Press, 2018); Charles C. Cole, Jr., *Lion of the Forest: James B. Finley Frontier Reformer* (Lexington: University Press of Kentucky, 1994); Jane Donovan, *Henry Foxall (1758–1823): Methodist, Industrialist, American* (Nashville: New Room Books, General Board of Higher Education and Ministry, UMC, 2017); Ashley Boggan Dreff, *Entangled: A History of American Methodism, Politics, and Sexuality* (Nashville: New Room Books, 2019); Robert Elder, *The Sacred Mirror: Evangelicalism, Honor, and Identity in the Deep South, 1790–1860* (Chapel Hill: University of North Carolina Press, 2016); Bridget Ford, *Bonds of Union: Religion, Race, and Politics in a Civil War Borderland* (Chapel Hill: University of North Carolina Press, 2016); Carol V. R. George, *One Mississippi, Two Mississippi: Methodists, Murder, and the Struggle for Racial Justice in Neshoba County* (New York: Oxford University Press, 2015); Alison Collis Greene, *No Depression in Heaven: The Great Depression, the New Deal, and the Transformation of Religion in the Delta* (Oxford and New York: Oxford University Press, 2016); Sam Haselby, *The Origins of American Religious Nationalism* (Oxford and New York: Oxford University Press, 2015); David Hempton, *Methodism: Empire of the Spirit* (New Haven: Yale University Press, 2005); Christine Leigh Heyrman, *Southern Cross: The Beginnings of the Bible Belt* (New York: Alfred A. Knopf, 1997); Reginald F. Hildebrand, *The Times Were Strange and Stirring: Methodist Preachers and the Crisis of Emancipation* (Durham: Duke University Press, 1995); April E. Holm, *A Kingdom Divided: Evangelicals, Loyalty, and Sectionalism in the Civil War Era* (Baton Rouge: Louisiana State University Press, 2017); Cynthia Lynn Lyerly, *Methodism and the Southern Mind, 1770–1810* (New York and Oxford: Oxford University Press, 1998); Jared Maddox, *Nathan Bangs and the Methodist Episcopal Church: The Spread of Scriptural Holiness in Nineteenth-Century America* (Nashville: New Room Books, 2018); Rex D. Matthews, ed., *The Renewal of United Methodism: Mission, Ministry, and Connectionalism, Essays in Honor of Russell E. Richey* (Nashville: General Board of Higher Education and Ministry, 2012); J. Gordon Melton, *A Will to Choose: The Origins of African American Methodism* (Lanham: Rowman & Littlefield, 2007); Peter C. Murray, *Methodists and the Crucible of Race, 1930–1975* (Columbia: University of Missouri Press, 2004); Joseph T. Reiff, *Born of Conviction: White Methodists and Mississippi's Closed Society* (New York: Oxford University Press, 2016); Russell E. Richey, *Methodism in the American Forest* (New York: Oxford University Press, 2015); Darius L. Salter, *"God Cannot Do Without America": Matthew Simpson and the Apotheosis of Protestant Nationalism* (Wilmore, KY: First Fruits Press, 2017); A. Gregory Schneider, *The Way of the Cross Leads Home: The Domestication of American Methodism* (Bloomington: Indiana University Press, 1993); Kevin M. Watson, *Old or New School Methodism? The Fragmentation of a Theological Tradition* (New York: Oxford University Press, 2019); John H. Wigger, *Taking Heaven by Storm: Methodism and the Rise of*

The Book's Organization and Major Themes

The first chapter will explore how race relations and particularly slavery took expression in three dimensions of Methodism's life: its connectional life, its formational processes, and its outreach dynamics. I will suggest that *connection, formation*, and *outreach* constitute rubrics under which to analyze, describe, and hence cover the denomination's (and denominations') everyday life (lives). The three rubrics provide a descriptive rather than formal, doctrinal way of treating American Methodism. They function as a lived ecclesiology or ecclesial approach to Methodism's on-the-ground way of being church. The three terms correspond to the Methodist ecclesiological and ministerial "trinity" of Word, Sacrament, and Order. These terms function formally, theologically, and descriptively. This study will suggest how Methodism has lived its ecclesiology (albeit in racially compromised terms): formation/Word, connection/Sacrament, and outreach/Order. After the first chapter, the three subsequent chapters will explore each of the three ways Methodism has been church.[16]

Suggesting that connection, formation, and outreach have constituted a lived theology takes the treatment of American Methodism onto a different level from what I have discerned and argued previously. An operational, descriptive, and somewhat evaluative treatment of connectionalism, as also of two terms parallel to formation and outreach, functioned in *The Methodist Conference in America: A History*.[17] There three rubrics—conference, fraternity, and revival—provided an overview of Methodist practices. Fraternity and revival pointed to Methodism's lived and effective formational and outreach efforts. Descriptive of conference activities, these two terms invited attention to the ways that men—and primarily those with full conference membership—shaped and implemented the church's formational and outreach endeavors. What of wider, deeper, daily, and ongoing conferencing, formation, and outreach outside of quarterly,

Popular Christianity in America (New York: Oxford University Press, 1998); John Wigger, *American Saint: Francis Asbury and the Methodists* (Oxford, New York: Oxford University Press, 2009); and Jeffrey Williams, *Religion and Violence in Early American Methodism: Taking the Kingdom by Force* (Bloomington: Indiana University Press, 2010).

16 For a similar schematization of Methodism undertaken collaboratively, see our *The Methodists* by James E. Kirby, Russell E. Richey, and Kenneth E. Rowe, *Denominations in America*, no. 8 (Westport: Greenwood Press, 1996). We provided an overview of American Methodism in three parts: Bishops (connection), Conference (outreach), Members (formation).

17 Russell E. Richey, *The Methodist Conference in America: A History* (Nashville: Kingswood Books/Abingdon, 1996).

annual, and general conferences; by women as well as men; haltingly across racial, ethnic, language, and nationality lines; beyond as well as in the USA? Nope! Early Methodism thought it ran and attempted to make it run under male, conferenced, top-down authority and governance.

To be sure, in various treatments of connectionalism, in an array of articles and several books,[18] I probed its nature and evolution. That same approach shaped repeated invitations to describe American denominationalism, doubtless inspired by several books of mine on the topic.[19] At several points, I did struggle toward interpreting denominationalism theologically.[20] However, more typically, I attended to the larger American ecclesial pattern and its evolution descriptively.

My first serious probing of connection, formation, and outreach came in *Marks of Methodism*—its subtitle pointing in that direction—*Theology in Ecclesial Practice*.[21] The chapter titles indicate four (rather than three) overarching themes—Connectional, Itinerant, Disciplined/Disciplining,

---

18 *Connectionalism: Ecclesiology, Mission, and Identity*, Russell E. Richey, primary co-editor with Dennis M. Campbell and William B. Lawrence, United Methodism and American Culture, vol. 1 (Nashville: Abingdon, 1997); *Doctrine in Experience: A Methodist Theology of Church and Ministry* (Nashville: Kingswood Books/Abingdon, 2009); and *Methodist Connectionalism: Historical Perspectives* (Nashville: General Board of Higher Education and Ministry, 2010).

19 Among the recent invited treatments of denominationalism are "United Methodism: Its Identity as Denomination" in *Denomination: Assessing An Ecclesiological Category*, Paul Collins and Barry Ensign-George, eds. (London & New York: T & T Clark, 2011), 67–85; "Religious Organization in the New Nation," in *The Cambridge History of Religions in America*, Stephen J. Stein, gen. ed., 3 vols. (Cambridge: Cambridge University Press, 2012), 2:93–116; and "Denomination," "Review of the Literature," "Primary Sources, Further Reading, and Links to Digital Materials on Denominations and Denominationalism," and "Summary" in the online *Oxford Encyclopedia of Religion in America*. My books on the topic are *Denominationalism*, editor and co-author (Nashville: Abingdon Press, 1977; WIPF & Stock, 2010); *Reimagining Denominationalism*, co-editor and co-author with R. Bruce Mullin (New York: Oxford University Press, 1994; paper edition 2010); and *Denominationalism Illustrated and Explained* (Eugene, OR: Cascade Books, Wipf & Stock, 2013).

20 "Church History from the Bottom Up: In Quest for the People of God," *The Drew Gateway*, 44, No. 1 (Fall 1973): 6–19; "Denominationalism: A Theological Mandate," *The Drew Gateway*, 47, Nos. 2 & 3 (1976–1977): 93–106; "Ecclesial Sensibilities in 19th Century American Methodism," *Quarterly Review*, 4 (Spring 1984): 31–42; "Methodism and Providence: A Study in Secularization," in *Studies in Church History, 7: Protestant Evangelicalism: Britain, Ireland, Germany and America, c. 1750–c. 1950*, ed. Keith Robbins (Essex, Engl.: The Ecclesiastical History Society, 1990), 51–77.

21 *Marks of Methodism: Practices of Ecclesiology*, with Dennis M. Campbell and William B. Lawrence, UMAC, vol. 5 (Nashville: Abingdon Press, 2005). Campbell and Lawrence served in advisory capacity on this volume. The writing was solely my responsibility.

and Catholic. The effort, however, retained the top-down, male-defined approach. Further, I was well along in this present volume, had finished a full draft of this introduction, and had much of the first chapter crafted before I realized that previously I had pursued Methodism's several lived commitments in this theological reading and in the several descriptive accounts. The trinity of connection, fraternity, and revival and the four themes of *Marks of Methodism* I had not been consciously revising as I launched this venture. Belatedly, I came to see that I am here enriching, broadening, and deepening my earlier Methodist studies.

Methodism's organizational processes and machinery have constituted our connectionalism—whether that is, at any given point, formally articulated and acknowledged. Annual and general conferences (once white men only) have been the most readily recognized connectional expressions. Those baptizing and serving at the Table and, often, those baptized and invited to the Table were white. Formational activities brought the faithful together regularly (daily, weekly, or quarterly), under different auspices (for worship, in Sunday school and colleges), and through changing delivery resources (Sunday school publications, magazines, weekly newspapers) to hear God's Word. Methodism found, over time, various ways of outreach to and ordering of new communities and peoples (circuit rider evangelizing, camp meetings, missionary societies). The ongoing value of the three rubrics for treating Methodism's everyday life as church will be illustrated in twenty-first-century terms and by contemporary denominational (UMC) organizational systems. Then the chapter will suggest their usefulness for a fresh look at Methodism divided over slavery, particularly in the Methodist Episcopal Church (MEC) and Methodist Episcopal Church South (MECS).

Chapters on Connection, Formation, Outreach; a Postscript and Appendix

The second, third, and fourth chapters will employ successively the three rubrics for treating MEC and MECS in the states of Ohio and Kentucky in the decade leading up to the Civil War.

A concluding chapter will return again to the three rubrics and ask whether the approach opens up fresh ways of interpreting Methodism. It should, I hope, invite reflection on whether the three rubrics serve adequately for interpreting Methodism in earlier and later periods and in other parts of the Methodist family. It will ask, in various

ways, how Methodism might have benefited from being more doc-
trinally aware, explicit, and public about its lived theology. And it may
well invite more friendly accounts, perhaps, by recalling that the New
Testament had not gifted us with a full-orbed doctrine of the Trinity. What the Gospels and Letters narrated, described, advocated, and
prescribed gifted "fathers" of the church with lived if not formalized
trinitarian beliefs. Creeds and confessions came eventually. So perhaps
Methodists need not be overly perturbed that its people have not the-
ologized their doings.

The postscript, as noted above, traces my own schooling in Methodist
racial practices and racist theologizing and in efforts to guide the church
and its people to a vibrant, inclusive, pluralistic, biblically grounded lived
theology, and to corporate life shaped accordingly. As I hope the autobiographical narrative will make clear, a Mason-Dixon life has been mine.
From an infancy in which both parents struggled against North Carolina
racism and through Southern schooling, not only segregated but often
implicitly if not explicitly racist and sexist, I went north for collegiate, seminary, and graduate schooling. But home remained Durham even while
studying, living, and teaching in New Jersey for two entire decades. That
personal Mason-Dixon experience was not, in my own mind, the rationale for undertaking this exploration of its nineteenth-century expressions. However, in crafting the postscript, initially as an introduction, I
became aware of the autobiographical in this study and its overriding
focus on Methodism and race.

An appendix includes documents to which reference is made at various points. Included there are:

- The First *Discipline* on Race Relations;
- Poetry on Race—*The Ladies' Repository*—1858;
- William Sasnett of MECS on Missions, 1855;
- Majority and Minority Reports on Slavery: 1860 General
  Conference of the Methodist Episcopal Church; and
- Address by the Confederate Clergy, 1863.

CHAPTER 1

Connection, Formation, and Outreach

Methodism's Way of Being Church

Our grand plan, in all its parts, leads to an itinerant ministry. Our bishops are travelling bishops. All the different orders which compose our conferences are employed in the travelling line; and our local preachers are, in some degree, travelling preachers. Everything is kept moving as far as possible; and we will be bold to say, that, next to the grace of God, there is nothing like this for keeping the whole body alive from the centre to the circumference, and for the continual extension of that circumference on every hand.[1]

Methodism *acts* first, as Bishops Francis Asbury and Thomas Coke so exclaimed. Then sometimes, only sometimes, it *thinks*. (That is even clearer in the longer citation of this episcopal declaration.) Frequently, American Methodism has opted to deal immediately with the then currently pressing cause, project, emphasis, commitment, direction, or ideal. It did/does so confident that gathered in conference, it would, should, must, did, or will act as God's agents of God. Implicit in what, to outsiders,

---

1   Thomas Coke and Francis Asbury, *The Doctrines and Disciplines of the Methodist Episcopal Church, in America with Explanatory Notes by Thomas Coke and Francis Asbury* (Philadelphia: Henry Tuckniss, 1798). Republished as *The Methodist Discipline of 1798, Including the Annotations of Thomas Coke and Francis Asbury*, Facsimile Edition, edited by Frederick A. Norwood (Rutland: Academy Books. 1979), 42. For an unpacking of this statement in relation to the themes of the book, see the conclusion of this chapter.

must appear to be impulsive action was/is confidence of being providentially guided.

Methodists act, trusting the Holy Spirit to lead them forward into an important decision, a new direction, a vital commitment. Sadly, the Spirit prompted/prompts action but without speaking loudly from heaven, supplying explanatory text, providing paragraphs of rationale, or contributing doctrinal specifics. Confident in divine guidance, Methodist conferences proceed to act, to legislate, to make a commitment, to launch new ministries. Thereafter and rarely did/does the church immediately ponder what it has done, attempt to make theological sense of its action, and modify or augment the *Discipline* or minutes accordingly. Often, much, much later, and perhaps reacting to another denomination's critique or to significant societal/political developments, Methodism awakes to the problems it has caused itself by acting before thinking. Belatedly, conference delegates add to the Journal or Minutes explanatory sentences. By then and frequently motivated by disputes over the actions taken previously, the debates, motions, amendments, postponements, and controversial resolutions look, at least retrospectively, to be quite earthly and evidencing nothing in the way of the Spirit's guidance.

With, perhaps, the grandest and most enduring and earliest of these under–Spirit-guidance-acts, John Wesley gifted American Methodists. How? With his adaptation of the 1780 British "Large Minutes" into an American Discipline. Wesley shoved together the (Anglican) orders of ministry (deacon, elder, bishop) and British Methodism's conference membership; used the "Large Minutes" as the framework; and decided to let the Americans figure out if, how, and when ministerial orders and conference membership function harmoniously (seldom) and when in tension with one another (most of the time).[2] Wesley's gift yielded conference membership fights and schism after schism in the nineteenth century; early and continuing struggles over racial and gender inclusion

2   For a useful exhibiting of the first *Discipline* and the *Large Minutes* in parallel columns see Jno. J. Tigert, *A Constitutional History of American Methodism* (Nashville: Publishing House of the Methodist Episcopal Church, South, 1908), Appendix VII, pp. 532–602. The title of that initial *Discipline* also suggests the indebtedness, "Minutes of Several Conversations Between the Rev. Thomas Coke, LL.D., the Rev. Francis Asbury and Others. At a Conference, begun in Baltimore in the State of Maryland, on Monday, the 27th of December, in the Year 1784, Composing a Form of Discipline for the Ministers, Preachers, and other Members of the Methodist Episcopal Church in America."

in orders and conferences; and decades of twentieth-century General-Conference-launched ministry studies. "Acting first" became Methodism's operational pattern.

Well into the twentieth century, American Methodism came to think of itself as *church* by capturing and formally delineating ministerial duties as *Word, Sacrament,* and *Order.* Here, we attempt to show that Methodists acted out such an ecclesial self-ordering from their earliest days. But again, they enacted faithfulness or fidelity to classic Protestant conceptions of church and ministry. The chapters that follow show Methodism's catholicity by exploring and explicating the ways preachers and laity enacted and lived a way of being church: connection/Sacrament, formation/Word, and outreach/Order. What follows immediately below explores the third motif outlined in the preface, namely, to track patterns, North and South or across both Mason and Dixon territory, thereby framing those for Ohio and Kentucky. Further, the national, sectional, and conference tensions are noted as the following sections highlight the overarching rubrics governing the next three chapters. Together, the chapters suggest ways nineteenth-century conflicts shape twenty-first-century United Methodism, the fourth motif of the preface.

From Connection to Church, Community, or Itinerancy

An important instance of such acting first occurred when American Methodism's first bishops, Thomas Coke and Francis Asbury, took it upon themselves to interlace extensive explanative and apologetic commentary **within** the *Discipline* (see the epigraph to this chapter). With explications frequently much longer than sections of the *Discipline* and in many cases carried over several pages, their *The Doctrines and Disciplines of the Methodist Episcopal Church, in America with Explanatory Notes by Thomas Coke and Francis Asbury* was too "Cokesbury" to be permitted again. Although published initially in 1798 and only again in 1979, the bishops' *Explanatory Notes* captured early Methodism's sense of being church, of its acting out an ecclesiology, and of its interlacing of connection, formation, and outreach. After a page and a half delineation of the episcopal office, this 1798 *Discipline* devoted six and a half pages, in much smaller type, to "Notes." The two bishops' explication of their duties went from Scripture, through John Wesley's practice, to their American and continental mandates as connectional, formational, and outreaching:

May we not add a few observations concerning the high expediency, if not necessity, of the present plan. How could an itinerant ministry be preserved through this extensive continent, if the yearly conferences were to station the preachers? They would, of course, be taken up with the *sole* consideration of the spiritual and temporal interests of *that part* of the connection, the direction of which was intrusted to them. The necessary consequence of this mode of proceeding would probably, in less than an age, be *the division of the body* and *the independence* of each yearly conference. The conferences would be more and more estranged from each other, for want of a mutual exchange of preachers: and *that grand spring, the union of the body at large*, by which, under divine grace, the work is more and more extended through this vast country, would be gradually weakened, till at last it might be entirely destroyed. The connection would no more be enabled to send missionaries to the western states and territories, in proportion to their rapid population. The grand circulation of ministers would be at an end and a mortal stab given to the itinerant plan. The surplus of preachers in one conference could not be drawn out to supply the deficiencies of others, through declensions, locations, deaths, etc., and the revivals in one part of the continent could not be rendered beneficial to the others. *Our grand plan*, in all its parts, leads to an *itinerant* ministry. Our bishops are *travelling* bishops. All the different orders which compose our conferences are employed in the *travelling line*; and our local preachers are, *in some degree*, travelling preachers. Everything is kept moving as far as possible; and we will be bold to say, that, next to the grace of God, there is nothing *like this* for keeping the whole body alive from the centre to the circumference, and for the continual extension of that circumference on every hand.[3]

Explicating the connectional, formational, and outreaching vision of this statement is a book in itself. The terms and their import do interlace, but note how the bishops point to each ecclesial dimension:

- **Connection**: the word *connection* itself, "plan," "extensive continent," "union of the body," "*that grand spring, the union of the body at large*," "grand circulation of ministers."

3   Coke and Asbury, *The Doctrines and Disciplines of the Methodist Episcopal Church, in America with Explanatory Notes by Thomas Coke and Francis Asbury*, 42.

- **Formation**: "yearly conferences," "station," "the spiritual and temporal interests," and the formational dimensions in the entire last section beginning "*Our grand plan*, in all its parts."
- **Outreach**: "extensive continent," "work is more and more extended through this vast country," "send missionaries to the western states and territories," "from the centre to the circumference, and for the continual extension of that circumference on every hand."

The terms *itinerant* and *travelling* carry tremendous weight in the above statement and effectively point to all three ecclesial activities—the connectional, the formational, and the outreaching. Sadly, the preachers in conference instructed the bishops not to reprint their *Doctrines and Disciplines . . . with Explanatory Notes*. Its richness on various aspects of Methodist policy and practice was lost, only to be recovered and used recently.

In 1816, General Conference instructed those editing the *Discipline* to replace generic use of the word *connection* with the terms *church, community,* or *itinerancy*. The *Journal of the General Conference of The Methodist Episcopal Church* did not specify reasons for substituting the more conventional terms.[4] Such ecclesial rethinking doubtless seemed necessary given the sense of crisis and of entering a new day for Methodism occasioned by the deaths of Bishop Coke in 1814, and Bishop Asbury in 1816. As we will see, General Conference laid plans for important initiatives of connection as well as formation and outreach, including that for the 1818 launch of *Methodist Review* (of which I am the twenty-first-century co-editor). And the *Discipline* continued to order ministerial sections with the older term:

3. Who are admitted into full connection? . . .
9. Who have been expelled from the connection this year?
10. Who have withdrawn from the connection this year?

The question of who would be admitted into full connection—indeed, who would be fully admitted into the church's life—very early became Methodism's quandary.

---

4   See *Journals of the General Conference of The Methodist Episcopal Church, 1796–1856,* 3 vols. (New York: Carlton & Phillips, 1856) and particularly vol. 1, 1796–1836.

Connected and *Dis*Connected

American Methodism named itself officially with "Minutes of Some Conversations between the Preachers in Connexion with The Rev. Mr. John Wesley, Philadelphia, June 1773."[5] In queries about "Connection" (or *Connexion* in early "Minutes"), the gathered preachers named those serving the Methodist cause in ministerial capacity and counted members. The defined "Society" numbered the adherents. The *Minutes* for 1785, the first for the newly constituted Methodist Episcopal Church, questioned, named, and numbered superintendents, elders, deacons, assistants, and those "admitted into full connexion."[6] The next year, "What numbers are in Society?" was answered with a column for "Whites" and one for "Col." (18,791 and 1,890, respectively). The columns included all whites and all black members. The *Minutes* did not distinguish free and slaves among the "Col." Nor did the numbers and names for those in the ministerial orders or those on trial and awaiting ordination to full connection capture black Methodists who were effectively ministering.

Neither Richard Allen nor Harry Hosier, black Methodists exercising critical leadership, make it into the *Minutes*. Harry had traveled with and preached alongside both bishops, Asbury and Coke. Allen had, in 1787, (by some judgments) effectively withdrawn his ministry and begun the trajectory that would culminate in his co-founding the AME Church and becoming its first bishop. By 1788, the preachers added yet another count, "Who desist from travelling in connexion with, and under the direction of our conference?"[7] In subsequent years, the *Minutes* numbered and named such with more explicit terms: expelled, withdrawn, dismissed. But black lives and ministry did not matter, except in Methodism's record-keeping.

---

5   *Minutes of the Methodist Conferences. Annual Held in America; From 1773 to 1813, Inclusive* (New York: Published by Daniel Hitt and Thomas Ware for the Methodist Connexion in the United States, 1813), 5. The 1840 version Americanized the title, *Minutes of the Annual Conferences of the Methodist Episcopal Church, for the Years 1773–1828*, vol. 1 (New York: T. Mason and G. Lane for the Methodist Episcopal Church, 1840). The second is the first of what would be the ongoing series of aggregated conference *Minutes*.

6   *MEC Minutes (1773–1813)*, 53.

7   *MEC Minutes (1773–1813)*, 71.

White and Black in Kentucky and Ohio

By 1824, the *Minutes* reported all the queries and counts by individual annual conferences. That year, the Ohio record preceded that for Kentucky in the *Minutes*. Quest. 3 of the, then, standardized question series asked: "Who are admitted into full connection?" To Quest. 13. "What numbers are in Society?" the *Minutes* responded by district and then totaled the numbers. For Ohio, the counts were Whites 36,348, and Col. 193. Kentucky reported numbers of 21,522 and 3,311, respectively.

Ohio did not, but Kentucky responded to Quests. 9 and 10: "Who have been expelled from the connection this year?" and "Who have withdrawn from the connection this year."[8] Those latter actions *explicitly* broke connectional bonds with named preachers and implicitly stripped those identified from offering the sacrament. *Implicitly*, the counts of Whites and Colored weakened or sundered the connectional bond and indicated who would offer and often also who could receive the sacraments. The *Minutes* provided a connection-side "General Recapitulation," listing numbers by race for thirteen conferences. For whites, the total for the year was 280,427, for "coloured," 48,040, and for Indians, 56. The latter number was for the Canada Conference whose overall pattern was 607,222 and 56. In the connectional body counts, the Holy Spirit slayed along racial lines!

Connexion posed the ecclesial question explicitly. For Methodism's formational processes, the "Society" queries and answers provided body counts, by then including Sunday schools. Of Connection, Formation, and Outreach—what pointed to the latter? The Ohio *Minutes* began Quest. 14, "Where are the preachers stationed this year?" by preceding the district-by-district listing of appointment with that for "Martin Ruter, book agent, Cincinnati." It concluded that question after the last district with "Conference missionary, David Young" and "Wyandot mission, J. B. Finley, Jacob Hooper." Similarly, Kentucky headed its list of stations with "Augusta College, John P. Finley," and concluded it with "Cumberland mission, Elisha Simmons" and "Jonathan Stamper, missionary to collect funds for Augusta College." So, the *Minutes* reported the church's outreach, as in a certain sense did also the identification of members by race.

Notable for their ongoing connectional, formational, and outreach activities in the 1824 Ohio and Kentucky *Minutes*, in addition to Ruter and Finley, were Charles Elliott and Henry B. Bascom of the Ohio Conference and Peter Cartwright of the Kentucky. Elliott had stints superintending

8   MEC *Minutes (1773–1828)*, 419–23.

the Wyandot missions, as faculty member and president of Iowa Wesleyan, and a longer one as editor of the *Western Christian Advocate*. He would be among the most outspoken critics of the southern church (MECS) and the slave cause. Then of Ohio, Henry B. Bascom was elected a bishop by the MECS in 1850. Later shifting sides as well was Peter Cartwright, in 1824, a presiding elder of the Kentucky Cumberland District. The two conferences met in September with the typical week-long and over-a-weekend pattern, Ohio beginning on the 2nd, Kentucky on the 23rd. Presiding over both were Bishops Robert Roberts, William McKendree, and Joshua Soule.[9] The first two died before the 1844 division. Soule later cast his lot with the MECS.

Connection/Sacrament, formation/Word, and outreach/Order—that trilogy provided nineteenth-century Methodism with a way of being church. What follows explores aspects of several of the motifs outlined in the preface; ways to employ three terms descriptive of Methodist life, work, and belief; and how such refreshing of classic and central theological rubrics yields fresh understandings of the nineteenth century and the current church.

Connection, Formation, and Outreach: American Methodism's Threefold Ordering, Then

Putting the three rubrics in this order—Sacrament/connection, Word/formation, and then Order/outreach—instead of in the traditional Word, Sacrament, and Order, permits the sequencing of treatment in this chapter. Here, glimpses of the three are descriptive of Methodism's everyday way of being the church, rather than in formal and doctrinal terms. The operational ecclesiology—living into connection, formation, and outreach ordering of life together—guided the faithful, the local, the regional, and the church as a whole. It has persisted from the seventeen hundreds into the twenty-first century.

Interestingly, the three terms—connection, formation, and outreach—had been selected for this study before discovering the nineteenth-century equivalents explicitly guiding an annual conference's work and as the threefold major commitment. The Kentucky Conference

---

9   *Journal of Kentucky Annual Conference* (1824), typescript held at Asbury Seminary Library and used with permission. William Warren Sweet, *Circuit-Rider Days Along the Ohio: Being the Journals of the Ohio Conference from its Organization in 1812 to 1826* (New York & Cincinnati: The Methodist Book Concern, 1923), 241–60.

(MECS) in the 1840s and 1850s elected three members to deliver sermons for the following year's conference (on ministry, education, and missions). In 1846, Bishop Joshua Soule announced sermons to be preached and committee members for the next conference meeting and year.[10] The list (and the visiting committees) illustrates the conference's commitment to connection, formation, and outreach:

- Annual Sermon on the Ministry
- Annual Sermon on Education
- Annual Sermon on Missions [Also for Education:]
  — Visiting committee for Transylvania
  — For Lexington Female Collegiate High School, three members
  — For Franklin Institute
  — For Science Hill Female Academy

Special evening sessions were dedicated to each. For 1849 they were:

- On the Ministry—H. H. Kavanaugh
- On Education—John G. Bruce
- On Missions—G. W. Brush

This threesome continued at least until 1855, appointed for the following year. For 1855, they were:

- On the Ministry—Thomas N. Ralston
- On Education—John G. Bruce
- On Missions—John M. Bonnell[11]

Kavanaugh would be elected bishop in 1854. Ralston exercised an episcopal-like office in publishing, including writing the *Elements of Divinity*, which remained as the doctrinal guide for southern Methodism from 1847 to 1924.[12] Regrettably, the talks do not seem to have survived, or,

---

10 Manuscript "Minutes" KY Wesleyan, *Journal of Kentucky Annual Conference* (1846–1850), typescript held by Kentucky Wesleyan and used with its permission, 1846, pp. 45–52. Other MECS Kentucky *Minutes* accessed at Asbury Theological Seminary and through the Duke Divinity School Library. The latter holds 1855–1870, 1872, and most subsequent years up to the 1939 unification of the three Methodisms.

11 For these actions, see Manuscript "Minutes" KY Wesleyan, *Journal of Kentucky Annual Conference* (1846–1850; 1851–1859).

12 See Louis Dale Patterson, "The Ministerial Mind of American Methodism: the Courses of Study for the Ministry of the Methodist Episcopal Church, the Methodist Episcopal

at least at this point, have not been uncovered. All three presentations doubtless hailed the progress made in relation to the major commitment, described present operations, outlined challenges that must be faced, and called the assemblage of those listening, laity (white men and women) and preachers (white men), to gird up their loins and face the animals and enemies.

Probably left unsaid was that little or nothing was being done connectionally (On the Ministry), in Sunday school formational activities (On Education), and in truly transformative outreach (On Missions) for the slaves. Doubtless numbers of slaves labored for the white laity, preachers, and bishops attending the evening sessions and listening. And though the MECS sustained a highly circumscribed (by law and church practice) ministerial outreach to the slaves, it did number them among adherents.

Perhaps surprisingly, the Ohio and Cincinnati conferences (MEC) in the 1850s routinely appointed preachers to deliver a missionary sermon for the following year but not one on ministry or education. They cared for those other two central concerns in other well-documented and lavish fashions, as we will see in subsequent chapters. Even so, the three concerns or causes interfaced so much that sermons alone would not suffice. In 1850, for instance, the Ohio Conference passed an eight-part motion with respect to the Missionary Society, committing to: raising of a specific amount; establishing a "monthly missionary prayer meeting"; recommending subscription to the *Missionary Advocate*; calling for preachers to take collections in May and appointing "missionary collectors in each charge"; the publishing "of a missionary report annually"; specifying collectors, amounts received, names of contributors; having a missionary sermon/service at each conference; and finally calling for maintenance of a *Missionary Advocate* subscription list in Cincinnati by the Book Concern.[13] Furthering outreach or missions for the next year required the lift from the conference's connectional and formational muscle.

In the 1850s, Ohio Methodism, as we will see in the next chapter, quit identifying blacks in their membership counts for ministry, education, and missions. There, state law counted African Americans as citizens

---

Church, South and the Methodist Protestant Church, 1880-1920," PhD dissertation, Drew University, 1984.

13 *Minutes of the Ohio Annual Conference of the Methodist Episcopal Church* (1850), 188–89. That conference convened September 17 in Chillicothe and "After uniting in the Holy Sacrament, Bishop Janes called the Conference to order," 179.

(albeit with limited prerogatives), and the MEC established churches or maintained balconies for them. But then the Methodists left ministerial, educational, and missional activities to whatever the small black congregations (and their white preachers) could muster on their own. In the white churches and for whites on district and conference levels, Ohio Methodism had created connectional, formational, and outreach mechanisms and machinery. Note below how the three are displayed in the index to the Ohio Annual Conference's 1859 *Minutes*. The italicized sections dealt with Formation/Education; the underlined with Outreach/Missions; much of the remainder with Connection/Ministry.

INDEX[14]

Journal
Appointments
Stewards' Report
    Total Fifth Collection
    Superannuated Preachers, etc.
Reports of Committees, Etc.

Report on Necessitous Cases
" " Finance
" " *Bible Cause*
" " *Sabbath Schools*
" of Committee on New York Accounts
" " Trustees of Allen Bequest

Report on Education—
    Ohio Wesleyan University
    Worthington Female College
    Coolville Seminary
    Wilberforce University,

Report on Temperance
" " Tract Cause
" " Slavery
" of Treasurer of SS Union

---

14   The index as printed included pagination, which is omitted here; it did not include the italicizing coding, which is added here for ecclesial emphasis.

Statistics pp. 22–27
Recapitulation by Districts

Resolutions—
    Delaware Excursion
    Transferring of Preachers
    Change of Boundary
Examining Committees

Ohio Conference MISSIONARY Society
    Business Meeting
    Anniversary
    Missionary Report
    Treasurer's Report

Constitution of the Mutual Aid Society
Ohio Conference Record

Detailed Missionary Report pp. 40–51[15]

Connection, formation, and outreach certainly constituted the conference's white business. The *Minutes* (both conference and general) documented the threefold business activities and expenditures. Those for the white ministry (connection) constituted much of the conference's activities; were upfront in the *Minutes*; and provided great detail on ministerial activities, salaries, and appointments. Some of the activities received descriptions, sometimes in detail, as for instance, on the colleges (formation). Other activities, also formational, including (regrettably) the Sunday schools and their extent, publications, and leadership, come to us in chart form as statistics and then in combination with overall membership and leadership numbers (pp. 22–27 and see figure 2 below). The Ohio Conference provided incredible detail on its missionary activities, expenditures, and funds raised (pp. 40–51/outreach) as we will show in detail in the chapter so devoted. Here, the summary for the conference illustrates:[16]

---

15 *Minutes of the Ohio Annual Conference of the Methodist Episcopal Church, 1852–1867* (1859), 52. HathiTrust Digital Library Rights, Public Domain, Google-digitized. Permanent URL: https://hdl.handle.net/2027/osu.32435053210050.

16 *Minutes of the Ohio Annual Conference of the Methodist Episcopal Church, 1852–1867* (1859), 27.

OHIO ANNUAL CONFERENCE. 27

RECAPITULATION BY DISTRICTS.

DISTRICTS.	Volumes in Library	No. of Scholars	No. of Officers & Teachers	No. of Sunday Schools	Amount for Sunday School Union	Amount for Bible Society	Amount for Tract Society	Amount for Missionary Society	Amount for Conference Claimants	Probable Value	No. of Parsonages	Probable Value	No. of Churches	No. of Children Baptized	No. of Adults Baptized	No. of Local Preachers	No. of Probationers	No. of Deaths	No. of Members
Columbus District	16,050	5,329	1,014	83	$19 53	$89 29	$9 95	$1,343 19	$286 59	$5,600	17	$104,700	82	285	216	78	277	48	4,698
Zanesville	14,890	4,705	919	75	39 97	119 56	49 19	1,200 43	196 57	5,900	6	74,000	62	164	243	38	994	65	4,955
Lancaster	13,554	3,440	747	72	43 45	116 15	19 74	1,545 55	173 23	10,350	13	74,300	73	130	114	38	234	46	3,958
Marietta	14,746	4,022	964	88	31 16	1 9 73	14 74	807 72	227 55	7,300	11	46,365	73	217	253	32	435	53	4,556
Jackson	13,034	3,650	1,076	86	8 75	1 89 49	16 50	989 39	179 60	5,203	16	43,840	68	909	332	54	620	49	4,235
Portsmouth	13,367	3,863	792	73	23 56	176 82	8 50	1,398 92	225 36	11,700	11	133,7-0	82	247	198	42	671	42	3,810
Chillicothe	12,563	4,1?-2	795	74	74 11	117 15	23 70	2,849 49	431 23	14,6?0	14	91,55 14	63	293	266	95	311	60	4,093
Total for 1859	98,454	31,331	6,237	561	$233 57	$841 15	$133 17	$10,042 91	$1,736 94	$63,765 84	84	$396,305 474	474	1,585	1,862	399	2,842	375	30,465 375
Total for 1858	98,111	29,391	5,590	533	118 52	802 33	67 68	9,669 83	1,082 15	66,190 78	78	445,385 408	408	1,563	1,740	216	4,978 246	3-5	29,049 3-5
Increase		1,940	647	28	$115 05	$38 82	$65 49	$483 08	$718 00		6				297			10?	1,416 10?
Decrease	323									$2,825		$129,920 6				4	2,136		29,049 3-5 4,978 2.6

The several pages prior to this recapitulation itemized the personnel, expenditures, assets, and numbers—the latter down to the penny.

Such records captured only that portion of the conference's work reported to the annual meeting and then published. The *Minutes* never attempted to explicate the way preachers traveling together to and from conference enhanced the *connectional* brotherhood. Nor did Minutes show the *formational* force of the preachers living, eating, and praying with the laity of the city during their stay for conference. Nor, for some reason, did the *Minutes* attend to Sunday doings, indicate which conference members preached and where, or describe the filling of the pulpits of the region. With such *outreach* the *Minutes* could not be bothered. Nor did the secretary describe the doings when, as frequently, a camp meeting gathered the faithful during the sitting of the conference and gave *outreach, formation,* and *connection* a wonderful venue.

Nor did the record indicate whether, when, how, to what extent, and by whom the conference's activities actually reached its black membership. To that issue, to conference minutes—and to similar nineteenth-century on-the-ground or in-the-lap or for-outreach-formation-and-connection— subsequent chapters will return again and again. Ministry/connection, education/formation, and outreach/missions in the 1850s constitute the heart of this study. Here it makes sense to indicate that the three rubrics encompass and describe today's Methodism as well. However, before so doing, the recent *distortion* of the threefold ordering of order and ministry should be noted.

What follows details the first portion of the second motif mentioned in the preface: exploration of today's social, economic, and political strains. The discussion here—for the remainder of the chapter—should, I hope, help the reader come to fresh understandings of the nineteenth-century national and regional conflict. It may as well aid in grasping why both preface and postscript frame this foray into the mid-nineteenth century in racial and personal terms. Most immediately, the following pages probe some of the problems created by United Methodism's relatively recent adding of terms to the classic Christian formula for interpreting and portraying ministry. The following section, then, makes a "defensive" argument for the use of formation, outreach, and connection to interpret American Methodism then and now.

Acting First into Successive Alterations of the Orders of Ministry

"Acting first" became Methodism's operational pattern, as we have noted. As the church more recently struggled over whether deacons were an operative and not just transitional order of ministry, twentieth-century United Methodism has decided that it needed to amend the classical way of conceptualizing ecclesial ministries in relation to that of Christ. From Anglicanism, American Methodism had inherited the threefold Christological pattern of prophet, priest, and king and the ordering of church as Word, Sacrament, and Order. Those male terms—prophet, priest, and king—wouldn't do, General Conference determined, even though initially applied descriptively and theologically to the man Christ Jesus. Nope. Add a fourth ministerial term, *Service*, and make it clear that the deacon belonged in the operative ecclesial order.

It would not suffice that a crown of thorns symbolized Christ's *service* as royalty, feeding the five thousand his *service* in priesthood, and cleansing the Temple his *service* of prophetic calling. Not that ministers and ministries of whatever gender, orientation, race, language, or nationality would be called into just such full-orbed ministries. Just add *service*.

That adding *service* to the historic, trifold ministerial scheme implicitly detracted from the Suffering Servant dimension of the royal office seemed not to matter. Bishops could continue—ignoring biblical imaging of true Christ-like ministry—to let earthly kingship guide their sense of how to conduct themselves. And if you add that fourth ordering of ministry and implicitly pull servanthood and service out of Order, wouldn't Christ's sacramental and feeding ministry be helped by adding *compassion* to our conception of ministry? And Christ's prophetic cleansing of the Temple and routing the money-grubbing priests couldn't adequately convey today's notions of *justice*. So, ignore compassion as an ingredient in the priestly office and justice in the prophetic. Glory be! Now United Methodism has "fixed"—doubled, as it were—the threefold Christological and perhaps even Trinitarian ordering of ministry: Service, Word, Sacrament, Order, Compassion, and Justice.[17]

Readers will doubtless recognize immediately that these six identities do not comprehend adequately and image appropriately the exploding

---

17 *The Book of Discipline of The United Methodist Church 2016* (Nashville: The United Methodist Publishing House, 2016), ¶224; ¶303.2.

twenty-first-century and online ministries into which we as a church are now plunging. What terms should be added to capture ministerial frontiers? Online? Global? Immediate? Or, if we are not thinking online but of urban and suburban congregations struggling with how best to image their welcome to prospective members, what about adding convenient parking and yet another identity, "Parking"? So, thorn-crowned, cleansed-temple, and loaves-fish-fed-5,000 AND prophet, priest, and king AND Word, Sacrament, and Order would not suffice. No. Add ministerial identities to capture the latest ecclesial agenda—Parking, Service, Online availability, Word, Sacrament, Order, Compassion, and Justice.[18] Or more tidily for the *Discipline*: "Parking, Service, Word, Sacrament, Order, Compassion, Justice, and Vision." What a future! United Methodists officially have abandoned the threefold Christological pattern of prophet, priest, and king and the ordering of church as Word, Sacrament, and Order. Here, in these chapters, we won't. Instead, in what preceded this aside and in subsequent chapters, we function with the three historical commitments, albeit with their lived equivalents.

Connection, Formation, and Outreach: American Methodism's Threefold Ordering, Now

The three rubrics, in fact, may be used to treat today's United Methodist lived ecclesiology, practice of church, and ordering of its ecclesial commitments. Methodists exhibit our connectionalism internally and externally. On the day of drafting this page, World Communion Sunday had just occurred, reminding us liturgically of our relationship with Christians across the globe.

Organizationally, Methodists have often led in the array of ecumenical organizations from the World and National Council of Churches to counterpart organizations on regional, state, and local levels. Methodists were on the ground floor in the several US efforts to bring an array of denominations into a common fold. Full communion agreements, again in the US, have been struck with the several Black Methodist denominations (African Methodist Episcopal, African Methodist Episcopal Zion, Christian Methodist Episcopal, African Union Methodist Protestant, and Union American Methodist Episcopal churches), achieved with Lutherans and Moravians and (at this writing) are in process with the Episcopalians.

---

18   See Matthew 15:13-21; Mark 6:30-44; Luke 9:10-17 for the feeding.

The UMC also enjoys full communion with the Uniting Church of Sweden. The World Methodist Council brings together the array of Wesleyan and Methodist communions as do Church World Service and other international ecumenical and Methodist connections. And, of course, United Methodism struggles to live up to its first name.[19]

Connectional bonding began/begins, perhaps, on a local level. There, World Communion Sunday, an array of other special days, weekly collections and annual pledges, regular baptismal and Communion services, and charge conferences remind parishioners of their connection to the larger Methodist and ecclesial families. However, Sunday mornings gather many congregations in largely, if not completely, racially defined communities. Annual conferences—South Carolina with its sizable black membership excepted—also show how little Methodism succeeded in evangelizing and churching across racial, language, ethnic, and tribal lines. On a denominational (and particularly US) level, distinct agendas, theological differences, and special causes take caucus form and have done so for half a century. Here, illustrating interested connectionalism but also *dis-connection* are caucus websites:[20]

- Affirmation: United Methodists for Lesbian, Gay, Bisexual, Transgender, and Queer Concerns
- Black Clergywomen of The United Methodist Church
- Black Methodists for Church Renewal (BMCR)
- Charles Wesley Society
- Concerned Methodists
- The Confessing Movement
- Good News
- Historical Society of The United Methodist Church
- Institute on Religion and Democracy
- Lifewatch (formerly Taskforce of United Methodists on Abortion and Sexuality)

---

19 United Methodism's ecumenical office provides a "List of UMC Partnerships." In the order of their listing and with the count for each category, they are Concordat Churches (4), Affiliated Autonomous Churches (18), Affiliated United Churches (8), Full Communion Relationships (8), Known Ecumenical Partner Churches Specific to European Central Conferences (7), and International Organizations (7). https://www.unitedmethodistbishops.org/ecumenicaldetail/list-of-umc-partnerships-12822590.

20 The list comes from Christopher J. Anderson, compiler, *United Methodist Studies: Basic Bibliographies*, Sixth Edition (Madison, NJ: Drew University Library, 2014), 190–92. Those pages also include the websites for each of the caucuses.

- MARCHA (Methodists Associated Representing the Cause of Hispanic Americans)
- Methodist Evangelicals Together
- Methodist Federation for Social Action
- Methodists United for Peace with Justice
- Mexican American and Hispanic Latin o/a Church Ministries Program
- Perkins School of Theology, Southern Methodist University
- Mission Society
- National Federation of Asian American United Methodists
- National Fellowship of Associate Members and Local Pastors
- Native American International Caucus
- Reconciling Ministries Network
- RENEW Network (A Woman's Ministry Network for United Methodists)
- Southern Asian National Caucus of United Methodists
- Transforming Congregations
- UMACTION
- United Methodist Association of Ministers with Disabilities
- United Methodist Rural Fellowship
- United Methodist Women
- Wesleyan Theological Society[21]

These organizations *divide* or *dis-connect* Methodism. Here is **Untied** Methodism—distinct communities within the denomination, each with distinctive identities, causes, campaigns, theologies, and agendas.[22] A few share cause and overlap membership with another caucus. A couple

---

21 A list of Affiliated Group Periodicals, strangely not including that for the Wesleyan Theological Society, exhibits United Methodist subgroups, many less discordantly related to the denomination than the caucuses. Here it follows: Aldersgate Renewal Ministries; Appalachia Service Project; Association for Couples in Marriage Enrichment, Inc.; Association of Annual Conference Lay Leaders; Christians Engaged in Faith Formation; Disciplined Order of Christ; Encounter; Fellowship of United Methodists in Music and Worship Arts; Foundation for Evangelism; Marriage Enrichment; Methodist Hour International; National Association of United Methodist Evangelists; National Association of United Methodist Foundations; National United Methodist Campers, Inc.; Order of Saint Luke; Professional Association of UM Church Secretaries; Renewal Ministries; Saint Brigid of Kildare Monastery; United Christian Ashrams; United Methodist Association; United Methodist Association of Scholars in Christian Education; United Methodist Camp & Retreat Ministries; United Methodist Network of Practice; Wesley Heritage Foundation.

22 On this theme, see note 13 in the introduction on the recent article and book.

might best not be included in the caucus category (as for instance United Methodist Women, the Historical and Charles Wesley societies, and Perkins School of Theology). Most of the above, however, provide community for those claiming such, as for instance: local pastor, gay, Asian American, Black, or rural Methodist. Typically, the groups maintain their own membership rolls. They issue documents, carry on campaigns, promote their cause, champion their distinct identities, press for denominational action on causes important to their membership, and publish with/for/to their members by phone, in print, by meeting, through the web, and by email.

Collectively, the caucuses exhibit, even champion, Methodism's **untied** character. Less obvious to most of the membership is the way that denominational agencies function in similar distinctive, competitive, caucus-like fashion:

- General Board of Church and Society
- Discipleship Ministries
- General Board of Global Ministries
- General Board of Higher Education and Ministry
- Wespath/General Board of Pension and Health Benefits
- General Commission on Archives and History
- General Commission on the Status and Role of Women
- General Commission on Religion and Race
- General Commission on United Methodist Men
- General Commission on Communication/UM Communications
- United Methodist Publishing House

Collectively, they represent the array of denominational concerns and speak for and to the church. Theoretically one, indeed meeting together, and sending key leaders to United Methodist gatherings, the agencies compete with one another over terrain, for money, and for attention. For the most part, each charts its own way. Illustrative is the fact that each agency functions as though it were a UM publishing house. As of this initial drafting, Discipleship put out, in print or online, *Alive Now, El Aposento, Devo'Zine, Pockets, The Upper Room, Walk to Emmaus*, and *Weavings*. Global Ministries offered five publications, Communications six, both Higher Education and Ministry and the Publishing House quite an array, and *United Methodist News covered them all*.

The general agencies collectively and competitively exhibit connection gone awry. Other central governing bodies do as well, at least sometimes. Among such—the Council of Bishops, the Judicial Council, the Connectional Table, and General Conference. Conflict between and within the Jurisdictions, between and within conferences, and between and within congregations also minimize and destroy our connectionalism.

More Quickly: Formation and Outreach

The formational and outreach dimensions of United Methodism's life and ministry can be treated much more briefly. They betray some of the same dis-unitive aspects described for our connectionalism, indeed shaped by our connectionalism, but also more unitive and less conflictual patterns. Formational Sunday schools invite, and formational community activities reach children and youth of various races and languages. So also, increasingly, do United Methodist Youth Fellowships (UMYFs) and church camps. Multiracial leadership in such operations aids the process. Methodist colleges, universities, and seminaries have made commitments to inclusion and staffing across racial, ethnic, gender, sexual orientation, national origin, and religious lines. On a denominational level, the General Board of Higher Education and Ministry (GBHEM), United Methodist (UM) Communications, the United Methodist Publishing House (UMPH), Discipleship Ministries, and Wespath function formationally and across the church's various lines.

United Methodism's outreach and ordering functions sustain Sunday schools and others of the above formational activities. Evangelization continues within families, between spouses, in neighborhoods, and among friends as it has for centuries. Urban congregations especially—those that survived the emptying out of many downtowns—invent outreach methods, programs, terms, goals, and ideals. New style congregations and ministries are touted for their missional effectiveness. Outreach figures prominently and programmatically, and in the UMC's boards, agencies, and commissions: Church and Society, Global Ministries, Status and Role of Women, United Methodist Men, Religion and Race, and United Methodist Women.

We noted above the competition between and among the agencies, that their programming typically is not coordinated and that their publications also do not cooperate and take advantage of one another. However, for formational and outreach purposes and for the ends for which those agencies were established, their regular and occasional publications, online programming, and websites and periodicals do serve. In this writer's experience, the outreach comes daily via email from the UM News Daily Digest. At this drafting (Oct. 15, 2019), it included "Providing news and information from around the church"; UMNS "News and Features" included "UMCOR, partners start asylum seekers project," "Central Texas Conference: Bishop calls for prayers and action," "South Carolina Conference: 2 years after fire, church returns to building," the press release "Council of Bishops: Full communion proposal is subject of videos," and under Resources—"United Methodist Communications: Ways to appreciate your pastor."[23]

Outreach might be argued for some of the caucuses and special interest groups who employ websites, news releases, meetings, and publications in efforts to reach out to the whole connection. They do not unite Methodism, but they reach out and help order the people(s) who are claimed by them and claim them.

Conclusion

United or **Untied** Methodism can and should live, perhaps through its connection, formation, and outreach, into the vision with which Bishops Coke and Asbury gifted us:

> *Our grand plan*, in all its parts, leads to an *itinerant* ministry. Our bishops are *travelling* bishops. All the different orders which compose our conferences are employed in the *travelling line*; and our local preachers are, *in some degree*, travelling preachers. Everything is kept moving as far as possible; and we will be bold to say, that, next to the grace of God, there is nothing *like this* for keeping the whole body alive from the centre to the circumference, and for the continual extension of that circumference on every hand.[24]

Connection? "*Our grand plan*, in all its parts"; "the different orders which compose our conferences"; the whole body.

Formation? "The different orders"; "*travelling* bishops"; "travelling preachers."

Outreach? "Everything . . . kept moving. . . . keeping the whole body alive from the centre to the circumference, and for the continual extension of that circumference."

---

23 A UMNS posting for October 18, 2019 featured a story about Uganda and clean water ventures, the burning of a historical Texas church, and updates from the Black Methodists for Church Renewal, Global Ministries, United Methodist Communications, and Church and Society.

24 Coke and Asbury, *The Doctrines and Disciplines of the Methodist Episcopal Church, in America with Explanatory Notes by Thomas Coke and Francis Asbury*, 42.

CHAPTER 2

Outreach

The missions to the slaves of the Southern plantations constitute the most interesting and important field for the missionary operations of the Church, South. The relations which this class of our population sustain to our members and ministers throw them more entirely upon our Church for sympathy and Christian instruction. The reasons which commend them to our Christian effort are sufficiently obvious without being distinctly stated. We regard these missions as the crowning glory of our Church. The good they have already accomplished is incalculable; but we have as yet very imperfectly entered into the work which God has assigned us. New fields are constantly inviting our occupancy, and if we could only properly occupy them, we believe that expansion to an almost illimitable extent is before us. If these missions could receive more of episcopal attention and supervision, it would be an important advantage to them, in more than one respect.[1]

---

1   *Journal of the General Conference of the Methodist Episcopal Church, South*, v. 4, 1858. HathiTrust Digital Library, *Journal of the General Conference of the Methodist Episcopal Church, South*, volume 4, 1858 (Nashville: Methodist Episcopal Church, South, 1858), https://hdl.handle.net/2027/osu.32435053208484, p. 395.

    NOTE: Here, as above and hereinafter, items from the HathiTrust Digital Library, https://www.hathitrust.org/, are routinely footnoted even when, as here, I own or Duke University owns, and I am using the hard copy. Some readers may lack access to the item, hence the addition to the note. HaithiTrust versions are accessed and used, often for correction purposes, according to its protocols and therefore with permission.

So MECS[2] Bishops Joshua Soule, James O. Andrew, Robert Paine, George F. Pierce, John Early, and Hubbard K. Kavanaugh exhorted the Southern preachers in 1858. Less embracive views of slaves and more defensive campaigns for slavery appeared regularly, as for instance, in *The Quarterly Review of the Methodist Episcopal Church, South* (see appendix for "William Sasnett of MECS on Missions, 1855" and treatment of slavery in that context). The prior year, the *Quarterly Review,* that official voice of the church, gave Southern outreach a more somber tone in review essays, apparently written by editor and MECS spokesperson, T. O. Summers, D. D.:

> The Scriptural Argument for Slavery
> Dr. Smith's Philosophy and Practice of Slavery[3]

By contrast, the bishops and, as illustrated below, Kentucky Methodists, could look through the slavery system toward the souls of the enslaved and urge outreach towards them.

The Bishops' Counsel

The episcopal address had, at least theoretically—since William McKendree's initiative in 1812—set the General Conference agenda. The bishops devoted five of the twelve pages explicitly to missions, and implicitly oriented much of their overall counsel to the subject. They began insisting, "The cause of Missions is so intimately connected with the vitality, enlargement, and prosperity of the Church, that it is proper for us in this address to call the attention of the General Conference to a critical scrutiny of our plans and operations in that direction." Continuing in that celebrative vein, they then pointed to specific missional imperatives: sparsely settled areas; large cities; the "large and rapidly increasing foreign population," specifically the Germans "crowding to our shores," and settling in Texas and Missouri; their "Church on the Pacific coast"; "missions to the Indians"; then the slave missions; and finally foreign missions, notably to China.[4]

---

2   Abbreviations for the Methodist Episcopal Church, South, and the Methodist Episcopal Church are MECS and MEC.

3   *The Quarterly Review of the Methodist Episcopal Church, South,* n. s., v. 11 (Louisville, Ky.: Published by John Early for the Methodist Episcopal Church, South, 1857), 30–43, 242–58 (January and April issues) HathiTrust Digital Library https://hdl.handle.net /2027/nyp.33433082273404.

4   MECS *Quarterly Review* (1857), 391–96. On missions to the slaves, the bishops had further insisted, "We regard these missions as the crowning glory of our Church. The

NOTE: Since this study focuses on Kentucky and Ohio, it tracks only passingly the exploding "foreign" missions, which both the MECS and MEC undertook and to which most studies of mission attend. It also attends to missions and other modes of outreach on a connectional level, as developments at a MECS or MEC level pertain to efforts within and/or by the conferences in Kentucky and Ohio.[5]

After two motions directing the printing of the address in the "Daily Advocate" and deeming the southern bishops' counsel as "appropriate and well-timed," the conference made customary referrals:

3. That so much of the Address as refers to the episcopacy be referred to the Committee on the Episcopacy.

4. That so much of it as refers to missions be referred to the Committee on Missions.

5. That so much of it as refers to books and periodicals, be referred to the Committee on Books and Periodicals.

6. That so much of it as refers to the publication and circulation of tracts be referred to the Committee on the Tract Society.

7. That so much of it as refers to education he referred to the Committee on Education.

---

good they have already accomplished is incalculable; but we have as yet very imperfectly entered into the work which God has assigned us. New fields are constantly inviting our occupancy, and if we could only properly occupy them, we believe that expansion to an almost illimitable extent is before us. If these missions could receive more of episcopal attention and supervision, it would be an important advantage to them, in more than one respect" (395).

5   For treatment of mission in and bibliography for the Methodist Episcopal Church, South (hereafter MECS), see Robert W. Sledge *"Five Dollars and Myself": The History of Mission of the Methodist Episcopal Church, South, 1845-1939* (New York: General Board of Global Ministries, The United Methodist Church, 2005), vol. 2 of *The United Methodist History of Missions* series. The seven volumes update the four-volume *History of Methodist Missions*. Pertinent to this study are the first three by Wade Crawford Barclay, *Early American Methodism, 1769–1844*, 2 vols. (New York: Board of Missions and Church Extension of the Methodist Church, 1949–50) and vol. 3, *The Methodist Episcopal Church, 1845–1939* (New York: Board of Missions of The Methodist Church, 1957). For an assessment closer to the time, see J. M. Reid, *Missions and Missionary Society of the Methodist Episcopal Church*, 2 vols. (New York: Phillips & Hunt. Cincinnati: Cranston & Stowe, 1879).

8. That so much of it as refers to lay-delegation, and any tendency toward congregationalism, or the weakening of the bond of our general union, be referred to the Committee on the Itinerancy.[6]

The MECS bishops had summoned, and the General Conference had determined to address, the church's missional, formational, and connectional calling. Missions constituted the fourth referral. Formation did for the fifth, sixth, and seventh; and connection for the third and eighth. (The formational and connectional will be addressed in subsequent chapters. Also, the chapter on formation will explore the pivotal role of women in Methodism, minimally treated below.)

The overall tone of the bishop's address was measured and self-critical. It presented a striking vision of/for the Southern church, a remarkable view of the world as within its missional charge, and the commitment to outreach in Africa *and* with its own/*owned* colored

---

6   MECS, *General Conference Journal* v. 4 (1858), 402–03. Previous to the bishops' address, the General Conference had established an operating structure to the programmatic committees of which the episcopal recommendations were then committed.

"John B. McFerrin announced that the book agents purposed to issue, during the session of the Conference, a *Daily Christian Advocate*, in which shall be published the proceedings of the Conference; whereupon, on motion of David R. McAnally, it was:

Resolved, That the General Conference approve the purpose of the Book Agents to publish a Daily Christian Advocate during the present session of the Conference and will give it a hearty support.

On motion of A. L. P. Green,

Resolved, 1. That the following Standing Committees be appointed, to consist of one member from each Annual Conference, and that each delegation appoint its own member on said committees:

1. On Episcopacy.
2. On Itinerancy.
3. On Books and Periodicals.
4. On Boundaries.
5. On Missions.
6. On Revivals.
7. On Sabbath-Schools.
8. On Education.
9. On the Tract Society.

Resolved, 2. That the following committees be appointed by the President: 1. On the claims of the American Bible Society. 2. On Temperance.

Resolved, 3. That a committee be appointed to ascertain from the records the exact vote, in each Annual Conference, on the Alabama and Holston Resolutions, and report to the Conference."

ranks.[7] Devoting almost half of their agenda-setting episcopal address to missions, the bishops balanced the "glory" of their estimate of slave missions with paragraph after paragraph demonstrating that the MECS had distances to go in care of the world. With such a tone, the paragraph prior to the one with which this chapter began briefly noted and called for an Outreach to Native Americans. On that, attention in this study will be given, for both the southern and northern churches, in the chapters on Formation and Connection:

> The missions to the Indians demand our special and earnest atten-
> tion. Much has been done for the salvation and improvement of
> these wandering tribes, for which we are grateful to God. But the
> work is not half accomplished, nor will it be till we can find a more
> abundant supply of efficient and faithful preachers and teachers,
> ready to labor among Indians, if they may but be the means of con-
> verting and saving them.[8]

That the Southern church could rise to such challenges, the bishops were confident. They had set that tone with their opening of the conference.

Fittingly, the General Conference session had convened under the leadership of the venerable senior bishop, once-Yankee, born in Bristol, Maine, Joshua Soule. He began "by reading Colossians 1; called the brethren into singing the 272d hymn—'And are we yet alive?'—and then offering an appropriate and impressive prayer."[9] Doubtless, the men (delegates) gathered would have experienced Paul's word to the Colossians as also to them celebrating their "faith in Christ Jesus" and love "ye have to all the saints":

> For the hope which is laid up for you in heaven, whereof ye heard
> before the word of the truth of the gospel;
>   Which is come unto you, as it is in all the world; and bringeth
> forth fruit, as it doth also in you, since the day ye heard of it, and
> knew the grace of God in truth. (Colossians 1:5-6, KJV)

---

7   On Methodism and slavery, see Donald G. Mathews, *Slavery and Methodism: A Chapter in American Morality, 1780-1845* (Princeton: Princeton University Press, 1965); H. Shelton Smith, *In His Image, But . . . Racism in Southern Religion, 1780–1910* (Durham: Duke University Press, 1972); J. Gordon Melton, *A Will to Choose: The Origins of African American Methodism* (Lanham: Rowman & Littlefield Publishers, 2007); and David Hempton, *Methodism: Empire of the Spirit* (New Haven: Yale University Press, 2005).

8   MECS, *General Conference Journal*, v. 4 (1858), 395.

9   MECS, *General Conference Journal* (1858), 379.

Similarly, for Southern believers who were upset, perhaps frightened, by the national racially driven chaos, Charles Wesley's verse in the hymn proclaimed Christ's guidance:

> And are we yet alive,
> And see each other's face?
> Glory and praise to Jesus give
> For his redeeming grace!
>
> . . . .
>
> What troubles have we seen!
> What conflicts have we passed!
> Fightings without, and fears within,
> Since we assembled last
> . . . .[10]

That hymn would gradually become a standard in conference openings, its selection North and South, in part, driven by the impending and then the actual breakage of civil as well as ecclesial unity.[11] In 1858, General Conference members could sing, hopeful, if not confident, in the Wesley promise to church and state from the following and last verse:

> Then let us make our boast of his redeeming power,
> Which saves us to the uttermost . . .

Southern Methodist church-state coziness was also indicated in that General Conference convened May 1 "in the Hall of the House of Representatives of the Tennessee Legislature, Nashville, Tenn."

---

10   "Part V *For the Society*, Section I, *Meeting*, 466," in *The Works of John Wesley*, The Bicentennial Edition of the Works of John Wesley, Vol 7, A Collection of Hymns for the use of the People called Methodists, Franz Hildebrandt and Oliver A. Beckerlegge, editors (Nashville: Abingdon Press, 1983). See there for the lines omitted from verses 1 and 2 and also verse 3. A note for this hymn affirms, "Ever since JW's later years this has been the opening hymn for the sessions of the British Methodist Conference."

11   On that motivation for the hymn's general adoption, *and* for manifold evidence that the Methodist conferences indeed came quite late to adopt this in conference opening ceremonies, see my "And Are We Yet Alive: A Study in Conference Self-Preoccupation," *Methodist History*, XXXIII (July 1995): 249–61.

Missional Outreach for the MECS

The conference rallied to the bishops' charge and gave substantial attention to mission, in its several aspects and targets, as the following entries
(with beginning pagination) in the 1858 *Journal* show:

INDEX TO THE JOURNAL OF 1858

Missions to Africa, resolutions concerning, 404, 415, 423, 429, 512.
Mission to Central America, or New Granada, 430.[12]

The "Annual Reports" of the Missionary Society of the MECS fed the
business of General Conference.[13] That, for 1855, illustrates the seriousness with which the Southern church took its outreach and on what it
targeted.[14] It dwelt on the then recent death of Bishop William Capers,
indicated what amounts had been raised in successive years since the
organization's founding (1847–1854), reported donations for that year as
$168,931.33, and then covered outreach. It did so under six rubrics:

1. Those in the destitute portions of our regular work.
2. Among the people of color.
3. Among the German population of our own country.
4. Among the Indian tribes.
5. China.
6. (California) the Pacific Annual Conference.

Before turning to each of those outreach agendas, the "Report"
encouraged missions at every level of the church's life, called for a
"monthly concern of prayer for missions," and urged Juvenile Missionary
Societies or Sunday School Mission Societies.[15]

"Missions in the Destitute Portions of the Regular Work"—on multiple
pages, 17–54—reported on outreach by conference, district, and charges.
For the Kentucky Conference and its first missions district, the breakdown
by race, Sunday school membership, and leadership was as follows:

Missions & Missionaries	W. M.	C. M.	Chs S.	Schs	Sch'rs
Highland	300	54	5	5	76
9 other charges	337		1	1	25
TOTALS	637	54	6	6	101

12   MECS, *General Conference Journal* (1858), 599–600.
13   For an overview of Southern Methodism, the place of missions therein, and slavery as
     one of its duties, see the appendix for "William Sasnett of MECS on Missions, 1855."
14   *Tenth Annual Report of the Missionary Society of the Methodist Episcopal Church, South*
     (Louisville, KY: Morton & Griswold, 1855). Here as elsewhere the year of the report has
     depended on what records remained of that organization in the libraries to which I
     had access.
15   *Tenth Annual Report of the Missionary Society*, 2–15.

In the Louisville District of that Conference with nine charges, a similar pattern:

Missions & Missionaries	W. M.	C. M.	Chs S.	Schs	Sch'rs
Louisville	405		4	6	450
Rough Creek	57	3			
TOTALS	973	3	4	7	510

The report on Missions among the People of Color (55–78), lacked Kentucky particulars, as did that for German Missions (79–81). Those for China Missions (109–124) and Pacific Conference (125–26) reported but lacked body counts. Indian Missions (82–108) did include the "Report of Indian Mission Conference" (101–07) by district, many with Indian names. Here are totals for four districts, each with five or more stations:

	Ind.	W.	Col.	Ch.	S. S.	Child.	P
Kansas	240	19	3	6	6	405	135
Cherokee	1359	30	117	7	13	285	
Creek	765	35	54		4	121	80
Choctaw	1206	68	209	4	14	550	235

The Report, of course, included a "Treasurer's Report" and then covered membership in the "Missionary Society of the Methodist Episcopal Church, South," listing two pages of "Life Members" who paid "twenty dollars at a time," about two hundred fifty donors. Twenty pages of donors, individually named, alphabetically and not by conference or district, identified some four thousand Southern givers to the church's outreach.[16]

Similarly, the MECS statistics for 1857–1858 show the MECS to be invested in missional endeavor, as the initial lines in this chapter's opening quotation had proclaimed: "The missions to the slaves of the Southern plantations constitute the most interesting and important field for the missionary operations of the Church, South." Overall, black and white membership had increased, but not Indian numbers (see figure 3).[17]

---

16 *Tenth Annual Report of the Missionary Society*, appendix, i–xx.

17 *Minutes of the Annual Conferences of the Methodist Episcopal Church, South, for the Years 1858–1865* (Nashville, Tenn.: Pub. by John Early for the Methodist Episcopal Church,

GENERAL RECAPITULATION.

CONFERENCES.	Trav. Pr's.	Sup'd Pr's.	Local Pr's.	White Members.	White Prob's.	Colored Members.	Col'd Prob's.	Indian Mem's.	Indian Prob's.	Total M'rs and Mb's.	Increase.	Decrease.
1. Kentucky	61	8	206	15,889	1848	4592	604	......	......	23,228	294	......
2. Louisville	86	11	215	20,001	2007	3745	415	......	......	26,540	1354	......
3. Missouri	84	5	152	15,295	2274	1508	347	......	......	19,725	1551	......
4. St. Louis	103	10	209	19,696	2378	1529	140	......	......	24,065	3256	......
5. Kansas Mission	24	1	11	510	80	18	......	138	......	782	17	......
6. Tennessee	190	10	371	31,111	6228	6868	926	......	......	45,704	3177	......
7. Holston	110	13	402	38,202	6775	2810	632	200	......	50,144	2231	......
8. Memphis	152	5	392	28,069	4084	7102	858	......	......	40,662	244	......
9. Mississippi	124	7	207	14,276	3881	12,013	3642	......	......	34,150	2109	......
10. Louisiana	74	3	112	6632	1736	4091	970	......	......	13,618	......	1098
11. Virginia	174	4	198	34,185	3901	6422	589	......	......	45,473	4743	......
12. Western Virginia	57	3	75	8096	2241	225	70	......	......	10,767	1822	......
13. North Carolina	117	7	192	27,805	3630	11,766	1429	......	......	44,946	......	317
14. South Carolina	150	9	209	32,108	4957	39,720	7929	......	......	84,201	2991	......
15. Georgia	197	26	579	44,513	9250	20,174	4992	......	......	79,831	6424	......
16. Alabama	202	17	536	36,418	9222	18,672	5414	......	......	70,481	4958	......
17. Florida	77	5	124	7891	1694	6459	1289	......	......	17,569	1193	......
18. Texas	130	7	193	10,643	3647	2547	1116	......	......	17,983	3171	......
19. East Texas	80	7	192	10,596	3570	1039	739	......	......	16,843	2049	......
20. Arkansas	53	2	159	9656	2522	865	309	......	......	13,566	1025	......
21. Wachita	66	3	159	7055	2477	1797	665	......	......	12,160	241	......
22. Indian Mission	34	......	55	88	......	251	......	2959	577	3964	......	81
23. Pacific	49	......	38	1457	1210	9	......	......	......	2763	1034	......
Total in 1858	2414	163	4984	419,592	80,102	155,932	32,104	3297	577	699,165	44,884	1496
Total in 1857	2267	167	4907	404,430	62,231	148,525	29,394	3389	467	655,777		
Increase	147		77	15,162	17,871	7407	2710		110	43,388	Net increase.	
Decrease		4						92				

[The transferred preachers are reckoned with those of the Conferences to which they now belong. The six Bishops are not counted. Their addition would make the number of travelling preachers, including those on the superannuated list, 2583. The preachers who located (77) are not counted; on the other hand, the preachers who were admitted on trial, (224,) and those who were readmitted, (58,) are counted among the travelling preachers, though many of them are also reckoned with the local preachers. The members in several charges in the Kentucky Conference, as well as those in China, are not counted, not being officially reported—these would make the total number of ministers and members about 700,000, and the increase about 44,000. The apparent decrease in the North Carolina Conference is accounted for on page 53. We have taken great pains to approximate correctness.]

Figure 3

The body counts, in themselves, do not describe the missional how, where, when, why, and what for. Nevertheless, in the table, the MECS declared its mission, what it was about, who labored, and for whom. The statistics indicate that the MECS leadership—at all levels—thought it imperative to report numbers by office, by membership status (full or probationary), and by race, and to indicate by conference and as a whole whether the church had gained or lost. A drop in Indian members had been offset by gains of probationers. The Kentucky and Louisville conferences boasted no Indian members but had substantial "Col'd" membership.

South, 1846–1923), 92. HathiTrust Digital Library Rights, Public Domain, Google-digitized. Permanent URL https://hdl.handle.net/2027/uiug.30112001348686.

Outreach for the Kentucky Conference

736   *Kentucky Conference, 1857.*

Harrodsburg District.

	White Mem's	White Prob's	Col'd Mem's	Col'd Prob's	Loc'l Pr's
Harrodsburg	116	6	60	20	6
Danville	184	17	193	11	.....
Perryville	358	8	8	.....	4
Lancaster	568	5	64	.....	3
Richmond	122	10	238	10	5
Madison	273	16	122	.....	1
Crab Orchard	185	.....	5	10	2
Somerset	557	46	46	3	18
Salvisa	281	6	110	6	2
Maxville	165	.....	.....	.....	2
	2639	114	846	60	43

Shelbyville District.

	White Mem's	White Prob's	Col'd Mem's	Col'd Prob's	Loc'l Pr's
Shelbyville	170	40	130	20	6
Shelby Circuit	231	26	114	4	.....
Simpsonville	136	2	73	.....	2
Taylorsville	162	9	46	.....	2
Bloomfield	252	13	95	32	1
Lagrange and Westport	163	15	22	.....	.....
Floydsburg	266	6	81	2	2
Newcastle and Bedford	683	35	180	2	9
Lockport	177	36	.....	.....	2
Lawrenceburg	207	.....	27	.....	2
Anderson	143	20	.....	1	1
	2544	202	770	62	27

Covington District.

	White Mem's	White Prob's	Col'd Mem's	Col'd Prob's	Loc'l Pr's
Covington	353	10	18	9	1
Newport	291	22	2	.....	1
Alexandria	400	35	10	.....	6
Falmouth	448	12	66	.....	2
Millersburg	193	.....	115	30	2
Cynthiana	161	6	188	15	1
Carlisle	463	60	15	.....	2
Carrolton	132	2	29	11	.....
Warsaw	98	3	2	.....	1
Owenton & Eagle Creek Miss	343	17	13	8	5
Crittenden	334	36	48	1	9
Burlington	369	.....	.....	.....	4
	3506	193	506	75	34

Maysville District.

	White Mem's	White Prob's	Col'd Mem's	Col'd Prob's	Loc'l Pr's
Maysville	117	3	11	.....	.....
Wash'ton & Germant'n	214	6	65	.....	1
Shannon and Sardis	170	.....	10	.....	2
Minerva	225	12	18	.....	1
Sardis Circuit	279	17	1	.....	1
Orangeburg	155	23	20	6	1
Lewis	268	19	17	3	3
Flemingsburg	377	15	115	4	5
Poplar Plains	561	31	13	3	6
Sharpsburg	168	4	79	6	3
Owingsville	232	25	.....	.....	1
	2706	155	390	23	23

West Liberty District.

	White Mem's	White Prob's	Col'd Mem's	Col'd Prob's	Loc'l Pr's
Pikeville	174	75	.....	7	.....
Prestonsburg	509	86	14	1	5
Jackson Mission	135	.....	2	.....	3
West Liberty Mission	145	10	1	.....	2
Irvine	433	80	20	10	3
Letcher and Perry Miss	230	40	.....	.....	7
Highland Mission	290	30	2	.....	7
	1882	321	39	18	28

Barbourville District.

	White Mem's	White Prob's	Col'd Mem's	Col'd Prob's	Loc'l Pr's
Barbourville and Manchester	198	5	2	.....	7
London Mission	287	50	19	5	4
Yellow Creek Mission	57	5	3	.....	1
Mount Pleasant Mission	190	15	15	.....	6
Williamsburg Mission	190	47	.....	.....	6
Mount Vernon Mission	60	3	1	5	1
	982	125	40	6	20

Recapitulation.

	White Mem's	White Prob's	Col'd Mem's	Col'd Prob's	Loc'l Pr's
Lexington District	2695	112	1935	238	57
Harrodsburg "	2639	114	846	60	43
Shelbyville "	2544	202	770	62	27
Covington "	3506	192	506	75	32
Maysville "	2706	155	390	23	23
West Liberty "	1882	321	39	18	28
Barbourville "	982	125	40	6	25
Total this year	16,585	1221	4626	479	235
Last year	15,850	1985	4859	639	238
Increase	535				
Decrease		764	33	200	3

Ques. 14. What amounts are necessary for the superannuated preachers, and the widows and orphans of preachers, and to make up the deficiencies of those who have not obtained their regular allowance on the circuits?

$3304.

Ques. 15. What has been collected on the foregoing accounts, and how has it been applied?

Collected, $839 00

Applied to superannuated preachers, widows, and orphans.

Ques. 16. What has been contributed for the support of Missions, what for the publication of Tracts and Sunday-school books, and what to aid the American Bible Society and its auxiliaries?

For Missions, $3734 35
" Tracts,   505 10
" Bible Society,   200 50
" Sunday-schools,   635 33

Ques. 17. Where are the preachers stationed this year?

LEXINGTON DISTRICT.

John G. Bruce, P. E.

Lexington, *John H. Linn.*
Frankfort, *John C. Harrison.*
Versailles and Georgetown, *Stephen Noland.*
Nicholasville, *Wm. J. Snively.*
Jessamine and Woodford, *Daniel W. Axline.*
Winchester and Mount Zion, *Henry C. Northcott.*
Vienna, John S. Coxe.
Paris and North Middleton, *Thomas F. Vanmeter.*
Mount Sterling, *Joseph Rand.*
Oxford, Seneca X. Hall.
Leesburg, *William G. Johns.*

HARRODSBURG DISTRICT.

George W. Merritt, P. E.

Harrodsburg, *Edmund P. Buckner.*
Danville, *Lewis G. Hicks.*

Figure 4

As for members and adherents in the several border and slavery-permitting states, Methodists in Kentucky had chosen in 1845 to go with the Methodist Episcopal Church, South. But there as well, critics and proponents of slavery lived uneasily together and found the ecclesial division especially tense close to the Ohio River boundary.[18] Slaveholding Kentucky Methodists did, however, bring "their" colored into the church. The Southern church's Kentucky Conference's sense of its mission—within itself, in outreach to and care for whites and the colored, to the wider world—is best captured as it talked to itself. The raw statistics show the conference's resolve to care for its members. For 1857, Kentucky circuits and stations reported as shown in figure 4.[19]

During the 1850s, the Kentucky Conference (MECS) moved, in various ways, to bring their black members into the fold. In 1850, the *Minutes* indicate "Christopher Garrett (a man of colour) having been duly recommended by the Quarterly Meeting Conf. of the Lexington Station was elected to Deacons Orders."[20]

In 1853, the conference's Committee on Missions submitted a long report, eight pages of the manuscript minutes, signed on behalf of the committee by H. H. Kavanaugh, two years later elected a bishop. Although the mission to California was included, the bulk of the report dealt with the rationale for missions, complaints about the handling of mission money, and the importance of outreach to the state's blacks. It noticed:

> that the statistics of our church show in some charges many more
> blacks than whites—and in some districts the numbers of each are
> nearly equal . . . that in many instances their spiritual interests are
> but nominally cared for. In many cases they are committed to the
> charge of ignorant, and unqualified preachers among themselves.

Continuing in this vein, the report concluded with two observations: 1. "Masters are at times, and in some places opposed to the assembling of large masses of Negroes without the presence of some responsible white man. 2. Masters, whether religious or otherwise, are exceedingly

---

18 For a layman's account of Kentucky life, politics, slave practices, and religious dynamics, see *The Heavens Are Weeping: The Diaries of George Richard Browder*, Richard L. Troutman, editor (Grand Rapids: Zondervan Publishing House, 1987).

19 *Manuscript Minutes of the Kentucky Conference, MECS* (Kentucky Wesleyan, 1857), 289.

20 *Manuscript Minutes of the Kentucky Conference, MECS* (Kentucky Wesleyan, 1850), 247.

anxious to have proper spiritual instruction and pastoral attention afforded their servants."[21]

Five resolutions followed. The first called for the increase of missionary money to $6,000; the second urged the bishop to consider missions to "the portions of interior Kentucky"; a third encouraged conference members to raise the needed money; the fourth called for support from the presiding elders for the cause; and the fifth affirmed "That if the Bishop can [appoint] a missionary or missionaries to the blacks, we will furnish the missionary funds to support them."[22] The conference went on then to recommend division of the $6,000 among the districts.

This came the following year: "Resolved that the subject of the religious instruction of the people of Color be referred to the several Quarterly Conferences of the Circuits and Stations that they may take such action on it as may be desirable."[23] The 1854 conference heard from "Rev. Charles Taylor, M. D. one of our missionaries to China" and decided that the missions cause warranted having the presiding elders constitute the "Committee on Missions."[24] In 1855, the conference recommended seven local preachers for deacon's orders, three of them "a man of color," and four local deacons for elder's orders, three "a man of color."

Bishop Paine took the chair and announced that the white preachers who had been elected to Deacon's orders would be ordained in the Methodist Church on tomorrow (Sabbath) at the close of the services in the forenoon, and that the white Deacons who had been elected to Elder's orders would be ordained in the same place at the close of the services in the afternoon of the same day, and that the colored preachers who had been elected to Deacon's or Elder's orders would be ordained at some suitable time in the African Methodist Church.[25]

In 1856, "A printed letter from E. W. Sehon, Missionary secretary of the M. Episcopal Church, South, was read and placed on file." Sehon reported that the enterprise was in debt, having borrowed $35,000. He

21 *Manuscript Minutes of the Kentucky Conference, MECS* (Kentucky Wesleyan, 1853), 68.
22 *Manuscript Minutes of the Kentucky Conference, MECS* (Kentucky Wesleyan, 1853), 68–70. The wording in square brackets is unclear.
23 *Manuscript Minutes of the Kentucky Conference, MECS* (Kentucky Wesleyan, 1853), 112.
24 *Manuscript Minutes of the Kentucky Conference, MECS* (Kentucky Wesleyan, 1854), 132, 142.
25 *Manuscript Minutes of the Kentucky Conference, MECS* (Kentucky Wesleyan, 1855), 204–05.

urged efforts on the missionary cause by the "pulpit and press," called attention to resolutions "adopted by the Bishops and Board at their last annual meeting," noted their importance as they determined "the specific amount of missionary money appropriated within the bounds of each Conference—how *much* to destitute white and how *much* to colored missions," indicated that the missions cause called for organization, support, and reporting, and finally suggested the amounts to be appropriated to each conference: $18,000 (SC), $14,000 (GA), $14,000 (Indian Mission), $13,000 (AL), . . . $1,700 (KY) . . . $1,400 (Holston).[26]

In 1857, the statistics summary, as usual (see above), counted the white and colored members, probationers, and local preachers. For the first time, the *Minutes* indicated by charge and district the numbers of white and colored Sabbath School "Scholars." For the Lexington District, the numbers were 658 white and 280 black, *but for Lexington* 130 and 90, respectively. Harrodsburg's ratio was 403:30; Maysville's ratio was 379:40; and one or two in the other districts. The conference's Scholar totals were Whites, 3,316, and Colored, 357.[27] In its report, the Sabbath School Committee was generally upbeat, judging "Many of the Sabbath-schools are in a flourishing condition," others acceptable, and "all are in a state [of] progress."[28] As we will note below, the Ohio and Cincinnati conferences, though counting the "Scholars," did not report any black "Scholars" or teachers.

Among its final actions, the conference dealt with a memorial from the Alabama Conference calling for striking the General Rule that prohibits "the buying and selling of men, women, and children with an intention to enslave them." A committee recommended non-concurrence; it was put to vote, the names of voters recorded, with 43 for and 18 against non-concurrence.[29]

Ironic, perhaps, given its overall missional commitments and actions, the conference voted "That hereafter we dispense with the Annual Sermons on Mission and the Ministry."[30] To that point, as we noted earlier, the Kentucky Conference had named three members, with alternates, to preach the Ministry, Education, and Missions sermons for the following year.

---

26 *Manuscript Minutes of the Kentucky Conference, MECS* (Kentucky Wesleyan, 1856), 241 ff.
27 *Manuscript Minutes of the Kentucky Conference, MECS* (Kentucky Wesleyan, 1857), 282–89.
28 *Manuscript Minutes* (1857), 298–99.
29 *Manuscript Minutes* (1857), 299–300.
30 *Manuscript Minutes* (1857), 298.

Southern Methodist Women

Males constituted the members of the Kentucky Conference and of the MECS General Conference, as with Northern annual and general conferences. The men at conference stayed, slept, ate in, and talked within the homes of the Methodists in the hostess city. The women of Methodism counted as providers of room, bed, meal, and listening ears for bishops, presiding elders, and conference members. Methodist women voiced and shared their faith, of course, in love feasts, class meetings, and especially in Sunday schools. By the 1850s, the Southern as well as the Northern church had established journals, which spoke to and for women, and sometimes gave them voice. The MEC, as we will indicate below, launched *The Ladies' Repository* in 1841, in Cincinnati. Over a decade later, the MECS launched its own serial. At the 1858 General Conference, the Committee on Books and Periodicals began one of its reports—that dealing with the church's papers and magazines—attending to outreach to Southern homes:

> *The Home Circle*—This monthly is generally approved, and is, so far as it has extended its circulation, a popular work. Yet your committee regret that it has not been more highly appreciated by the Church generally. It should have at least twenty thousand subscribers. Being the only periodical especially designed for the female members and friends of our Church in the South, it should find a broad and untrammelled circulation. Your committee recommend its continuance, with the hope it will in future be more highly appreciated.

> *The Sunday-School Visitor*—This excellent child's paper should have fifty thousand subscribers. Your committee regret, however, that many Methodist families and communities do not extend to it a more liberal patronage. Your committee regard it as an indispensable publication and recommend its continuance.[31]

Southern women, like their MEC counterparts, served as hostesses and exercised their home-based leadership, doubtless with even greater subtlety and with regionally nuanced, interactive gestures: nodding, smiling, frowning, or stepping out of the room or away from the table. They

---

31 *Journal of the General Conference of the Methodist Episcopal Church, South,* v. 4 (1858), 493.

gained a connectional medium in 1855 with *The Home Circle: A Monthly Periodical Devoted to Religion and Literature*. The Rev. L. D. Huston served as editor[32] and produced, elicited, or accepted material that must have appealed to women as well as men. It apparently lasted up to the Civil War, appeared monthly, and delivered six hundred+ pages each year for Southern men, and at least some women, to peruse.[33] An entry in the October 1860 *Quarterly Review of the Methodist Episcopal Church, South* sought just such readership:

> THE HOME CIRCLE. L. D. BOSTON, D.D., Editor. Nashville: Southern Methodist Publishing House. $2. The September number contains a good likeness of our excellent friend, Col. Chambers, and the usual supply of reading matter. The Agent has been devising liberal things for the next year. Let the ladies give it a deserving patronage—why not twenty thousand subscribers?[34]

The names of the Northern and Southern journals indicated something of what the respective general conferences and their male editors thought women would and should read. More so than *The Ladies' Repository, The Home Circle* divided its attention between purposes conveyed by its title and subtitle. A regular feature of each month's issue was what could be a dozen or so pages listed under the "Editorial Department." An array of single articles was spread throughout the volume, well described by their titles: The Centre-Table, The Closet, The Garden, the Key-Basket,

---

32 "General Conference Periodicals and Editors—The General Book Agent shall publish a Quarterly Review, to be called the 'Quarterly Review of the Methodist Episcopal Church, South;' a monthly magazine, to be called 'The Home Circle;' a child's paper, to be called the 'Sunday-School Visitor;' and a weekly newspaper, to be called 'The Christian Advocate.' There shall be an editor of books and tracts, who shall also be editor of the Quarterly Review; an editor of the Home Circle, who, shall also be editor of the Sunday-School Visitor; and an editor of the Christian Advocate, all whom shall be elected by the General Conference. VI. Newspapers and Editors—1. The General Conference shall also elect, quadrennially, an editor for each of the following weekly papers, to Wit: the Richmond Christian Advocate, . . ." (MECS *General Conference Journal* [1858], 497).

33 *The Home Circle: A Monthly Periodical Devoted to Religion and Literature* (Nashville: E. Stevenson & F.A. Owen for the Methodist Episcopal Church, South, [1855–57]). HathiTrust Digital Library, Permanent URL: https://hdl.handle.net/2027/njp.32101074718287.

34 *The Quarterly Review of the Methodist Episcopal Church, South*, n. s., v. 14 (Louisville, Ky: Published by John Early for the Methodist Episcopal Church, South, 1860), 620. HathiTrust Digital Library, https://hdl.handle.net/2027/nyp.3343308227451. Other similar, brief endorsements occurred in the January and July *Quarterly Review* issues, pp. 140, 463.

The Library, The Sick Room, and The Toilette. The contents pages for 1855 listed pages for the topics as follows:

> The Centre-Table, 37, 83, 130, 177, 228, 276, 322, 371, 418, 466, 614, 663; The Closet, 89, 150, 187, 282, 332, 429, 523; The Garden, 46, 140, 189, 235, 284, 331, 381, 477, 522, 567; The Key-Basket, 42, 137, 180, 281, 379, 473, 621, 668; The Library, 40, 94, 141, 191, 237, 289, 336, 382, 430, 479, 627, 669; The Sick-Room, 328, 427; The Toilette, 91, 474.[35]

In 1857, an additional category was added, "The Poultry Yard," its contents even more expressly filled with content appealing to women.

The Home Circle

Over its brief pre–Civil War years, *The Home Circle* increasingly reached out to and sought to engage women. It did so with these rather direct communications in the "Editorial Department." It did so with regular articles and the overall feel, as will be shown in the Connection and Formation chapters. And it did so graphically, with pictures and depictions serving as frontispieces for each month's issue. In 1855, *The Home Circle* depicted a woman for only one of the twelve months. Entitled "My Wedding," it would be used in subsequent years. In 1856, five women's depictions appeared, along with a Resurrection scene with three women and a guard. In 1857, Bishop Early's picture served as frontispiece of the volume. Eight more men, including other bishops, appeared, but eight women as well (some months featuring two pictures).

The Home Circle: A Monthly Periodical Devoted to Religion and Literature lived into its subtitle, offered outreach, and reached out in bidding women further into the world with articles that ranged through time, across the world, over an array of topics, into various genres, and with serious as well as light-hearted content. The A–D entries for 1856 illustrate that range:

> A Camp-meeting Sermon by Bishop George, 661; A Character which some one else has taken a Pen to, 100; A Dumb Sunday, 671; A Mother's Portrait, 595, 647; A Sketch from Life, 66; A Sketch from Real Life, 373; A Sketch with a Moral, 675; A Valedictory Address, 310; Advice to a Young Husband, 376; American Poets, 665; An Auto da Fe before Philip I, 208; Artificial Light, 439; Astronomical Discovery, 288; Athenian Houses and Entertainments, 78, 122; Autumn Loaves,

35 *The Home Circle*, 1 (1855): Table of Contents, no page number.

15, 73, 102, 167, 205, 282, 322, 409, 458, 521, 601, 637; Bascom's Lectures on Infidelity, 100; Beautiful Extract, 327; Belshazzar's Feast, 159; Benjamin Northcutt, 667; Bishop Asbury, 632; Brilliancy and Vigor of Christian Experience, 69; Buncombe, 309; Campbell's "Exile of Erin", 573; Character of Bishop M'Kendree, 63; Characters that I have taken a Pen to, 1, 60, 106, 162, 301, 377, 449; Chatsworth, 6; Christian Fortitude, 643; Christmas Evans, 219; Coronation of Charles II, 211; Croakings about Music, 200; Dante's Paradise, 214; Death of Queen Mary, 107; Declaration of Independence: New Version, 513; Don John of Austria, 653; Dr. William Sherlock, 328; Dress, No. II, 48; Dust.[36]

For a journal geared for *The Home Circle*, for women as well as men, it dealt out serious fare. That invitation to the larger world is indicated in the array of biographical treatments. That for Bishop Asbury is short. "The Character of Bishop M'Kendree" extends over five pages and had been crafted by his surviving colleague, no less than Bishop Soule.

An even longer essay, on "Slavery," appeared in the February issue of that volume.[37] Close to five thousand words and extending over six pages, it ranged over the Atlantic and over time to portray slavery, not abolition, as the humane way to bring Africans into civilization. Reflecting on travels through Domingo, the author proclaimed:

> I believe, and must not hesitate to confess my belief, the negro race is incapable of self-government; and I suspect its present condition in the United States is practically the best that the character of the negroes admits of. It is for their happiness and interest to remain in tutelage—at any rate for two or three generations. Is there any part of Africa, the West Indies, or South America, where three millions of negroes are to be found as comfortable, intelligent, and religious, or as happy, as in the Southern States? The most practical mode of improving a semi-barbarous race is to place it in the proportion of one to two in the midst of a civilized people.[38]

"The Pious Slave," taken "From Confessions of an Infidel. By Rev. John Bayley," struck a different tone, crediting "a colored man, bowed down with the infirmities of age," as responding to a plea from his mistress, praying

---

36 *The Home Circle*, 2 (1856): Contents, iii.
37 *The Home Circle*, 2 (1856): 274–80. The essay, at least in part, drew from *From Letters from the United States, Cuba, and Canada. By the Hon. Amelia M. Muray. New York: G. P. Putnam & Co.*, which is footnoted.
38 *The Home Circle*, 2 (1856): 274–80.

for his "master . . . at the very point of death," and effecting the latter's cure and conversion.[39]

The latter short entry typified the tone of the strikingly infrequent attentions to slavery and slaves in the years that *The Home Circle* spoke to Southern women, increasingly, if gradually so. Here follow the D–I entries for 1857:

> Death of Aunt Molly, 673; Deaths of Little Children, 732; Difficulties of Alpine Climbing, 540, 588, 660; Dreams—Visions—Second-Sight, 665; Eleanor Maywood's Waking Dream, 728; European Impressions, 525, 648, 705; Extravagance and Economy, 237; Father Webb's Talk In Class-Meeting, 551; Female Education, 553; Female Pioneers of Methodism, 120; Flowers, 215; George Crabbe, 668; Going to Paris, 166; Her Silence Saved Me, 347; Human Longevity, 231; Impressions of the Sandwich Islands, 175; Indian Women, 221; "I wouldn't be a Preacher's Wife," . . .[40]

The Home Circle invited its readers to outreach doubtless mapped by gender. Women could mourn at the "Death of Aunt Molly" and "Deaths of Little Children." The men might travel for "Alpino Climbing," aspire to "Going to Paris," or revel in "Impressions of the Sandwich Islands." Outreach pointed to different, quite different for some, prospects for Southern white men, white women, and slaves. Southern Methodism counted bodies.

The Ladies' Repository

From its base operation in Cincinnati, Ohio, Northern Methodism published in various genres catering to women and women's life, concerns, and work (see, e.g., appendix for "Poetry on Race—*The Ladies' Repository*—1858"). The long, long "Report of the Book Agents at Cincinnati" provided readers of the 1860 *Journal of General Conference* with statistics on "Circulation of Periodicals at the Close of 1859." Most of the offerings below, save perhaps for the modestly subscribed-to *Quarterly Review*, served home or Sunday school on a weekly or monthly basis. The book agents reported the following, with gains in readership indicated (as reported) with the second figure:[41]

---

39 *The Home Circle*, 2 (1856): 464.
40 *The Home Circle*, 3 (1857): iii.
41 *Journal of the General Conference of the Methodist Episcopal Church, Held in Buffalo, NY,* 1860, Rev. William Harris, DD., Editor (New York: Carlton & Porter, 1860), also accessed

From Cincinnati—
Western Christian Advocate 31,000; 2,282
Ladies' Repository 33,400; 3,820
Sunday School Advocate 80,509; 49,317
Missionary Advocate 6,000; 945
Good News 6,500
Quarterly Review 625; 183
Christian Apologist 9,166; 2,199
Sunday School Bell 12,000
From St. Louis—
Central Christian Advocate 8,016
From Chicago—
Northwestern Christian Advocate 13,300; 3,267
Ladies' Repository 8,200; 1,000
Sunday School Advocate 36,500; 23,200
Quarterly Review 510; 292
Missionary Advocate 6,700; 3,700
Good News 6,500

With more than forty thousand subscriptions and doubtless even larger readership, *Ladies' Repository*,[42] like its Southern counterpart, catered to women and men across the connection. However, both its main and subtitle differed in interesting and telling ways from those in *The Home Circle*. The later-launched Southern journal had inverted those of the *Repository—A Monthly Periodical, Devoted to Literature and Religion*. Literature indeed constituted the regular and dominant fare.

Nor did the *Repository* coop up its ladies by garden fence or household doors; nothing like *The Home Circle*'s The Centre-Table, The Closet, The Garden, the Key-Basket, The Library, The Sick Room, and The Toilette. The *Repository*, in its articles, but especially in its "Editor's Repository," differed radically from its Southern counterpart. The latter provided its women the following typical array of subsections: Scripture Cabinet; Notes and Queries; Items, Literary, Scientific, and Religious; Literary Notices; New York Literary Correspondence; Sideboard for Children; An Editorial Paper;

---

online with HathiTrust Digital Library, Permanent URL: https://hdl.handle.net/2027/wu.89077109460, 350.

42 *The Ladies' Repository: A Monthly Periodical, Devoted to Literature and Religion*, vol. XVIII (1858), Edited by Rev. D. W. Clark, D. D. (Cincinnati: L. Swormstedt and A. Poe [also New York, Chicago, and Boston], 1858). HathiTrust Digital Library. Permanent URL: https://hdl.handle.net/2027/nyp.33433104825652.

and Editor's Table. In many months, but not January, the *Repository* also offered "Mirror of Apothegm, Wit, Repartee, and Anecdote."

In the January *Repository*, each of the above received two pages of entries. A page, with its two columns, provided much for women to peruse. The two columns of the first page of the three-page "Literary Notices" for August gave readers over a thousand words to ponder. One of the shorter entries sounded an anti-slavery note that could be *heard* over a hundred times in that year's issues:

> *Aunt Sally; or, the Cross the Way of Freedom*, published by the same, is a narrative of the slave life and purchase of the mother of Rev. Isaac Williams, a Methodist preacher in Detroit, Michigan. This is one of those narratives that will implant in the heart of the young an implacable hatred of the system of slavery. It is an unveiling of real life in bondage. 18mo. 216 pp.[43]

A longer item, a review of close to five hundred words, offered Methodist women equally serious fare. Here are lines from the beginning and ending of that critical assessment:

> *The Source of Power; or, The Philosophy of Moral Agency.* By Rev. S. Comfort, M.A. [Since the publication of this work Mr. C. has received the degree of Doctor of Divinity from the Ohio Wesleyan University.] 16mo. Pp. 416. New York: Carlton & Porter.—Doctor Comfort's book is not happily named. What is meant by "The Source of Power" we are not certain that we have been able to discover, and after having gone through the book we are satisfied that the second part of the title is a sufficient, and the only appropriate index to the contents. The volume treats of "the nature and grounds of man's original and present moral agency." . . .
>
> Dr. Comfort reviews and defends the old, exploded, scholastic idea of an Eternal Now, and insists that in the divine Being, it is correlate to an "Immense Here," as he names the idea of ubiquity; that God's knowledge embraces eternity in the same defensible sense that his presence fills space. The concluding chapter treats of man as a moral agent under Divine and human governments. The book is thoughtful and suggestive, and will interest and profit men, of whatever name, who are inclined to metaphysical subjects. Even

---

43 *The Ladies' Repository*, 18 (1858): 502. The publisher referenced was The: American Reform Tract and Book Society.

those readers who do not accede to all of Dr. Comfort's views, will
still recognize the honesty and ability with which he presents and
elaborates them.[44]

Such serious entries occurred in much of the Editor's Repository except
for the occasional "Mirror of Apothegm, Wit, Repartee, and Anecdote."
"Scripture Cabinet" and "The "Sideboard for Children" could be descriptive, reflective, instructional, or meditative. In the February issue, the
"Sideboard" began:

> WE give space again to the talk of the little ones. If any of our read-
> ers think it is not worthy of their attention, they can pass over the
> page. That is by no means an enviable moral or intellectual condi-
> tion, when the lively prattle, sparkling wit, and quaint expressions
> of a bright little child have no charm for us. In the spontaneous
> outgushings of its little thoughts, childhood often suggests the
> gravest and profoundest lessons to age and experience. We must
> not always expect wisdom, or gravity, or even the strict proprieties
> of expression in them. . . .

In the second of the notes from readers, a child offered the following
spiritual guidance:

> *Don't Like Them Preachers.*—"Little Bell" is three years old. When
> praying she sometimes begins to rise without saying amen, but
> she soon thinks of it and says, "O, I forgot!" then kneeling again she
> says very seriously, "Amen." A few days ago two ministers visited
> her father; when they were gone she said, "Ma, I don't like them
> preachers." "Why, Bell?" "Because they didn't talk to me." One eve-
> ning she seemed quite thoughtful, and, as her mother was prepar-
> ing her for bed, all at once she said, "Ma, why can't we go where
> God is?" J. A. P.[45]

Similarly, other portions of the *Repository* could range, month to
month, in the topics or concerns to which they gave attention. For example, the May "Items, Literary, Scientific, and Religious" devoted paragraphs
of various length to the following notices:

---

44 *The Ladies' Repository*, 18 (1858): 502.
45 *The Ladies' Repository*, 18 (1858): 123.

- Drs. M'Clintock and Strong
- The Baltimore Christian Advocate
- Death of Rev. Dr. Cook
- Signification of Ladies Names
- Origin of Meteoric Bodies
- Hypothesis Respecting the Solar Spots
- Atmosphere in Dwelling-Houses
- Facts for Growers of Wheat
- Cultivation of the Peach
- The Pitcairn Islanders
- Telegraphing Storms
- Life of Bishop Asbury
- Public Schools in Maine
- Maine Wesleyan Seminary and Female College
- Bishop of Africa

The first entry celebrated the forthcoming *Cyclopedia of Biblical, Theological, and Ecclesiastical Literature*. The second, and longest, noticed a new Methodist paper and worried that it might deviate from "the old Methodistic antislavery platform." The last acclaimed the MEC's first black bishop:

> *Bishop for Africa.*—The Liberia annual conference, at its late session, elected the Rev. Francis Burns bishop, subject to the provisions made by the last General conference. Mr. Burns has long been one of our prominent missionaries in Africa and has been for several years superintendent of the mission. The redemption of Africa is to be effected by the instrumentality of the colored race; and we are glad that our work in Liberia can be safely committed to the superintendence of a colored man as bishop.[46]

The attention here to the *Repository*'s attention to race and slavery should not be taken as indicating that it dominated the journal. Although editor D. W. Clark, D.D. had sprinkled notices, articles, and even verse (see the appendix for "Poetry on Race—*The Ladies' Repository*—1858") on that concern throughout, he stayed the journal's course and ranged the 1858 *Repository* over an incredible array of topics, issues, biographies (current and earlier), reviews, information, and inspirational matters. Women figured as topics, as poets, as authors. The following are illustrative:

46 *The Ladies' Repository*, 18 (1858): 307–08.

Literary Women of America. Number XII. Mrs. Harriett Beecher Stowe. By the Editor. 171–74

The "Five Points" Mission, by Rev. N. Mead, Missionary. 200–02

The Imprisoned Mind, by Imogen Mercein. 212–16

Passages in the Life of a Country Pastor, by Ellen Bligh [4-part essay]. 297–300; 326–29; 401–04; 729–33

Methodism and the Moravians, by Rev. A. Stevens, LL. D. [3-part essay]. 333–36; 392–95; 460–63

Florence Nightingale: Editorial. 358–64

Mrs. Elizabeth Fry. First Paper by Imogen Mercein. 417–29

Female Philanthropy. Second Paper by Imogen Mercein. 477–80

Mrs. Garrett, Founder of the Garrett Biblical Institute: Editorial 427–30

Note that the 1858 *Repository* carried three articles by Imogen Mercein. Further, one of the "Literary Notices" for September reported on articles in the most recent *Methodist Quarterly* (for July), among them, "Faith, the Everlasting Bond," by Miss Imogen Mercein. Then "Notices" commented: "It is a rather novel thing for a *lady* contributor to appear in the Quarterly. We are glad to see Miss Mercein here and hope this article will be followed by many more from the same prolific pen."[47]

Articles by and about women appeared far, far less frequently than the above selection might suggest, but the *Repository*, in the range of its essays and variety of matters covered, clearly catered to readership signaled by its title. Further, these entries cannot do justice to the range of topics covered and to the way in which it bid Methodist women out of the domestic and into the political, literary, economic, and ethical. In a couple of years, into just such wider world endeavor, the Civil War and later temperance would invite them.

Now available online, the *Repository* lasted four decades with a national and substantial readership. It lost its first editor, L. L. Hamline, in 1844, when he was elected to the episcopacy. Under similar able leadership, it drew submissions from all levels of Methodist life. The journal reached *out* to Methodist women, but its outreach doubtless invited others *into* the fold.

---

47 *The Ladies' Repository*, 18 (1858): 569.

Missional Outreach in the Northern Church

The *Thirty-Ninth Annual Report of the Missionary Society of the Methodist Episcopal Church* reported for the society's 1857 meeting, listing officers, managers, and standing committees for 1858. The MEC's seven bishops, of course, were listed first as both officers and managers. Among the officers, a who's who for the Northern church and its publishing enterprises, were Nathan Bangs, Abel Stevens, John M'Clintock, Daniel Wise, J. B. Wakely, James Porter, and J. P. Durbin as corresponding secretary.[48]

The committees indicated the Society's horizons, agenda, and duties: Auditing, Legacy, Finance, Estimating, and Publishing cared for the business of missions. Domestic, Foreign Population, and Indian, then African, China, Pacific and Island, Spanish, India & Turkey, and Western European indicated horizons. Not included in the Society's outreach, at least as it surveyed missionary endeavor, were American black populations. The Indian Missions, by contrast, were specific as to conference responsibility and people to be reached: Oneida Conference—Oneidas and Onondagas; Black River Conference—St. Regis Mission.; Genesee Conference—Senecas; Wisconsin Conference—Oneidas; Detroit Conference; Michigan Conference, Kansas and Nebraska Conference.[49]

German Domestic Missions—the next mission covered—noted the spread of that outreach in nine annual conferences, with two or three districts in each. Also mentioned were Scandinavian Domestic Missions, Welsh Domestic Missions, French Domestic Missions, and English Domestic Missions, a cute way of putting the rest of American Methodism into missionary targets. "This class of missions," it observed, "is at present the most valuable of all our missions, in the estimation of many of our most intelligent brethren."[50]

A section of the report covering "The Providential Rise of Our Missions" provided an overview of the Society's history and its various missions. Among matters discussed were African Missions, noting the spawning role of the American Colonization Society, recognizing the purposes for which that Society operated, and positing that "it is not within our present purpose to inquire whether this project was justifiable; but

---

48 *Thirty-Ninth Annual Report of the Missionary Society of the Methodist Episcopal Church* (New York: Printed for the Society, 1858).

49 MEC, *Thirty-Ninth Annual Report of the Missionary Society*, 80–89.

50 MEC, *Thirty-Ninth Annual Report of the Missionary Society*, 90.

simply to show how our missions in Western Africa arose." That report then recalled MEC missions, especially that of Melville R. Cox.[51]

Organizing the whole church for missions—from the bishops out to each and every circuit or station, and from preachers down to children—required constituting "Sunday-School Missionary Societies" and adopting the then primary mode of fundraising. So the report charged:

> In every principal Church the whole Sunday should be devoted to the missionary cause. A sermon in the morning, followed by collection and subscriptions; a conversational missionary meeting, or a Sunday school or juvenile missionary society anniversary at three o'clock, collection and subscriptions continued; and a formal missionary meeting, or a sermon in the evening, and collection and subscriptions concluded. Experience has shown that the giving the whole Sunday in this way to the missionary case is not only best for the funds, but for the spirit and life of the Church also. In this case, the committee should invite help to their pastor.[52]

The report required ninety-six pages. Eighty additional pages surveyed the results and other mechanisms for funding outreach. Specified were receipts from the annual conferences, individual donors, and then the big givers.[53] Patrons had given $500, and the list included a few names at the bottom as "Patrons on account of valuable services rendered the Missionary Society." Among the six named was the Rev. Dr. N. Bangs. Life Directors had contributed $150. Life Members were "Constituted in 1856, by the payment of twenty dollars at one time" and Life Members for 1857 similarly.[54]

How much had come in? For what had that money been expended? And for whom? The budget overview indicated the limits on outreach. In the appropriations for 1858, Foreign—benefiting the countries identified above ($60,081); Domestic—including Germans, "foreign" populations in the US, English speaking, under the care of the several conferences, and Indians ($125,812.50). The Society's other, namely operating, expenses came to $75,000.

---

51   MEC, *Thirty-Ninth Annual Report of the Missionary Society,* 21–22.
52   MEC, *Thirty-Ninth Annual Report of the Missionary Society,* 34–35.
53   MEC, *Thirty-Ninth Annual Report of the Missionary Society,* index, 65–68.
54   MEC, *Thirty-Ninth Annual Report of the Missionary Society,* index, 68–70, 71–73, 74–79.

Unnamed? African Americans did not figure in the Missionary Society of the Methodist Episcopal Church's outreach or, at least, in whom it counted.

The following year, 1859, the Society celebrated its "Fortieth Anniversary." "After devotional services, led by Rev. William Livesey, the corresponding secretary, in the absence of the Treasurer, made a verbal statement of the financial condition of the society..."

> Bishop Janes, after excellent singing by the choir, addressed the audience on the essential elements of the missionary cause, showing that every legitimate movement of the Church at home, as well as abroad, was really missionary.
>
> Dr. Crooks followed, after singing by the choir, on *Our missions in Western Europe*, particularly in Germany....
>
> Dr. Haven followed Dr. Crooks, having for his topic *Our missions in the East*....
>
> [T]he Corresponding Secretary made a few remarks on the sudden rise and expansion of our missions, and the great extent of the work at home and abroad.[55]

In 1860, the first major speaker, the Rev. F. H. Newhall of New England, reported on missions to Africa and among Africans, focusing on efforts among the Hottentots of South Africa. They represented "a second species of our race ... yet by the power of the Gospel they are redeemed and saved." He continued:

> Another paradox on the continent of Africa we now call your attention to. We have presented to us the offers of Christianity, with the uplifted Christian hands, standing face to face with the greatest enemy of Africa's reformation. When we look at the foreign slave-trade, it seems as if all hell had disgorged itself for the accomplishment of its evil purpose. We have the slave-dealer with his work of death, and the missionary offering life to save their souls. While we sympathize with the poor victims of the slave-trade, we see that by an over-ruling Providence these victims have become the commencement of a colony on the coast of Africa, and we now have African Churches.[56]

---

55 *Fortieth Annual Report of the Missionary Society of the Methodist Episcopal Church* (New York: Printed for the Society, 1859), 1–8.

56 *Forty-First Annual Report of the Missionary Society of the Methodist Episcopal Church* (New York: Printed for the Society, 1860), 13–15.

Bishop Matthew Simpson,[57] Methodism's "Pope," and to gain national papal status for his funeral rites for Abraham Lincoln, continued in that vein, asking, can heathen be converted? He identified three challenges or trials. The first were differences of language and dialects. Second, the "trial" of addressing challenges as "among the Hottentots and South Sea Islanders; among the savage cannibals." He touted successes with "the Indians of our own country, and the Africans, among whom were some of the lowest and most degraded of our race." "A third point is to enlist such nations as can best aid us in sending the Gospel to the heathens. And has not our Church done this in her missions among the Germans in this country and in Europe?" He then went on about other missions, including Europe and America as peopled through and by missions, mentioning the Pilgrims. "The downfall of the missionary spirit," he concluded, "would be the downfall of the Church and the downfall of the world. There is but one imperative duty resting on Methodism. We have no restrictive creed. We can offer salvation to all; our system is adapted to the wants of the world."[58]

The Southern church's white leadership included blacks in their missionary visions and membership counts but defended slavery as a system. The Northern church, as will be shown below, tracked the steps of its Missionary Society, gradually backing away from expulsion of blacks through colonization, spoke more decisively against slavery as a system, did little missionizing of black neighbors, and just about ignored those who had joined the church.

---

57   On Simpson, see Darius L. Salter, *"God Cannot Do Without America": Matthew Simpson and the Apotheosis of Protestant Nationalism* (Wilmore, KY: First Fruits Press, 2017).

58   *Forty-First Annual Report of the Missionary Society*, 16–18.

Outreach, Missions, and Racial Counting in the MEC

GENERAL RECAPITULATION.

Page	CONFERENCE.	NUMBER OF MEMBERS.					Total Memb'z	No. OF PREACHERS.			
		Whites Mem.	Whites Pro.	Colored Mem.	Colored Pro.	Ind		Trav.	Sup.	Local	Total.
413	Baltimore	46,620	6,433	14,779	1,023	....	68,855	251	25	303	579
419	Philadelphia	36,668	5,031	8,406	532	....	50,637	166	6	319	491
427	Providence	11,940	2,059	....	....	....	13,999	114	19	86	219
430	New-Jersey	27,594	5,435	641	....	....	33,670	159	10	194	363
437	New-England	11,459	1,782	....	....	....	13,641	113	27	80	220
440	New-York	22,609	4,002	255	2	....	26,868	168	8	132	308
447	New-Hampshire	8,107	1,016	....	....	....	9,123	82	19	80	181
450	New-York East	19,022	2,346	....	....	....	21,368	134	16	109	259
455	Troy	22,640	2,996	....	....	....	25,636	197	16	140	353
461	Western Virginia	12,202	1,597	382	....	....	14,181	55	....	119	174
463	Vermont	7,079	770	....	....	....	7,849	69	13	58	140
465	Pittsburg	31,429	3,864	118	....	....	35,411	165	15	213	393
471	Black River	15,838	2,566	....	....	....	18,404	120	12	141	273
474	Wisconsin	6,205	1,796	6	....	169	8,176	75	5	184	264
477	East Maine	8,342	1,678	....	....	....	10,020	69	14	62	145
480	Maine	9,654	1,354	....	....	....	11,008	88	19	91	198
483	Erie	18,852	2,553	45	8	....	21,458	137	19	210	366
486	Rock River	14,035	3,094	19	....	....	17,078	107	....	253	360
490	North Ohio	24,325	3,108	26	1	....	27,460	140	13	250	403
494	Oneida	23,639	3,137	....	....	....	26,776	180	25	194	399
499	Iowa	9,183	1,897	15	....	....	11,095	62	....	134	196
501	East Genesee	15,769	1,941	....	....	....	17,710	121	16	148	285
504	North Indiana	25,598	4,782	10	7	....	30,397	137	12	279	428
508	Missouri	4,262	790	197	....	225	5,474	51	....	86	137
510	Michigan	14,377	1,912	....	....	638	16,927	128	11	182	321
513	Ohio	58,116	6,474	324	22	....	64,936	283	11	482	776
520	Genesee	9,860	881	....	....	....	10,741	91	5	118	214
524	Illinois	26,784	5,058	27	....	....	31,869	160	9	483	652
529	Indiana	31,747	5,874	177	....	....	37,798	141	7	290	438
534	Liberia Mission	....	....	882	235	....	1,117	14	....	....	14
	Total this year,	574,355	86,156	26,309	1,830	1,032	689,682	3,777	352	5,420	9,549

White Mem. & Prob., 660,511; Col'd.,'28,136; Ind., 1,032; total 689,682.   Of Preachers,.....9,549
Total of Members last year,...................................662,315.   Of Preachers,....9,138
Increase this year,................Members and Probationers, 27,367........Preachers, 411

Figure 5

Counting the bodies had been, and to this day remains, a Wesleyan inheritance. The first American gathering of preachers, that in 1773, ended its *Minutes* with "Quest. 2. *What numbers are there in the Society?*[59] The Southern church proclaimed its mission by detailing numbers, leadership status, and race. By contrast, conferences in the Northern church ended their racial counts in the 1850s. The denominational level, in 1850, the last year the MEC published its membership by race, boasted far fewer black and Indian members. That General Recapitulation shows that Baltimore, Philadelphia, *and* Liberia had the largest black counts and Wisconsin, Michigan, and Missouri the Indian members (figure 5).[60]

---

59   *Minutes of the Methodist Conferences, annual held in America from 1773 to 1784, inclusive* (Philadelphia, 1795), 5–7. Reproduced in *Methodist Experience in America: A Sourcebook*, 56–57.

60   *Minutes of the Annual Conferences of the Methodist Episcopal Church, for the years, 1846–1851*, vol. IV (New York: Carlton & Phillips, 1854), 540 (1850).

The Northern conferences' black membership reflected, in part, over-all racial patterns. Again, note that Baltimore and Philadelphia boasted over 24,000 of the 28,000 "Colored" members.

Methodists from the middle Atlantic had flooded Ohio. Methodist-friendly, by selecting lay-preacher Edward Tiffin as its first governor, the state had labored from its launch to inhibit blacks from settling. Its orga-nizing convention and later General Assembly passed various acts dis-couraging in-migration and severely limiting citizenship rights of those who succeeded. The black population in 1800 numbered 337, whites 45,365. By 1820, the ratio was 4,723 to 581,434. Ten years later, black num-bers reached 9,586 but were still 1 percent. Its white leadership and peo-ples treated Native Americans similarly, leading to the virtual exits of the Wyandot, Miami, Shawnee, and Delaware tribes.[61] The pitiful number in Ohio and North Ohio were owed, in large part, to the state's unwelcome policies and stance and the consequent very small black population in the state.

Gradually, the MEC conferences gave up counting by race. Ohio did so after 1851. That year it boasted 66,674 white members and 6,846 probationers. Its colored count? Members 365 and probationers 50, for a total of 415.[62] The next year, the two charges that supplied almost all of that count—New-Street/East Cincinnati Mission (151/50) and Augusta (106/0)—belonged to other conferences.[63]

The Cincinnati Conference continued reports until 1854. Cincinnati as a city, one authority notes, "was an uncongenial place for blacks," despite its black population increasing from 433 in 1820 to 3,237 in 1850.[64] Con-ference statistics bear that out. In 1853, its nine districts reported a total of 32,407 whites and 156 "colored." Of that the New-Street/East Cincin-nati Mission claimed 137 black members, 9 probationers, and 37 white members. None of the three German Mission Districts reported any. In the other districts, three charges reported 3; two, 2; and six, only 1 mem-ber.[65] In the next year, 1854, of a conference total of 132, New-Street claimed 113. Three other charges in that district each had one "Colored."

61   Andrew R. L. Cayton, *Ohio: The History of a People* (Columbus: Ohio State University Press, 2002), 5, 9–11, 15.

62   Cayton, *Ohio: The History of a People*, 26.

63   *Minutes of the Ohio Annual Conference of the Methodist Episcopal Church* (1851), 234–38.

64   Cayton, *Ohio: The History of a People*, 26. For Cayton's treatment of Cincinnati as a whole and white hostility toward blacks, see 21–29, 83–84.

65   *Minutes of the Cincinnati Annual Conference of the Methodist Episcopal Church, The Year 1853* (Cincinnati: The Methodist Book Concern, 1853), 28–31.

The conference had lost 24 "Colored" members from the year before.[66] Interestingly, Cincinnati, like other MEC conferences, did not report racial numbers for its Sunday schools. In other respects, conferences generally counted everything about their Sabbath school efforts. Here's Cincinnati's numbers by district for 1854 (figure 6):[67]

CINCINNATI ANNUAL CONFERENCE.   13

RECAPITULATION OF SUNDAY SCHOOL STATISTICS.

Districts.	Schools.	Officers and Teachers.	No. of Scholars.	Volumes in Library.	Bible classes.	No. in Infant classes.	Expenses for this year.	Collection for S. S. Union.	S. S. Advocates taken.	Conversions.
East Cincinnati,....	62	890	4390	17104	76	808	$1234 07	$ 96 00	913	230
West Cincinnati,...	46	597	3111	15019	94	578	823 75	10 00	670	106
Dayton,	41	453	2454	13820	34	131	435 75	41 13	396	32
Urbana,	44	640	3395	9202	45	190	591 75	33 88	621	73
Xenia,	43	648	3928	10620	40	417	373 75	28 98	370	179
Hillsboro,	89	945	4554	12876	117	559	516 41	56 48	486	81
Cincinnati, German,	15	165	602	2347	18	189	198 47	27 13	65	32
Pittsburg, "	16	142	697	1572	6	173	108 87	... ..	10	12
North Ohio, "	28	212	929	2832	15	21	120 28	18 19	...	19
	385	4692	23360	85492	447	3066	$4403 10	$311 79	3531	760

The foregoing is a recapitulation of the statistics of Sunday schools in the bounds of the Cincinnati conference, for the year 1854.

JNO. T. MITCHELL, Sec'y.

Figure 6

Cincinnati's Racial Mission: Colonization, People of Color Among Us, and Slavery

In 1853, the Cincinnati Conference added a committee "On Slavery" to the twenty-plus it had established in its organizational opening. Doubtless stimulated by the passage of the Fugitive Slave Law and recognizing the issue to be pressing, the bishop and conference made it among the largest of the committees, with fourteen members. Headed by Granville Moody, the Civil War's "fighting parson," the committee charted Cincinnati directions—condemning slavery and viewing Liberia as a new home for freedmen and perhaps their own conference's members. After a long series of *whereas*-es, reciting Methodist stances against slavery and rationales for such (in paragraph form), the committee

---

66 *Minutes of the Cincinnati Annual Conference of the Methodist Episcopal Church, The Year 1854*, 9–12.

67 *Minutes of the Cincinnati Annual Conference of the Methodist Episcopal Church, The Year 1855* (Cincinnati: The Methodist Book Concern, 1855), 13 (17 in another printing of the *Minutes*).

1. Resolved, That all slaveholding for gain is sinful, and all per-
    sons guilty of so doing should neither be received into nor
    retained in the Church.
2. Resolved, That we deem it indispensable duty to use all
    proper means for the extirpation of the great evil of slavery.
3. Resolved, That we recommend our people to memorialize
    Congress to repeal or modify the Fugitive-slave law.
4. Resolved, That the establishment of the republic of Liberia,
    under the fostering care of the Colonization Society, and the
    various missionary associations, has, under God, conferred
    immense advantages upon the emancipated slaves of our
    own land, and upon the continent of Africa, in planting
    civilization and Christianity in the midst of its darkness and
    misery, affording an effectual barrier to the prosecution of
    the slave-trade along a large proportion of its western coast,
    and securing the medium of missionary communication to
    the millions of that unhappy people.
5. Resolved, That we recommend the people committed to
    our care, to petition the Congress of the United States to
    recognize the nationality.[68]

The conference's commitment to destroying "the great evil of slavery" by shipping the freedmen to Africa and so "planting civilization and
Christianity in the midst of its darkness and misery" showed Methodists
shared general Ohioan white attitudes. As Cayton observes, "Most whites
wanted neither slavery nor African Americans in Ohio, believing that both
threatened their growing sense of their state as a land of freedom, indus-
try, and morality."[69]

The following year, Cincinnati heard back-to-back reports—or at
least published them back-to-back—from committees on Colonization, People of Color Among Us, and Slavery. By the first, the conference
pledged to cooperate in the establishment of "a colonization society for
the state of Ohio." The report recommended the cause as supporting
the emigration of "the more intelligent free people of color in this country." Its first resolution urged support so as to undercut the trans-Atlantic

---

68 *Minutes of the Cincinnati Annual Conference of the Methodist Episcopal Church, The Year 1853* (Cincinnati: The Methodist Book Concern, 1853), 20–22.
69 Cayton, *Ohio: The History of a People*, 118. His chapter, "Defining Ohio," traces race-relation activities and attitudes through the Civil War.

slavery-based economic system. A second argued that colonization would deter the export of the institution of slavery to Africa. The third commended involvement in the American Colonization Society for "the effect it must have upon slavery in this country": as it adds "strength, respectability, and importance to a republic whose Constitution frowns upon and prohibits slavery forever within its jurisdiction. Any thing that we can do for the promotion of this free nation must weaken the chains of their brethren in this country—an object dear to every Christian heart." The Report ended by calling for the "appointment of an efficient man from our conference to act as agent of this organization."[70] An agent? By establishing an agent, the conference employed the then operative system for advocacy, membership recruitment, and fundraising—so connection—but also missional and formational!

Striking is the length, detail, vigor, and directions of the Report of the People of Color Among Us. Extending over six pages and over two thousand six hundred words in length, the report called for more care for its black members and neighbors: ongoing, programmatic, within communities and state, substantive, and deliberate.[71] While nodding to colonization, within the Americas as well as Africa, the report focused on education as an imperative. Further, the mandate extended up the formational ladder: common schools, Sunday schools, and "a literary institution of high order for the education of the colored people generally, and for the purpose of preparing teachers of all grades to labor in the work of educating the colored people in our country and elsewhere."[72] That latter commitment would lead the conference two years later into establishing Wilberforce University. The committee acknowledged how "very few colored people immediately connected with us in Church fellowship" and then called for collaboration with the African Methodist Episcopal Church.[73] Interestingly, the Cincinnati Conference communicated with the Ohio Conference on this cause. The latter, in its Report of Education of Free People of Color, affirmed:

> The committee to whom was referred certain documents, forwarded to this conference by a committee of the Cincinnati

70 *Minutes of the Cincinnati Annual Conference of the Methodist Episcopal Church, The Year 1854*, 27–29.

71 *Minutes of the Cincinnati Annual Conference* (1854), 29–34.

72 *Minutes of the Cincinnati Annual Conference* (1854), 34.

73 *Minutes of the Cincinnati Annual Conference* (1854), 31.

> conference, relative to the education of the free people of color in the west, beg leave to report:
>
> We highly approve of the views of said committee, and desire to co-operate in the very worthy object of elevating both intellectually and morally, the free people of color in the west.
>
> 1. Resolved, That we recommend the Ohio conference to take the most efficient measures to carry out these views as soon as practicable.
>
> 2. Resolved, That we recommend the appointment of a committee of one—J. M. Jameson—to co-operate with committees that may be appointed by other conferences.
>
> 3. Resolved, That we concur in the opinion, that a general agent should be appointed to carry out the views expressed in the above named report.[74]

We will return to this development and other educational matters touched on in this report in the chapters dealing with formation and connection. Here, we underscore the missional tone that runs through. So we have formation as education (but clearly connection and outreach as well)!

The third of the committees, on Slavery, rehearsed the difficulties that church, state, and nation had suffered. "For fifty years," the committee recalled, "the standing inquiry of the Church has been, What shall be done? and practically the answer has been, Nothing. For it cannot be denied, that instead of any thing toward the extirpation of this evil being effected by the Church, slavery has made large encroachments upon the Church and upon the country." After more in that vein, the committee called conference members "to memorialize Congress, asking the repeal of the Fugitive-Slave law, and the re-enactment of so much of the late law known as the Missouri Compromise, as excluded slavery from Kansas and Nebraska and other territory of the United States." Its second action sought enforcement of the MEC's and conference's exclusion of slaveholders from membership.[75] So we have outreach, but also formation and connection!

---

74 *Minutes of the Ohio Annual Conference of the Methodist Episcopal Church* (1854), 15.

75 *Minutes of the Cincinnati Annual Conference (1854)*, 34–36.

Mission: Methodism's Imperative

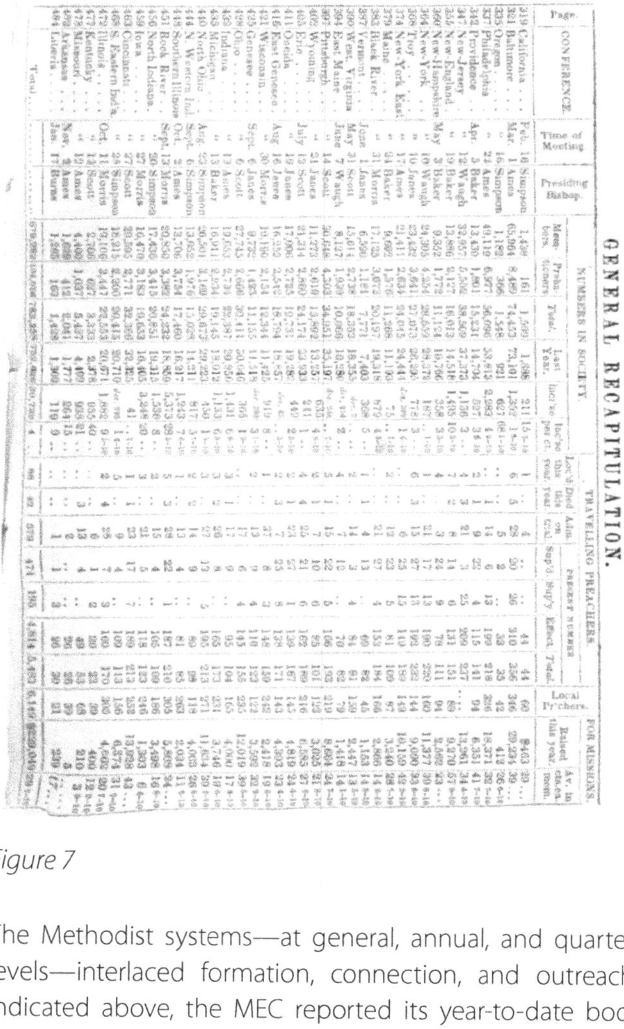
GENERAL RECAPITULATION.

Page. | Conference. | Time of Meeting. | Presiding Bishop. | Numbers in Society | Travelling Preachers. | Local Pr'chers. | For Missions.

Figure 7

The Methodist systems—at general, annual, and quarterly conference levels—interlaced formation, connection, and outreach. In 1850, as indicated above, the MEC reported its year-to-date body and money numbers for members and preachers. By the mid-1850s, that General Recapitulation provided the year's counts under three formational, connectional, and outreach categories—"Numbers in Society, Travelling and Local Preachers, and For Missions." The report, that for 1854 attached above (figure 7), provided those with access to the *General Minutes* with a sense of how Methodism had grown in membership, by conference, nationally plus Liberia; of where, how, if its leadership prospered; and of how much it had raised for missions.[76]

Cincinnati, in only its third year as a conference, had raised the third largest amount, exceeded only by the two older and larger conferences, Baltimore and Philadelphia. The church wanted to know, by conference, the dollars raised for missions and therefore the average contribution by membership.

In a couple of years, the MEC would need three pages for its General Recapitulation. As we will see in other chapters, the church thought its ministerial body count ought to acknowledge deaths and baptisms (of adults and of children). It also arrayed by conference, on a second page, the number of churches and parsonages and "Probable Value" of both. The third page featured columns indicating "Benevolent Contributions" for Conference Claimants, Missionary Society, Tract Society, American Bible Society, and the Sunday School Union. The latter conference-by-conference columns counted schools, officers and teachers, scholars, and volumes in libraries. While, then, other causes had joined Missions in report-ing their outreach-like contributions, the Missionary Society retained its prominence. The MEC total for the Missionary Society that year, $226,697, approximately equaled those for the other four causes combined. Mem-bers of the Cincinnati Conference, interestingly, gave three times as much to Missions as to the others collectively ($11,052/$3,388), and Ohio four times as much ($10,435/$2,526). Methodism reported its doings by counts. And it clearly thought much about missions, its outreach.

Mission in Conference Minutes

What Methodism said to itself about its purposes and how to meet them is also striking—indeed far more striking—in the pages of an annual conference's *Minutes* devoted to missions. A Missions Committee sum-marized the concerns, issues, activities for the year. The *Minutes* carried its report along with those of the array of other committees. In the 1854 Cincinnati summary of actions, the following indicated the centrality of missions to the conference's life:

76 *Minutes of the Annual Conferences of the Methodist Episcopal Church, for the Year 1854* (New York: Carlton & Phillips, 1854), in *General Minutes of the Annual Conferences of the United Methodist Church in the United States, territories, and Cuba* (Chicago: Council on World Service and Finance, Methodist Church (U. S.), 1852–55, 487. HathiTrust http://hdl.handle.net/2027/uiug.30112048866450.

Annual Missionary Collection. The month of May was agreed upon as the time when the annual missionary sermons shall be preached, and the public collections for missions taken within our bounds.[77]

Conference Sermon on Missions. Brother C. Brooks was appointed to preach the annual sermon on missions, before the conference, in 1855; brother M. Dustin, alternate.

. . . .

The session of the conference was protracted somewhat beyond the usual length, and was closed at one o'clock on Friday, October 6th. Much good feeling prevailed throughout, and the bonds of Christian union between brethren were knit more closely. Some most painful duties devolved on the conference; but these were met with a firm and yet tender spirit. Bishop Scott, who was on his first visit to the conference, in his presidency, preaching, and social intercourse, endeared himself to all. Doctors Durbin and J. T. Peck represented the missions and tract interests, with which they are charged, with addresses before the conference and the public in their usual felicitous style; and we were favored with visits from several beloved brethren from other conferences.[78]

Report of the Mission Committee. The Mission Committee of the Cincinnati conference met September 27, 1854. Members present. . . . The following missions in the German work were continued, and the sums annexed were appropriated for their support the ensuing year. . . [Then followed three pages itemized by district and charge showing the thousands expended for German stations and circuits from the year's mission receipts.][79]

Even more striking, however, the Cincinnati Conference devoted the **last third** of the *Minutes,* pages 61–96, to missions. The index so listed: Cincinnati Conference Missionary Society, 61; Report of the Secretary of Missionary Society, 62; Report of the Treasurer of Missionary Society, 68; Detailed Missionary Report, 68; List of Life Members, 95. Stunning when first encountered is the *Minutes* list—page after page (68–98), district

77 *Minutes of the Cincinnati Annual Conference* (1854), 5.
78 *Minutes of the Cincinnati Annual Conference* (1854), 6.
79 *Minutes of the Cincinnati Annual Conference* (1854), 37.

after district, charge after charge—of the names of the Methodist individuals and the amount each had given. And the List of Life Members,
the major donors, pages 95–98, arrayed in three columns, add up to more
than five hundred.

Similarly, the Ohio Conference, like other Northern conferences,
devoted comparable attention to missions. The *Minutes* carried terse
summary reports on the Ohio Conference Missionary Society, Business
Meeting, Annual Sermon, and Anniversary on a page (17). The secretary's
and treasurer's reports covered pages 18–22 and 22–23. The total collected that year was $12,019.63. The reports concluded as follows:

> The people were then addressed by Bishop Scott, his speech being
> principally in relation to Africa, and by Rev. Joseph M. Trimble, at
> the close of whose remarks a basket collection was taken up. A call
> was made for subscriptions to make life members to the Parent and
> Ohio Conference Missionary Societies. To these a liberal response
> was given. On motion, the Society adjourned.[80]

Prior to page 17 and the above missions topics, the *Minutes* index indicated that the conference had attended to Undergraduates, Ordina-
tions, etc., Committees of Examination of Local Preachers, Visiting and
Examining Committees of Literary Institutions, and heard reports on the
Bible Cause, the Committee on Education, its Tract Committee, Education of Free People of Color, Temperance, and the Committee on Sunday
Schools. To its other business, following the Missions Committee's, Ohio
also devoted a few pages in its *Minutes*:

---

80 *Minutes of the Cincinnati Annual Conference* (1854), 23.

On its last page (80), the *Minutes* provided the index and the twelfth itemizing of donations to Missions from the charges on the Chilicothe District. The conference devoted over half of its *Minutes* to the Missionary Society and the cause of missions. Incredibly striking—for almost forty pages—the conference put on record the names of its members who gave to the Missionary Society.

The amounts range from twenty dollars down to twenty-five cents. Names of the children in the Sabbath School did not make the *Minutes*. But by naming their parents and other adult members, the *Minutes* and the Missionary Society Report identified the people called Methodist. Printing these lists, the annual conferences gave history the fullest count and actual naming of membership. Individual charge or circuit records, quarterly conference reports, and membership lists have bit the dust. By publishing the givers, conferences called the roll. And Google and Hathi Trust now share that who's who with any who want to know. Here follows the first page of the Missionary Society Report, with the women's names underlined:

OHIO CONFERENCE MISSIONARY SOCIETY, DETAILED REPORT

The committee appointed to publish the *Minutes*, have, with no small labor, rewritten and arranged part of the reports of missionary collections in the stations and circuits. This was done partly as a matter of economy, but principally with the design of presenting the preachers an example of the style in which, in the judgment of the committee, the reports should be made out. We hope that our labor will be appreciated, and this printed report become the model for future ones.

JOSEPH M. TRIMBLE,
BENJAMIN ST. JAMES FRY.

COLUMBUS DISTRICT

Wesley Chapel—*Columbus*—<u>Hannah Neil,</u> Thomas Walker, each $10; J. T. Bartlett, Ann Bartlett, E. N. Boothe, J. E. Rudisell, Joseph Butler, W. Royce, M. Goodling, <u>Julia Gooding,</u> <u>Jane A. Minor,</u> L. Wilson, each $5; smaller sums and public collection, $19.62; collected in the Sabbath school, $64.45; contents of missionary box of Wilber C., S. H., and Morris S. Booth, $3,113 . . . $177.20. Worthington Circuit—*Worthington*—Stephen L. Peck, collector: Rev. O. M. Spencer, $20; Rev U. Heath, Rev. A. B. See, William Bishop, each $10; S. J. Peck, <u>Mrs. P. Peck,</u> Rev. J. T. Miller, each $5; <u>Mrs. A. Hubbard,</u> N. H. Hoyt, each $3; <u>Mrs. E. A. R. Miller,</u> H. Pinney, W. Young, S Peck, each $2; <u>Mrs. L. Andrews,</u> E. Stiles, <u>Miss Groome,</u> E. W Foster, E. Gray, L. Young, J. P. Mills, Dr. P. Goble, S. Hoyt, G. G. Wilcox, T. Heath, H. Stiles, J. D. Fuller, W. Peck, L. W. Leaf, J. Hubbard, E. Lewis, D. Weaver, J. N. Budge, <u>Mrs. C. Weaver,</u> J. W. Scanland, J. H. Hammond, each $1; A. Wilcox, J. Martin, P. Kemp, <u>Mrs. P. Kemp,</u> A. Lewis, <u>Mrs. M. Bod,</u> E. Lewis, Jr., <u>Mrs. J. Prentice,</u> each 50 cts. *Clintonville*—J. Bull, collector: A. Wilson, $5; A. Webster, W. C. Tripp, each $3; T. Bull, J. Webster, T. H. Cue, each $2; G. P. Whip, P. Rhoades, J. W. Smith, A. Bull, a friend, Rev. J. Bull, F. Bull, C. Wilson, M. Webster, S. M. Westervelt, <u>Miss A. Bull,</u> C. Bull, J. B. Cline, each $1; T. Beach, 75 cts.; W. Fetridge, P. R. Hunt, M. Webster, E. Landon, J. Webster, D. R. Cook, T. Lane, S. Coe, A. Brevort, L. Rhoades, each 50 cts.; J. Webster, C. Webster, each 25 cts.; sundries, $1.90. *Alum Creek*—E. R. Williams, collector: E. R. Williams, <u>Mrs. R. Williams,</u> S. Dalzell, E. Harris, each $1; <u>Mrs. M. A. Herlocker,</u> S. Barklow, <u>Miss S. Folkner,</u> J. Dalzell, C. Holt, each 50 cts.; cash, 37 cts. *Williamsburg*—B. F. Smith, collector: B. F. Smith, W. Ward, each $1; M. Gooding, Dr. Mercer, <u>Mrs. W. A. Mercer,</u> <u>Mrs. P. Gooding,</u> each 50 cts; sundry persons, $1. *Liberty*—W. Wilcox, collector: W. Wilcox, S. Moses, T. R. Hall, each $2; J. Pennell, D. Clark, F. Moses, each $1; J. T. Gardiner, $1.50; E. Humphrey, 75 cts.; J. Clark, R. B. Moses, W. Andrews, L. Neda, W. A. Armstrong, each 50 cts.; sundry persons, $5.20. *Asbury*—H. M. Cryder, collector: H. M. Cryder, $3: J. B. Crum, E. Matthews, each $2; <u>Mrs. L. Lane,</u> $1.20; L. T. Lane, <u>Mrs. M. Matthews,</u> L. Lane, <u>Miss S. Perry,</u> each $1; <u>Mrs. P. Meteer,</u> S. O'Hara, <u>Mrs. Cryder,</u> each 50 cts. *Fletcher Chapel*—<u>Mrs. M. Wright, collector:</u> <u>Mrs. M. Wright,</u> $3; J. Matthews,

$2; W. Armstead, W. Gray, J. Wright, W. Meleer, E. Matthews, each $1; A. Belsford, P. Bower, G. Penny, <u>Mrs. J. Matthews</u>, E. A. [Davis][81]

Outreach

What each and all these folks thought when they contributed their dimes and dollars, the conferences did not compile and have not told us. Missions doubtless meant different things to different women, men, and children. Clearly, some outreach efforts and expenditures were welcomed. Others not so much. Certainly embraced were an array of missional but also formational and connectional efforts to causes and peoples to which we turn attention in those chapters. Among them, the outreach—financially, organizationally, and significantly—to Midwestern Germans. Wilhelm Nast, appointed initially as "Missionary among the German immigrants in and near Cincinnati," championed that outreach, as we have noted, by preaching across the region; organizing Germans into congregations, circuits, and conferences; establishing educational and other denominational systems; and by publications, including the paper *Der Christliche Apologete.*

Native Americans? Having been chased further west, they did not figure in Kentucky, Ohio, and Cincinnati conference giving. Africans, certainly through support (in print if not significantly in dollars) of Colonization and of the Liberia Conference. Black Methodists? The MEC and MECS differed radically and paradoxically on their outreach to blacks.

The Northern church had done little to make the Midwest an accommodating environment and the church as the agent of that welcome. The Southern church, at least in the upper South, took missions to and among slaves to be a mandate for political as well as religious reasons. And a *southern* portion of the Northern church lived with and sanctioned the system. The Northern church launched its own *Kentucky* conference in the 1850s. By its third session (1855), its outreach needed two districts and fourteen charges serving 2,424/320 members/probationers and 201/50 "Col'd" members/probationers.[82] Its *Minutes* did not indicate whether any of the latter were freedmen. But it committed itself, as was typical in other conferences, North and South, to assessment of slavery.

---

81 *Minutes of the Ohio Annual Conference of the Methodist Episcopal Church* (1854), 42.
82 Typescript. Duke Divinity School, p. 9. "The Kentucky Annual Conference of the M. E. Church commenced its third session in the City of Maysville, October 11, 1855, Bishop Morris, presiding; *Minutes of the Kentucky Annual Conference* (1855).

Among its nine committees—On Divine Service, Conference Stewards and Necessitors Cares, On Mission, Sunday School, Bible Cause, Tract Cause, Post Offices, On Temperance—was that On Slavery.

That Northern conference (MEC) in Southern church (MECS) terrain behaved *Yankee* on some matters, *Rebel* on others. On the Slavery Committee's recommendation, the conference voted non-concurrence twelve and thirteen to zero on two resolutions on slavery, the first from Wisconsin against "buying, selling or holding a human being as a slave"; the second from N. Ohio changing the General Rule forbidding that "when emancipation can be effected without injury to the slave."[83]

Fifteen years later, in 1860, the MEC Kentucky Conference dealt with slavery amidst the considerable resolving, petitioning, and advocating by its sister conferences in the Northern church. It did so chaired by Bishop Matthew Simpson, soon to add national acclaim to his stature within the MEC. The Committee on Slavery's report, unanimously accepted, rehearsed the stance of the MEC on slavery. It conceded that:

> The founders of Methodism in this country, and in this Common-wealth, were decidedly anti-slavery men. Two facts, however, are alleged against this: First, they never made slaveholding a bar to membership; and secondly, they did frequently, both in the General and annual conferences, declare against *abolitionism*, and against all exciting agitations of the subject of slavery. These allegations are true; but they do not prove our fathers to have been pro-slavery, or even indifferent in their feelings upon the subject. They only prove the conservative character of the Church. The men who laid the foundations and built the walls of our noble superstructure were not fanatics. They knew that slavery was one of the fixed institutions of the state, protected by law, and sustained by the interests and convictions of a large portion of the people; and that factious, declamatory opposition to it would be unwise, irritating, and injurious, and, therefore, incompatible with their duties as neighbors, citizens, and Christians.[84]

Then the committee quoted, with appreciation, a report by Henry B. Bascom "late Bishop" of the MECS, and by Bishop H. H. Kavanaugh of the Southern church and once an extraordinarily active member of the

---

83   Minutes of the Kentucky Annual Conference (1855), 9–10.

84   *Minutes of the Kentucky Annual Conference of the Methodist Episcopal Church* (1860), Duke Typescript, 17.

Kentucky conference.[85] The Southern bishops had insisted that the attacks on slavery threatened the church's "institutions and welfare, not less than the peace and stability of our whole country." Further, the Southern bishops declared that "we are not the advocates of slavery. We believe it to be morally wrong, and relatively mischievous in all its tendencies. We consider it an evil, even in its most tolerable aspects," and then that though "a chronic disease in the body politic . . . the remedy must be gradual."[86]

The Kentucky statement moved on to urge caution in a long argument and with elaborate points like this: "Our Church government is indebted to its simplicity for its efficiency [long paragraph]. . . . We love it as it is, and wish to withhold our consent from any change or innovation, till the necessity for the modification is clearly demonstrated." After considerable further argumentation, the report insisted, "Finally. We do not believe that the demand for more stringent legislation is sustained by any Scriptural precept or example." The Northern church's Kentucky conference then affirmed:

1. Resolved, That we do not concur in any of the propositions submitted to us by sister conferences, recommending the suspension of the fourth Restrictive Rule, with a view to altering the General Rule on the subject of slavery.
2. Resolved, That in refusing our consent to any additional legislation on the subject, we do not base our action upon any disposition to countenance slavery in the Church, further than is necessary on account of the difficulties attending emancipation; but, on the contrary, "we are much as ever convinced of the great evil of slavery," and anxiously await

---

85 In 1875, the *Minutes of the Forty-eighth Session of the Kentucky Annual Conference of the Methodist Episcopal Church* indicated that the conference met in Trinity Church, Louisville, Kentucky. "Rev. Bishop H. H. Kavanaugh, D. D. and twelve members of MECS entered. . . . Chairing Bishop Foster made remarks appropriate to the presence of our brethren of the Church, South, and was followed in fraternal expressions by Bishop Kavanaugh and nine from MECS and six from MEC." The second day, "Bishop Kavanaugh appeared and was invited to a seat on the platform." The third, "Bishop Kavanaugh again occupied a seat on the platform" (6–7, 9, 11, 16–17).

Among its closing resolutions: "Resolved, That a committee be appointed by the bishop to draft resolutions expressive of the sentiments of the Conference concerning the special manifestations of fraternal regard made by Bishop H. H. Kavanaugh, D. D. of the M. E. Church, South, and the presiding elder and pastors of that church in this city, and report the same at our next sitting" (28–29). Adopted that evening unanimously. Bishop Kavanaugh gave the benediction a little later.
86 *Minutes of the Kentucky Annual Conference* (1860), 18.

the openings of Providence for its removal in a just, peaceful, and Christian manner.

3. Resolved, That when our fathers pronounced in favor of "extirpating the evils of slavery," they did not intend any interference with the rights of those legally connected with the institution.[87]

Conclusion

Methodists in Kentucky and Ohio reached out, door-to-door, in Sunday school and church services, on camp meeting grounds, through legislation, in their programs, and via an array of publications. Much of that outreach, to be sure, focused on the insiders in the two churches and several conferences. But even Methodist-specific occasions and resources looked beyond conference, denominational, state, and national boundaries to larger publics and the world. Missions constituted Methodism's business. And outreach entangled with and depended on the day-to-day, weekly, monthly, and yearly formational and connectional apparatus of the two churches and several conferences.

---

87 *Minutes of the Kentucky Annual Conference* (1860), 20.

CHAPTER 3

Formation

Methodism's Churching Its Members

What are our Sunday-schools? Are they not the nurseries of the Church? And are we not to look to them for the best materials for supplying the ranks of our membership? We say the best materials, because those who enter the Church from the Sunday-school, have been already trained from early childhood in the knowledge of the Holy Scripture. We must not look wholly to the conquests of Methodism in the broad field of the world for recruits to fight the battles of the Lord. We must, in our midst, and under the guidance of veteran soldiers of the cross, bring up our trained bands to fight and conquer the armies of the aliens. . . .

We are of opinion that there is no enterprise of the Church to which our people would more fully and promptly respond. The hearts of the best men and women in our communion are deeply interested in this cause, and we firmly believe that it would not be difficult to make this interest general through-out our Zion.[1]

These affirmations, albeit in a minority report of the Committee on Sunday-Schools, led the General Conference (hereafter GC) of the Methodist Episcopal Church, South (MECS) to reaffirm commitments:

- to protect its nurseries and their formational activities,

---

1   *Journal of the General Conference of the Methodist Episcopal Church, South,* volume 4, 1858 (Nashville: Methodist Episcopal Church, South, 1858), HathiTrust Digital Library, Permanent URL: https://hdl.handle.net/2027/osu.32435053208484, 571–72.

- to train thereby more "soldiers of the cross" through its Sunday-schools,
- to commit to preparing leadership "to fight and conquer the armies of the aliens,"
- to select a general to lead Zion's cause, and so
- to authorize the election of a Corresponding Secretary of the Sunday-School Society.

On a third ballot, Charles Taylor was elected Zion's *general*, more officially, modestly, and typically titled "Corresponding Secretary." He was charged "to travel through the conferences to encourage the formation of Sunday-schools, and to take collections for the cheapening and distribution of Sunday-school literature.[2] Formation from the bottom up—churching the young and old members. Churching, then, at least for white southerners.

Before reviewing the operation and impact of Sunday schools and before turning to the array of other formational activities and institutions—colleges, the Course of Study, magazines, popular literature, newspapers—note should be taken of how the Southern church shaped its nonwhite members in bondage. For them, the MECS guided masters in the use of a subset of its catechisms.

Catechisms for Slaves

The title and authorship of this frequently republished and apparently widely used catechism indicated how the Southern church viewed its publication:

Catechism for the use of the Methodist Missions. First Part by William Capers, D.D., One of the Bishops of the Methodist Episcopal Church, South. Published by order of the General Conference.

Capers had earned his responsibility and prerogative to guide the church in caring for its black members. The MECS recognized his formational strengths early. Holder of a M.A. from South Carolina College and having studied law as well, he vaulted successively through key church assignments. Then, from 1821 through 1825, the MECS entrusted him with outreach to the Creek Indians in Georgia and Alabama. From 1825 to 1840, he

---

2   MECS, *General Conference Journal* (1858), 573.

oversaw mission to plantation slaves, while successively holding a presiding eldership and then a pastoral charge. During that saga, specifically in 1833, he published the first version of what is represented above, initially and tellingly entitled *Catechism for Little Children and for Use on the Missions to the Slaves in South Carolina*. Not viewing him as a man for a single task, the MECS assigned Capers the responsibility in 1836 of launching and editing what became the *Southern Christian Advocate*. In 1840, the national church (MEC still), made him secretary of the southern division of the Missionary Society. At the 1844 General Conference, he urged conciliation but defended slaveholder Bishop Andrews. The MECS elected him to the episcopacy at its organizational General Conference in 1846.

Capers prefaced the 1853 edition of the catechism noted above with four words of counsel to those instructing slaves, the first two of which indicate its tenor:

> The author of this humble work begs leave to accompany it with a few brief remarks to those of his brethren who may think proper to use it.

> 1. It is believed that a Catechism for the mass of colored people, whether children or adults, had better be confined to the rudiments of Christian knowledge, simply, than diffused through a wide range of Scripture topics, doctrinal, historical, biographical, &c.; our object being not barely to communicate knowledge, but such as tends most to the glory of God—the knowledge of salvation.

> 2. The present little work has been composed under a persuasion that the persons to be instructed can more easily conceive the truth than comprehend the terms in which it is apt to be expressed. We have therefore discarded all hard words and aimed to present truth in a guise so simple as to suit their capacities. This, however, is very difficult; we can only say, we have done what we could.[3]

The catechism dealt with the various duties, roles, and relationships (husband, wife, child, sibling, fellow slave, etc.) of slaves. Here, for instance:

---

3   William Capers, *Catechism for the Use of the Methodist Missions*, 3rd ed. (Charleston: John Early, 1853), HathiTrust Digital Library, Rights Public Domain. https://hdl.handle.net/2027/nc01.ark:/13960/t9960rb16, 3.

The Duty of Servants

Servants, be obedient to them that are your masters according to the flesh, with fear and trembling, in singleness of your heart, as unto Christ. Not with eye-service as men pleasers, but as the servants of Christ, doing the will of God from the heart. Ephesians vi, 5, 6.

Let as many servants as are under the yoke count their own masters worthy of all honor, that the name of God, and his doctrine, be not blasphemed. And they that have believing masters, let them not despise them because they are brethren, but rather do them service because they are faithful and beloved, partakers of the benefit. These things teach and exhort. 1 Tim. vi, 1, 2.[4]

Four years after Bishop Capers oversaw the republication of this catechism and two years after his death, two other Southern Methodist heavyweights, M'Tyeire and Summers, issued the following guidance to the church: H. N. M'Tyeire, D. D., *Duties of Christian Masters*, edited by Thomas O. Summers, D. D.[5]

M'Tyeire had the prior year assumed the editorship of the Southern church's leading paper, the Nashville-based *Christian Advocate*, continuing that office into the Civil War. In the 1866 General Conference, the first after the war, he was elected bishop. He continued various publishing and writing activities thereafter, among them a *History of Methodism*. British-born Summers succeeded M'Tyeire as editor of the *Christian Advocate*. Indeed, Summers "edited" the Southern church, serving for decades as its chief spokesperson, theological guide, publisher, formational spirit, and teacher (for all ages). From 1850 till his death in 1882, he was the book editor for the church and the secretary of General Conference. For most of that period, he edited the *Quarterly Review*, *Sunday School Visitor*, *Minutes of Annual Conference*, and General Conference minutes. His name appeared on title pages of more than five hundred works of diverse sorts. At Vanderbilt, he served as dean of the theological faculty and professor of Systematic Theology.

---

4   Capers, *Catechism*, 21–22. For further illustrations of the Capers catechism, see our *Methodist Experience in America*, 2:231–35.

5   H. N. M'Tyeire, D. D., *Duties of Christian Masters*, ed. Thomas O. Summers, D. D. (Nashville, Tenn.: Southern Methodist Publishing House, 1859). HathiTrust Digital Library, Public Domain, Google-digitized. Permanent URL: https://hdl.handle.net/2027/njp .32101037454806.

In their *Duties of Christian Masters*, M'Tyeire and Summers gave far more specific advice to the church than Capers. Further, they honored slave codes in detail, making it clear that the Christian faith embraced, if it did not enhance and encourage, slavery. The titles of and topical entries in the three sections lay that out clearly (the number indicating where a topic begins). The sections—As Property, As Social Beings, and As Religious Beings—made clear how white society viewed slaves and slavery. And under those rubrics, the sequence of topics fleshes out the thought processes, the actual and encouraged relationships, and the day-to-day activities toward which masters were encouraged to head.

Contents

HUMBLE ANNALS
  Happy death of a servant 267
  The word precious 268
  Light in dark places 271
  A native African 272[6]

At 170 words a page and over 280 pages, the bishop-to-be and intellectual governor gave Southern Methodists schooling on forming and reforming their black servants. And they added words of counsel from Bishop James O. Andrew, whose slaveholding by marriage and inheritance had sparked the fires that inflamed the 1844 General Conference and divided the church. Andrew exhorted masters to permit the church to reach slaves as this introduction to the Four Letters indicates:

> **The Religious Instruction of Negroes**. [The following Letters were first published by Bishop Andrew in the *New Orleans Christian Advocate*, in the year 1856, and are reproduced in this form by the consent of the venerable author.] FIRST LETTER. The Southern States contain a population of several millions of slaves, many of whom are cut off from the opportunity of attending the Sabbath ministrations of those pastors who attend to the religious instruction of the white population.[7]

After explaining that slaves are not reached because white population density calls for few preachers, their itinerating through an area when slaves are in the field, and the lack of room for blacks in small preaching houses, Andrew encouraged masters to permit the religious instruction of Negroes:

> Now we wish to lead all masters, and especially those who call themselves Christians, to a careful consideration of their obligations to their slaves in this respect. We regard it as a settled fact that the gospel of God is for all, in the extent of its provisions and its adaptation to the wants and peculiarities of man, under every possible variety of circumstances. No matter what his country, what his color; no matter under what laws or usages he has been reared; no matter at what shrine he has knelt; no matter what his civil or social position, the blood of the incarnate God has redeemed him: he is a man, he is immortal, and is invited to an heirship of hopes and consolations which point him to a home in a happy world where

---

6   M'Tyeire, *Duties of Christian Masters*, v–vii.
7   M'Tyeire, *Duties of Christian Masters*, 219.

all is life, and purity, and beauty. The negro is no exception to the far-reaching extent of this glorious provision.[8]

Such counsel, though "colored" in assumptions and commitments that are odious today, encouraged treatment of blacks as deserving of formation, at least on basic levels (for later guidance on "Colored" instruction framed within an overview of southern organization, see appendix for "William Sasnett of MECS on Missions, 1855"). For whites, the Southern church and its Kentucky leadership sought formation through educational institutions.

Schools, Colleges, but Not a Seminary

Another committee of the MECS General Conference (GC), "On Education," addressed formation at all levels, including college and high school, formation from the top down.[9] It celebrated the progress that the church had made in founding and sustaining these institutions, but worried, at some length, that members and communities enthralled by their importance might launch more than could be sustained:

> The increase for the last four years has been very encouraging. Eighteen institutions and nearly two thousand pupils additional have been reported; while the value of property and endowment has probably increased in a greater ratio.
>
> Of the institutions reported, there are twenty-one Colleges and institutions for young gentlemen; twenty-eight Colleges for young ladies; twenty-seven High Schools for young ladies; sixteen mixed schools, and four Academies for young men. It will be seen that the whole number of collegiate institutions is too great in proportion to the schools of lower grade. It is true that most of these Colleges have preparatory departments; but even with this arrangement the number of preparatory schools bears too small a proportion to that of the higher schools.
>
> The whole value of the property owned or used by the Church, for educational purposes, including libraries, apparatus, and buildings, is $1,509,000. And as this report is not full, the value of the

8   M'Tyeire, *Duties of Christian Masters*, 222.
9   MECS, *General Conference Journal* (1858), 523–38.

property of many schools being omitted, it is reasonable to suppose that the whole value is in the neighborhood of $2,000,000.[10]

More constructively, devoting half of its 15-page report to conference-by-conference inventory of the schools, the committee took note of these for whites in Kentucky and for Native Americans across the MECS connection:

KENTUCKY CONFERENCE

This Conference has no actual ownership of any institution of learning; but extends its patronage to the following institutions:

1. Science Hill Female Academy. Rev. J. Tevis, Principal. It was founded in 1825. Present number of pupils, 250.
2. Shelbyville High School, for boys, is a comparatively young but very flourishing school. Number of pupils, 75.
3. Millersburg Collegiate Institute, male and female. Rev. George Savage, M. D., President. A very successful school, with 135 pupils. . . .

LOUISVILLE CONFERENCE

1. Bardstown Female Institute, Rev. J. Atkinson and wife, Principals, has 80 pupils, and property worth $5,000.
2. Russellville Female Institute, Rev. J. E. Carnes, President, has 100 pupils, and property to the value of $4,000.
3. Louisville Conference Male High School, Rev. G. Gardner, President, has 50 students, and property worth $5,000.
4. Hardinsburg Female High School.
5. Camden Seminary, Rev. J. P. Murrell, President, with 60 pupils, is under the patronage of the Louisville Conference.

INDIAN MISSION CONFERENCE

The following Government schools are under our control:

1. Asbury, Creek Nation, a mixed school, has 80 students.
2. Fort Coffee, a Choctaw school for boys, has 50 students.

10   MECS, *General Conference Journal* (1858), 532–33.

3. New Hope, a Choctaw school for girls, has 50 pupils.
4. Chickasaw, a school for boys, has 12 students.
5. Colbert Institute is a mixed school, having 65 pupils.
6. Bloomfield Academy, for girls, has 45 pupils.

These schools have often been blessed with revivals of religion.[11]

Identifying schools by name, president, gender, student count, and even assets, GC claimed education as its enterprise. The long report recognized in various ways the importance of these to the well-being of the church, of formation at all levels, of schools shaping its women and men, of the necessity of strong leadership, and especially of the equipping of its ministry. Its recommendations, which GC affirmed by adopting, included as well that the church form itself and its people with the revealed Word, and voice that commitment in praise:

1. Resolved, That it is matter of devout gratitude to the great Head of the Church that we have had such increase and general prosperity in our literary institutions, and especially that the spirit of revival has been so generally manifested among the pupils of the various institutions under our care and patronage.
2. Resolved, That, in view of the great interests involved, we set apart the second Friday in October of each year as a day of fasting and prayer to Almighty God, for the more abundant outpourings of his Holy Spirit upon the teachers and pupils of our literary institutions.
3. Resolved, That we recommend to the Church the increase of primary and preparatory schools wherever it is practicable.
4. Resolved, That the Bible be recommended as a text-book in all the schools connected with our Church.
5. Resolved, That sacred music be introduced into all our schools as far as possible.

B. M. DRAKE, Chairman.

. . . .

Resolved, That we earnestly exhort all our people to sustain and patronize their own institutions of learning, and to consider the painful consequences that have befallen some who have most

---

11   MECS, *General Conference Journal* (1858), 531.

unwisely allowed their children to be placed in Roman Catholic and kindred schools.[12]

The last resolution, added to the committee's report by an amendment, reminded Southern Methodists of the dangers posed by Roman Catholicism.

Another danger, or perhaps temptation, was for the church to form and shape its ministry by authorizing the establishment of an institution providing post-collegiate theological education. The Committee on Education gave such a proposal very deliberate and cogent response. It acknowledged differences of opinion on the church's undertaking such an endeavor, one already launched by their Northern counterparts and functioning for half a century by more upscale denominations. The committee affirmed, secondly, "Of one fact we are fully persuaded, and one of no little significance: the wide-spread demand amongst all our churches for a higher degree of intellectual cultivation in those who minister at their altars than was made in the earlier years of our history."[13] After giving that point considerable elaboration, the committee concluded that it did not "believe that the Church is prepared to adopt or to establish theological institutions, nor do they think that such institutions are necessary; nor do they suppose that any real infraction of our cherished system is demanded."[14]

The Course of Study

Cherished system?—the Course of Study (COS). Established by the 1816 General Conference and launched at least by 1817, the COS functioned as the norm for ministerial formation for a century, has continued to this day, and increasingly reclaims its place as United Methodism's dominant formational pattern. The MECS Committee on Education then urged "the expansion and improvement of our existing platform." To that end, it claimed a "happy adjustment between our ecclesiastical principles and our actual necessities" and proposed five enabling recommendations. The committee called for annual conferences to require candidates for ministry to achieve expected formational standards and to evidence such in examinations. Second, needed were "different and better textbooks . . . corresponding with the advancement of knowledge." Third,

---

12 MECS, *General Conference Journal* (1858), 537–38.
13 MECS, *General Conference Journal* (1858), 550.
14 MECS, *General Conference Journal* (1858), 551

the committee recommended "a faculty or board of examiners," and candidates passing "a satisfactory examination on the required subjects." Fourth and finally, "We propose, 5, that there be in all the colleges and universities under our care a chair of Biblical Literature, accessible to all students without exception, as a department of general education, in which the Bible, with collateral branches, shall be the text-book."[15]

To address these concerns, the committee then followed with another five points mainly specifying how operational procedures should be adjusted at quarterly and annual-conference levels. The fifth recommendation addressed the matter that had prompted the report, namely establishing theological seminaries. "In the opinion of the committee," the journal indicates, "the present course of study for deacons' and elders' orders should be immediately revised, so as to elevate the standard for graduation to orders."[16]

The counsel and reforms strengthened what had been and would remain for another half century a connectionally vitalizing but conference-administered formational system. Across the whole Methodist Episcopal Church, South, a common reading list indicated, by year of candidacy, what must and ought to be read to advance toward ordination and life-long annual conference membership. The white fraternity ordered itself thus and provided, as well, procedures for recognition of Native American leadership. Some conferences, Kentucky included, opted for the provision to ordain black preachers, as is noted here below and in the outreach chapter. At any rate, the whole of the church's white preachers-to-be labored over the very same books. But to annual conferences belonged the administration of that system with the procedures hinted at above. A conference-based but connectionally shared ministerial library shaped ministry. Southern and Northern Methodism doctored the mandated list—deleting and adding—to arm preachers with each church's political, social, ethnic, and racial agendas. A similar highly orchestrated operation program reached the white membership.

Churching Southern Reading Members

American Methodism slowly and gradually launched the printed weekly and monthly formational ventures that John and Charles Wesley had

---

15   MECS, *General Conference Journal* (1858), 552.
16   MECS, *General Conference Journal* (1858), 553–54.

adapted to shape and reshape the British faithful. By the 1850s, the Southern as well as Northern churches had become publishing empires. In "Report Number Four," the "Committee on Books and Periodicals" reviewed the business side of the operation and then turned to the array of formational "Periodicals."

> Your committee have inquired into the condition of the periodicals authorized by the General Conference. The result of this investigation is very unsatisfactory with respect to some of these publications; while others exhibit a healthy and prosperous state.
>
> *The Quarterly Review*—This work, though ably conducted, has failed by some eight thousand dollars, in the last four years, to meet the expenses of its publication. With a list of less than fifteen hundred paying subscribers, it has been a constant drain upon the funds of the Church. Reluctant, however, to abandon the enterprise, your committee recommend its continuance upon a plan which may possibly greatly diminish its cost. . . .
>
> *The Sunday School Visitor*—This excellent child's paper should have fifty thousand subscribers. Your committee regret, however, that many Methodist families and communities do not extend to it a more liberal patronage. Your committee regard it as an indispensable publication and recommend its continuance.[17]

The report continued with the committee's assessment of the various publications that served the whole or parts of the church. Among its concluding recommendations was the following, which covers the various serials and also indicates that General Conference stamped MECS approval on their editorial leadership:

> V. The General Book Agent shall publish a Quarterly Review, to be called the "*Quarterly Review of the Methodist Episcopal Church, South*;" a monthly magazine, to be called "*The Home Circle*;" a child's paper, to be called the "*Sunday-School Visitor*;" and a weekly newspaper, to be called "*The Christian Advocate*." There shall be an editor of books and tracts, who shall also be editor of the *Quarterly Review*; an editor of the *Home Circle*, who shall also be editor of the *Sunday-School Visitor*; and an editor of the *Christian Advocate*, all of whom shall be elected by the General Conference.

---

17   MECS, *General Conference Journal* (1858), 492–93.

VI. Newspapers and Editors.—1. The General Conference shall also elect, quadrennially, an editor for each of the following weekly papers, to Wit: the *Richmond Christian Advocate,* published at Richmond; the *Southern Christian Advocate,* published at Charleston; the *St. Louis Christian Advocate,* published at St. Louis; the *Memphis and Arkansas Christian Advocate,* published at Memphis; the *New Orleans Christian Advocate,* published at New Orleans; the *Texas Christian Advocate,* published at Galveston, and the *Evangelische Apologete,* published at the same place; the *Pacific Methodist,* published at San Francisco, California; and the *North Carolina Christian Advocate,* published at Raleigh; and in case of vacancy in the editorship of any of these papers, its Publishing Committee may fill the vacancy, with the approval of one of the Bishops.[18]

See the Outreach chapter for attention to *The Home Circle,* and to some extent to the *Quarterly Review.* Each appealed to a selected Southern readership. Through the array of *Christian Advocates* and *Sunday-School Visitor,* the MECS addressed its white adults and the men and women who furthered formation of children. Note that general conferences selected the editors of these communication devices for both Methodisms, South and North. Editors spoke to and for the whole church (whites at least). They possessed, as the connectional voice, what bishops, collectively as well as individually, could only wish for.

Serving Kentucky's Readers

Methodists in Kentucky most probably availed themselves of the serials listed under V above. The conference's *Minutes,* available in text form at Kentucky Wesleyan, show how the MECS and its publishers engaged the preachers and, through them, the church's reading members. Those for the 1850s generally follow a similar pattern, as the *Minutes* for 1853 should illustrate.[19] After Bishop Capers led the opening "divine service" and committee members "were appointed" (with later substitutions or

---

18 MECS, *General Conference Journal* (1858), 497.
19 Manuscript "Minutes" KY Wesleyan, *Journal of Kentucky Annual Conference* (1851–1859), typescript held by Kentucky Wesleyan and used with its permission, 1853, pp. 76–122. Other MECS Kentucky Minutes accessed at Asbury Theological Seminary and through the Duke Divinity School Library. The latter holds 1855–1870, 1872, and most subsequent years up to the 1939 unification of the three Methodisms. [NOTES: Page numbers can be provided, if needed, but are ignored here and in the following

additions referred to as elections), "A published letter on the subject of Sabbath Schools from the Rev. Thos O. Summers was read and referred to the Committee on Sabbath Schools." The three annual sermons occurred upfront, setting forth a substantive agenda for the conference and the Kentucky faithful. "J. [?] Bruce delivered the sermon on the ministry at 11 O'clock, A. M. L. D. Huston, the sermon on Education at 3 O'clock P. M. & J. S. Bayles the sermon on Missions at night."

Soon-to-be bishop H. H. Kavanaugh preached a funeral sermon to be sent to the *Lexington Observer and Reporter,* the *Kentucky Statesman,* and the *Shelby News.* He effectively presided much of the day. A publication, "Notes on the twenty-five Articles of Religion" by Rev. Dr. [?Jameson?] was referred to Committee on Books & Periodicals. A motion passed expressing appreciation for the three sermons and requesting that they be "forwarded" to the Nashville and Louisville *Christian Advocate.* Introductions of visitors included Edward Stevenson, head of the Book Concern, Louisville. A motion followed, expressing appreciation for Dr. Stevenson's management and success, and then came a short report of the Book Committee. The array of reports that followed—Bible Cause, Temperance, Sabbath Schools—should indicate, as other chapters show, that the conference routinely dealt with connectional and outreach interests. But striking, again, is how routine, regular, manifold, and substantive attention to formational matters dominated.

The report for Sabbath Schools called for creation of Methodist schools rather than participating in Union Schools and lamented difficulty in getting members to subscribe to the *Sunday School Visitor.* The conference's Education Committee announced the establishment of a new society, the "Ministerial Education Society of the Kentucky Conference." It also exhibited a Constitution for a Young Men's Aid Society to assist such folk to gain the "literary qualifications" needed for ministry. A report followed on Augusta College.

The conference statistics show the attention to formational matters, particularly in regard to Sunday schools: 18,319 Whites; 6,204 Colored; 81 Sabbath Schools; 93 Superintendents; 626 Teachers, 4,382 Sunday Schools; 17,389 Volumes in Library; Sunday School Money; Missionary Money $3,137.68; Bible Money $210.80; 213 1/3 Churches; 19 Parsonages; and 193 Local Preachers.

---

paragraphs. Bracketed question marks in quoted text indicate where a name or initial proved hard to read.]

The conference then "Resolved. That the subject of the religious instruction of the people of Color be referred to the several Quarterly Conferences of the Circuits and Stations that they may take such action on it as may be desirable."

Reports were heard about, and visiting committees of three were appointed for, Science Hill Female Academy and Lexington Female High School. No action was taken for a school dealt with the prior year, Albion Female Institute, Newport. Of the four instructional actions taken at the close of the Kentucky Conference that year, two dealt with formation. One expressed concern over the "alarming deficiency . . . of ministerial supply" and called in two resolutions, that God "would thrust out more laborers into his vineyard," and that a committee be established to help *poor* God in His work. The other instructed five members, but specifically Kavanaugh and Thomas Ralston, as "Commissioners on the subject of Education" to pursue support for & location of a "Conference High School."

The charges to Kavanaugh and Ralston show the Kentucky Conference to be committed to matters formational. That the conference boasted the two as members should indicate that they played important roles in shaping the whole church. Kavanaugh would soon become bishop.[20] Ralston, a delegate to the 1845 Louisville Conference that created the MECS and to subsequent general conferences, had headed the Methodist Female High School, edited the *Methodist Monthly*, and published his *Elements of Divinity*, long featured on the Course of Study for the MECS.

The *Minutes* for the later 1850s evidence similar preoccupation with formation for Kentucky whites. At points, they show the conference moving with the whole Southern church to empower its black members. In 1855, the conference identified its seven "Local Preachers for Deacon's Orders," three of them "a man of color." Similarly, among four "Local Deacons for Elder's Orders," three were "a man of color." Then

> Bishop Paine took the chair, and announced that the white preachers who had been elected to Deacon's orders would be ordained in the Methodist Church on tomorrow (Sabbath) at the close of the services in the forenoon, and that the white Deacons who had been elected to Elder's orders would be ordained in the same place at the close of the services in the afternoon of the same day, and

---

20 On Kavanaugh, see *Life and Times of H. H. Kavanaugh* by Albert H. Redford (Nashville: [n. pub.], 1884), HathiTrust Digital Library Rights: Public Domain, Google-digitized. Permanent URL: https://hdl.handle.net/2027/mdp.39015064339271.

that the colored preachers who had been elected to Deacon's or Elder's orders would be ordained at some suitable time in the African Methodist Church.[21]

In 1857, the *Minutes* indicated, for charge and for district, the numbers of white and of "colored" Sunday School "Scholars." The conference boasted 3,316 white and 357 "Colored" Scholars. Of the latter, most were in the Lexington (280), Maysville (40), and Harrodsburg (30) districts.[22]

For some formation of "colored" members, the MECS, or at least Kentucky Methodists, could look to black preachers and doubtless also Sunday school teachers. And they could avail themselves of an incredible array of publications published by the Southern church. Most of it clearly went to white readers. A particular basic formational device, the catechism, the MECS redesigned for its black members.

The Church's Publishing Vatican

Certainly, Kentucky Methodists and their reading counterparts across the MECS availed themselves of the huge number of books, tracts, and Sunday school materials. For that, they could, after the 1858 General Conference, look to J. B. M'Ferrin. Throughout that conference, he had been active again and again as the chairman of the Committee on Books and Periodicals. Thereafter, as noted above, the election made M'Ferrin the church's General Book Agent. The next year he showed his hand in pressing Southern Methodists to continue, increase, or launch their serious and formative reading. He did so with the *Catalogue of Southern Methodist Books and Miscellaneous Publications, On sale at the Publishing House, Nashville Tenn., and also at the Depository, New Orleans, LA., J. B. M'Ferrin, Agent.*[23] It showed what Southern Methodist readers had and had had available. With two pages, he specified the "Business Regulations for the Publishing House at Nashville." Then came a "General Catalogue" which listed books alphabetically, 41 pages (5–46; see figure 8 for a sample page issued two years later). Then came books by category or topic:

21   Manuscript "Minutes" KY Wesleyan, *Journal of Kentucky Annual Conference* (1851–1859), 1855, 204–05.
22   Manuscript "Minutes," 1857, 282–89.
23   J. B. McFerrin, *Catalogue of Southern Methodist Books and Miscellaneous Publications, On sale at the Publishing House, Nashville Tenn., and also at the Depository, New Orleans, LA.* (Nashville: Southern Methodist Publishing House, 1859).

Sunday-School List (47–52), Tract List (53), Church Registers (56), Appendix (57–66) with various publications:

- 1st the Acts of the Apostles, Notes on. By Pierce 75¢
- Last Winans's Discourses on Fundamental Religious Subjects, 589 pp., $2.00

Appendix, Part II, pp. 67–73

- 1st Abbott's Illustrated Histories column of titles for 60¢
- Last Will, Philosophical and Practical Treatise by T. C. Upham, $1.25

Then the catalogue carried books from other publishers or of other types (73–77), then School Books (78–79), *The Home Circle* for 1860 (80–81), *The Christian Advocate* (82), and *The Quarterly Review of the Methodist Episcopal Church, South* (83). Finally, the *Catalogue* featured advertisements for various Conference Depositories (84–85), recommendation for, and a sample constitution for, conference Book and Tract Depositories, various state and conference book operations as advertisements, *and* a final promotion for what to use when tired of reading—a sewing machine. So the Southern church provided 83 pages of reading material for all ages and an array of purposes.

A couple of years later, M'Ferrin's colleague, Summers, took only 10 pages to display and itemize the MECS's formational publications. The first page should suffice to indicate that reading had become important to and for the church and its white members.[24]

Southern white readers could start their acquisitions on the first page of "Books for Sale" with an "Abyssinian Boy"; purchase a page's worth to digest and be reassured in their thinking with Adam Clarke's *Christian Theology*, Harris's *Christian Liberality Explained and Enlarged*, James's *Christian Father's Present to his Children*, and John Wesley's *Christian Perfection*. The year prior to publication of the *Almanac*, the MECS Publishing House gathered catechisms for children of all ages. The eight were entitled:

24   *The Confederate States Almanac for the Year of Our Lord 1862, Being the 2d after Bissextile, or Leap Year, the 86th of American Independence, & the 2d of the Confederate States,* calculations made at the University of Alabama, ed. T. O. Summers, D.D. (Nashville: Southern Methodist Publ. House, 1862), 23. Hathi Trust http://hdl.handle.net/2027/nc01.ark:/13960/t2f77gv9s.

BOOKS FOR SALE

BY J. B. M'FERRIN, AGENT,

PUB. HOUSE M. E. CHURCH, SOUTH, NASHVILLE, TENN.

TWENTY-FIVE PER CENT. DISCOUNT TO WHOLESALE DEALERS. ON CASH PURCHASES, TEN PER CENT. ADDITIONAL ON NET AMOUNT OF BILL.

Abyssinian Boy.	$0 25
Advice to a Young Convert. By L. M. Lee, D.D.	0 65
Alexander the Great. Life of.	0 30
Alfred the Great, Life of.	0 35
Alleine's Alarm to Unconverted Sinners.	0 30
Alleine's Alarm and Baxter's Call.	0 40
Analysis of the Principles of Church Government: particularly that of the M. E. Church. By Henkle.	0 40
Ancient British Church. By Wm. Lindsay Alexander, D.D., F. S. A. S.	0 30
Anglo-Saxons, Lives of Eminent.	0 60
Annals of Southern Methodism. By Dr. Deems.	1 00
Apostolical Succession, Essay on. By Powell.	0 65
Apostolic Succession. By Abbey.	0 50
Apostolic Succession, End of. By Abbey.	0 30
Appeal of the Southern Commissioners. By Dr. Bascom.	0 25
Arminius, Life of James, D.D. By Brandt: trans. by Guthrie.	1 00
Australia and its Settlements.	0 30
Ball we live on.	0 25
Baptism. By Summers.	0 65
Baptism, Infant. By Chapman.	0 50
Baptismal Demonstrations. By R. Abbey.	0 10
Baxter's Call to the Unconverted.	0 25
Bereaved Parents Consoled. By Thornton. Gilt.	0 40
Do. do. Muslin.	0 30
Do. do. do.	0 25
Better Land. By Jeremiah Dodsworth.	0 75
Bible in Many Tongues.	0 30
Bible, Our English.	0 30
Bible Gleanings. By Mrs. Cross.	0 25
Bible Expositor.	0 40
Bible Readings for Every Day in the Year. Six vols.; per set,	2 50

Bible Christian: A View of Doctrinal, Experimental, and Practical Religion. By the Rev. Josephus Anderson.	0 50
Boatman's Daughter. By Barrett.	0 30
Buds and Blossoms. Two vols.	0 60
Biblical Atlas, (the New,) and Scripture Gazetteer.	1 00
Biographical Sketches of Eminent Itinerant Ministers. Muslin,	1 50
Muslin gilt,	2 00
Bramwell, William, Memoir of.	0 45
Bible Stories. By Rev. Daniel Stevenson, A.M., of the Kentucky Conference.	0 25
Browning on Perseverance.	0 55
Carvosso, Memoir of.	0 45
Catacombs. By Selina Bunbury.	0 25
Ceremonies of Modern Judaism. By Herman Baer.	0 40
Chapters for Children. By Old Humphrey.	0 30
Charity Superior to Knowledge. By Winans.	0 10
Charlemagne, Life and Times of.	0 30
Cheerful Chapters. By Old Humphrey.	0 35
Childs, Life of. By Edwards.	0 75
Christianity in Earnest, as Exemplified in the Life and Labors of the Rev. Hodgson Casson. By A. Steele.	0 35
Christian Theology. By Adam Clarke. Selected from his published and unpublished Writings. With a Life of the Author. By Dunn.	0 75
Christian Liberality Explained and Enforced. By Harris.	0 10
Christian Father's Present to his Children. By James.	0 50
Christian Perfection, Plain Account of. By John Wesley. 18mo, pp. 172.	0 30
24mo, pp. 172.	0 25

Figure 8

- Wesleyan Catechism, No. I.
- Wesleyan Catechism, No. II.
- Wesleyan Catechism, No. III.
- Scripture Catechism, No. I.
- Scripture Catechism, No. II.
- Catechism for the Methodist Missions, Part I.
- Catechism for the Methodist Missions, Part II.
- A Manual for Infant Schools.[25]

The third of these, "Adapted to the Use of Families and Schools," ran answers to standard queries over several pages and would tax twenty-first-century readers, even seminarians. The two for slaves, described above, allowed Capers to offer instruction from his grave. It had acquired a gentler name "For the Methodist Missions" and had been reshaped to serve "the mass of colored people, whether children or adults," and so "had better be confined to the rudiments of Christian knowledge."[26] Race figured materially in the agenda of the MECS (though attention here is needed to show that necessarily but perhaps disproportionately).

The Southern Church's Self-Portrayal

The *Journal of the General Conference* and conference *Minutes* depict Southern Methodism as it sought to govern itself, as much of the above indicates. A similar self-assessment can be found in the various communications devices with which the church kept readers informed, as for instance the *Quarterly Review* and *Christian Advocate*. Useful as well are less-official publications including *Annals of Southern Methodism*,[27] another communicative device over which M'Ferrin exercised his leadership. That, for 1857, typified the church's formative commitment.

The *Annals* devoted a third of its 430 pages to formation: Colleges and Schools, Sunday-schools, and Southern Methodist Literature. Of course, Southern Methodism, as Connection, received attention in separate short sections on individual annual conferences, Historical Sketches

25 *Catechisms of the Methodist Episcopal Church, South*, revised by T. O. Summers, D.D.; with an introduction by Bishop Pierce (Nashville: Southern Methodist Publishing House, 1861), HathiTrust Digital, Library Rights Public Domain. Permanent URL: https://hdl.handle.net/2027/dul1.ark:/13960/t3902xg8g.
26 MECS, *Catechisms*, 3 (separately paginated).
27 See *Annals of Southern Methodism for 1857*, Charles F. Deems, D. D., editor (Nashville: Published by J. B. M'Ferrin, Agent, for the Methodist Episcopal Church, South, 1858).

(individuals, institutions, and overviews), and "In Memoriam" (death notices). It also contained outreach sections on missions, "Dedication of Churches" (individual churches), obituaries, and "Our People of Color" (a very short section). But, if showing its slavery colors, at least the Southern church attended to its black members. Did the Northern church?

Churching Readers in the Northern Church

Cincinnati hosted the MEC's Sunday-School Union in 1857.[28] Its first business on Sabbath, October 18th, was worship in the morning and an afternoon of Children's Meetings, led by Ohio and national leaders:

SUNDAY MORNING SERVICES

The services began on Sabbath morning, October 18, when sermons bearing on Sabbath schools were preached as follows:

Wesley Chapel: Rev. JAMES BAUME, Chicago, Illinois. Deut. vi, 6–8
Asbury Chapel: Rev. T. M. EDDY, Chicago, Illinois. Psalm lxxviii, 3–8
Union Chapel: Rev. F. G. HIBBARD, Auburn, New-York. John xxi, 15–17
Ninth-Street: Rev. DANIEL WISE, New-York. John xxi, 16
Morris Chapel: Rev. S. L. YOURTEE. Prov. xxii, 6
Christie Chapel: Rev. MOSES HILL, Cleveland, Ohio. Matt, vi, 22, 23
Park-Street: Rev. J. F. CHALFANT. Isa. xliv, 3
Raper Chapel: Rev. ADAM POE.
M'Kendree Chapel: Rev. C. FERGUSON. 1 Peter iii, 8
Walnut Hills: Rev. MR. WARREN.
Mount Auburn: Rev. T. S. DUNN. Prov. xxii, 6
Greenup-Street, Covington: Rev. G. BATTELLE.
Main-Street, Covington: Rev. S. S. BELLVILLE.
Finley Chapel: Rev. M. SMITH. Isa. lxiv, 9, 10, 13
York-Street: Rev. T. D. CROW.

---

28 *Annual Report of the Sunday School Union of the Methodist Episcopal Church*, 1857–1858 (New York: Lane & Scott, n.d.), HathiTrust Digital Library, Permanent URL: https://hdl.handle.net/2027/uiug.30112112399610. Initially printed as *Annual Report of the Sunday School Union of the Methodist Episcopal Church*, 1858 (New York: Printed for the Union, 1858) but covering the 1857 meeting.

Collections were taken up in three or four of the churches only, it being the opinion of the friends of the "Union" that the prevailing financial panic made it inexpedient to attempt the raising of funds at that moment. We are assured, however, that the Cincinnati Churches will not fail to do nobly for our treasury during the year.

CHILDREN'S MEETINGS

In the afternoon very large meetings of children and teachers were held, and addresses to the children delivered at half past two o'clock, by the persons named, in the following churches:

Wesley Chapel: D. WISE, T. M. EDDY, J. J. THOMPSON. Rev. William Herr presided.
Ninth-Street: J. F. CHALFANT, J. F. FORBUS, C. FERGUSON
Morris Chapel: BISHOP MORRIS, DR. COMEGYS, A. M. SEARLES, J. G. L. M'KOWN
Christie Chapel: DR. E. B. STEVENS, THOMAS COLLETT, W. H. SUTHERLAND
M'Kendree Chapel: S. H. BURTON, E. P. JAMES
Finley Chapel: T. D. CROW, M. SMITH, C. F. BROOKE
Greenup-Street, Covington, Ky.: M. M. BENTON, G. BATTELLE, S. S. BELLVILLE

. . . .

. . . The singing in all of the afternoon meetings was exceedingly fine. It would be invidious to particularize.[29]

Neither the morning Sunday worship nor the afternoon Children's Services included New Street, Cincinnati's black church. Nor did the MEC's Sunday School Union—it covered the whole church's Sunday School operations, activities, or programming—deign to mention colored, black, or Negro membership or their interests. The *Report* did deal with anti-slavery as a political issue, a cause, and a concern for the church. But it did not deal with black members and blacks generally. To be sure, among its several hundred children's books, five dealt with the overall issue:

---

29 *Annual Report of the Sunday School Union of the Methodist Episcopal Church* (1858), 7–8. On American Sunday schools, see the classic but still pertinent studies: Robert W. Lynn and Elliott Wright, *The Big Little School: Sunday Child of American Protestantism* (New York: Harper & Row, 1971), and Anne M. Boylan, *Sunday School: The Formation of an American Institution, 1790–1880* (New Haven and London: Yale University Press, 1988).

Children's Anti-Slavery Book, illustrated. [in preparation]
Missions in Western Africa
Converted Slave—selected from our Youth's Library
Pious Negroes—Among the "German Sunday-school books"
The Hottentots—Western Book Concern.[30]

The next year, as anti-slavery boiled more through the MEC, the early pages of the *Report* recalled the development of the Sunday school cause among Methodists generally. About its planting on American soils, it noted "In 1790 the Methodist Conference formally resolved on establishing Sunday schools for poor children, white and black."[31]

The *Report* contained actions by the various conferences on matters before the church, including a published declaration by the editor, Daniel Wise, that the *Sunday School Advocate* would speak out against slavery and the deterioration of the nation's stance thereon. A section of the *Report*, "Annual Conferences: Resolutions and Sunday-School Committees," consuming pages 11–35, reproduced declarations from the conference societies on issues before the church. Some, but not all, spoke on slavery and its being addressed in Sunday school. The Delaware Conference offered four resolutions, the fourth:

> Resolved, That this conference fully approve the antislavery course of the Rev. Drs. Whedon and Wise, in the conduct of the Methodist Quarterly Review and of the Sunday School Advocate, and that we will endeavor to promote the circulation of those periodicals among our people."

Ohio had a more evasive stance in the fourth of its five:

> Resolved, That we approve of the editorial course of Rev. Dr. Wise, in making the Sunday School Advocate the true representative both of the doctrine and morals of our Church, and trust that it will continue to speak out prudently against every sin, whether individual or national.[32]

---

30 *Annual Report of the Sunday School Union of the Methodist Episcopal Church* (1858), 74–77. NOTE: *Children's Anti-Slavery Book* and *Missions in Western Africa* were among the "One Hundred Books."

31 *Annual Report of the Sunday School Union of the Methodist Episcopal Church* (1858), 8; pagination in the published volume followed the complete 1858 Report. Initially printed as *Annual Report of the Sunday School Union of the Methodist Episcopal Church*, 1859 (New York: Printed for the Union, 1859), but covering the 1858 meeting.

32 *Annual Report of the Sunday-School Union of the Methodist Episcopal Church* (1858), 13, 26.

Although vocal on slavery, neither the 1858 nor 1859 long *Report* showed the national Sunday School Union to have had any substantial, ongoing, relevant programmatic involvement with the nation's black population—slave or free. At the conference level, the Sunday school sections of Ohio and Cincinnati *Minutes* also showed little specific engagement with, interest in, or strategy for its black membership. However, both conferences had, five years earlier, increased attention to formational challenges they needed to address for black people more generally and, of course, those within the fold. And their hopes, as expressed in annual *Minutes*, did attend to Sunday schools, their status and progress.

The Sunday School Enterprise

The MEC made available quite ample and substantial resources for the formation of its youth. That was true on a national level but also for, by, and within the conferences. The "Report of the Board of Managers" for the Sunday School Union for 1859 (covering 1858 doings and numbers) required over 20 pages and provided these national statistics, interesting in part for the Cincinnati and Ohio data:[33]
The totals in figure 9 are striking:

•	Sunday Schools	11,834
•	Officers & Teachers	131,344
•	Scholars	695,302 [increase from the prior year of 56,182]
•	Volumes in Library	2,146,264
•	Bible Classes	12,320
•	Scholars in Infant classes	79,157
•	Expenses of schools	107,786
•	Amt. Raised for SSU	11,300
•	SS Advocates	152,641
•	No. Conversions	33,315 [prior year 14,669]

Here, as elsewhere, the church paid careful attention to counts: schools, teachers, students (scholars), materials, classes, money, serials, and *conversions*. In a study focused entirely on Christian education, each of the above would deserve comment. Particularly striking is the figure of 187,000 for circulation of the *Sunday School Advocate*. Of that production, 115,000

---

33 *Annual Report of the Sunday School Union of the Methodist Episcopal Church* (1858), 50.

SUMMARY OF SUNDAY-SCHOOL STATISTICS

Of the Methodist Episcopal Church.

1858.

CONFERENCES.	No. of Sunday Schools.	No. of Officers and Teachers.	No. of S. Scholars.	No. of Volumes in Library.	No. of Bible Classes.	No. of Scholars in Infant Classes.	Expenses of Schools this Year.	Amount raised for the S. S. Union.	Sunday-School Advocates taken.	No. of Conversion.
Arkansas (1853)	25	131	652	1,984	15	131	$11	....	....	....
Baltimore	300	4,139	20,852	56,443	385	1,545	2,981	$9	2,234	757
Black River	339	3,278	14,638	39,647	179	873	2,086	152	4,965	545
California	73	624	3,185	20,336	54	420	3,330	297	2,290	115
Cincinnati	386	4,891	29,307	100,521	613	4,014	3,832	436	9,659	1,344
Delaware	270	3,114	15,688	50,635	°166	1,724	1,888	149	389	....
Detroit	282	2,544	11,027	36,661	137	824	1,382	78	2,670	530
East Baltimore	476	6,267	31,782	99,210	523	3,635	5,165	43	3,590	1,208
East Genesee	363	3,860	19,553	47,901	229	2,126	2,740	124	5,445	767
East Maine	166	1,494	7,931	25,428	217	616	1,118	113	2,331	521
Erie	445	5,010	23,712	75,884	444	1,946	2,926	319	4,917	1,224
Genesee	231	2,384	11,203	34,655	°143	1,029	2,361	187	3,544	....
Illinois	418	3,529	20,643	66,030	315	2,801	2,800	224	5,010	1,530
Indiana	229	2,027	11,519	31,273	194	1,204	1,081	84	2,305	803
Iowa	318	3,130	16,234	40,823	260	1,401	1,661	5	2,014	837
Kansas & Neb.	73	524	1,823	7,777	36	172	346	12	452	68
Kentucky	32	268	1,478	4,472	°31	173	157	1	316	....
Maine	111	1,332	7,983	26,157	236	506	1,376	118	2,464	743
Michigan	264	2,254	9,754	27,079	125	606	1,015	74	1,794	325
Minnesota	49	426	1,993	5,667	°15	130	336	20	292	....
Missouri	20	163	875	1,955	°11	35	121	...	221	....
Newark	248	3,398	18,000	53,951	323	2,380	3,787	750	3,968	895
New-England	148	2,639	17,618	55,873	655	2,364	3,265	417	5,618	973
New-Hampshire	107	1,436	9,373	29,322	504	780	1,285	197	3,013	991
New-Jersey	262	3,661	19,050	59,915	291	2,081	2,928	536	3,423	861
New-York	429	5,187	28,128	69,153	288	3,306	3,355	893	7,052	1,577
New-York East	220	3,646	22,264	77,115	322	4,112	5,809	1,050	6,375	1,825
North Indiana	360	3,479	18,639	55,840	131	1,643	1,074	47	1,387	787
North Ohio	320	3,659	17,945	55,237	360	2,800	2,404	196	4,112	842
N. W. Indiana	237	2,122	11,918	36,306	226	1,758	1,343	36	1,763	808
Ohio	532	5,851	30,216	99,418	593	3,690	2,953	190	4,833	1,431
Oneida	268	2,578	12,605	39,165	168	1,138	1,828	116	4,332	720
Oregon	49	324	1,480	8,754	°27	103	527	70	277	....
Peoria	273	2,525	14,068	44,496	311	2,303	2,432	84	3,784	1,054
Philadelphia	519	8,225	47,184	138,988	401	6,361	10,827	1,061	8,469	1,893
Pittsburgh	475	5,908	30,117	86,876	962	3,742	4,759	416	4,018	1,847
Providence	140	2,106	12,611	56,974	391	1,808	2,253	319	6,876	1,023
Rock River	323	3,315	17,149	48,434	°175	1,569	3,432	531	3,454	....
South E. Indiana	250	2,356	13,626	42,612	°204	1,383	1,637	91	2,994	....
Southern Illinois	288	2,633	12,493	38,980	252	1,765	2,119	89	2,620	513
Troy	409	4,478	24,572	77,080	410	2,599	5,138	447	8,139	1,150
Upper Iowa	215	2,125	10,300	30,870	174	1,041	1,488	57	2,735	509
Vermont	82	828	5,488	18,416	320	461	906	69	1,554	313
Western Virginia	209	2,104	9,504	24,072	197	1,805	941	58	719	443
West Wisconsin	129	1,096	5,744	14,945	68	330	521	9	997	247
Wisconsin	163	1,663	9,742	21,642	109	601	815	7	1,394	296
Wyoming	263	2,346	11,450	38,369	°130	1,323	1,248	156	2,149	....
German Mission	19	137	1,190	916	...	....	....	...	....	....
Liberia do.	26	115	862	1,719	...	....	....	...	....	....
Buenos Ayres.	1	15	134	....	...	....	....	(982 from sundries)		
Total	11,834	131,344	695,302	2,146,264	12,320	79,157	107,786	11,300	152,641	32,315
Last year	11,229	120,421	639,120	2,054,253	11,405	71,645	115,559	11,269	145,755	14,669
Increase	605	10,923	56,182	92,011	915	7,512	....	31	6,886	17,646
Decrease	...	....	......	......	...	....	7,773	..	......	....

* The figures marked with an asterisk, and those in the columns on the right of the asterisks, are from the returns of 1856.

Figure 9

Advocates went out from the New York, and 72,000 from the Cincinnati offices.[34] Midwestern German kids doubtless also shared the 11,900 copies of *Die Sontag Schul Glocke,* then boasting a circulation of 11,900.[35]

---

34 *Annual Report of the Sunday School Union of the Methodist Episcopal Church* (1858), 58.
35 *Annual Report of the Sunday School Union of the Methodist Episcopal Church* (1858), 55.

At the conference level, as well as at the national and regional, reports on the Sunday schools and the layers of the conference society did not attend to black children or indicate whether the resourcing their formation constituted agenda. The reports do show, as just noted, that German American kids received attention. And the tables carried in the minutes indicate the overall seriousness of the endeavor. Those for Cincinnati in 1854 are reproduced in the Outreach chapter. Those for 1858 (figure 10) provide a glimpse of the Sunday school enterprise, for white children (German and English speaking).[36]

Counting, as already noted, has preoccupied Methodists ever since Wesley, for virtually all purposes, at every ecclesial level, for signs of progress or decline, and to assign credit or blame. The first five counts were explicitly Sunday-school related. The next three organizations served multiple purposes, formation among them. And the last seven identified what the Sunday schools had yielded in human terms. Notably absent in the recapitulation was attention to gender, ethnicity, and race. However, the Ohio conferences became ever more vocally committed to ending slavery.

The People of Color Among Us

The 1854 Cincinnati *Minutes*, as noted in the Outreach chapter, carry successively a Report on Colonization, a Report on People of Color among us, and a Report on Slavery. (For assessment of these reports for their missional significance, consult that chapter.)

In the first report, the conference committed itself to collaborating in the establishment of a colonization society for Ohio and furthering its cause. The several-page report echoed the Colonization Society's longstanding arguments (since 1817) that planting willing émigrés in Africa would provide them a viable future, would abate practices of slavery within Africa, and would similarly undercut slaveholding in the US.[37] The third of these reports, that on slavery, recalled that the MEC had, from its birth, sought its "destruction by all wise and prudent means." Briefly charting the church's steady and substantive retreat from that commitment, the committee observed:

---

36 *Minutes of the Cincinnati Annual Conference of the Methodist Episcopal Church, For the Year 1858* (Cincinnati: Printed at the Methodist Book Concern, 1858), 45.

37 *Minutes of the Cincinnati Annual Conference* (September 1854), 27–29.

CINCINNATI ANNUAL CONFERENCE. 45

RECAPITULATION.

Districts.	Volumes in Library.	Scholars	Officers & Teachers.	Schools	Amount for Sunday School Union	Amount for Bible Society	Amount for Tract Society	Amount for Missionary Society	Amount for Conference Claimants	Probable Value	Parsonages	Probable Value	Churches	Children Baptized	Adults Baptized	Local Preachers	Probationers	Deaths	Members
East Cincinnati District	10,281	2,001	416	29	$132 42	$164 24		$1,669 18	$291 66	$10,400	4	$126,700	32	70	145	31	241	43	2,599
West "	16,829	4,633	638	48	36 12	280 50	$14 00	3,590 64	609 20	4,600	6	162,510	40	277	994	28	518	43	3,506
Dayton District	12,031	3,015	524	37	64 70	233 10	2 00	1,078 79	100 65	11,600	7	78,900	48	196	337	21	431	34	3,180
Urbana "	10,218	3,532	633	48		112 47		1,475 82	171 70	8,2??	10	81,900	56	149	176	37	405	41	4,622
Xenia "	10,987	3,202	62?	45	38 24	129 74	16 04	1,286 61	118 69	12,300	9	62,775	55	78	307	28	394	39	3,585
Hillsboro "	14,049	4,799	615	65	24 97	236 75		1,584 11	102 41	9,550	12	74,325	71	168	398	41	549	72	4,908
Georgetown District	13,335	4,54?	699	74	24 25	129 64	16 25	1,558 77	166 91	7,300	10	63,100	71	160	324	40	636	77	5,136
Cincinnati German District	4,694	858	219	19	24 74	49 58	33 30	605 55	103 29	2,850	4	45,850	18	183	1	10	134	15	1,114
Ohio "	3,981	843	224	25	33 67	50 79	45 24	548 31	114 64	2,050	7	21,510	24	175		13	2?3	12	1,306
Total for 1858	95,718	27,975	4,593	390	$378 41	$1,409 81	$126 83	$13,287 80	$1,706 45	$68,850	69	$717,560	41?	1,392	1,969	253	3,441	376	29,749
Total for 1857	89,303	25,516	4,244	367	280 67	1,431 71	210 44	12,911 98	1,459 74	76,500	63	648,940	404	892	943	236	2,016	292	97,401
Increase	13,325	2,459	349	23	$97 74			$1,175 82	$246 71		7	$68,620	7	500	1,019	17	1,425	84	2,348
Decrease						$21 90	$83 61			$7,650									

Figure 10

For fifty years the standing inquiry of the Church has been, What shall be done? and practically the answer has been, Nothing. For it cannot be denied, that instead of anything toward the extirpation of this evil being effected by the Church, slavery has made large encroachments upon the Church and upon the country.

To change the church and return to its formative cause, and in recognition of then current realities, it recommended:

1. Resolved, That we earnestly recommend our people to memorialize Congress, asking the repeal of the Fugitive-Slave law, and the re-enactment of so much of the late law known as the Missouri Compromise, as excluded slavery from Kansas and Nebraska and other territory of the United States.
2. Resolved, That persons holding slaves for gain, or for their own convenience in any way, or with the intention of perpetuating the bondage of the slave, should not be received into the Methodist Episcopal Church, nor suffered to continue therein.[38]

Between those two reports, the "Report of People of Color Among Us," at least symbolically, looked across the Ohio River and offered hopeful views for and about American black folk. The report beckoned Ohio's colored people toward the horizon, not just the few black Methodists.

What can best be done to promote the welfare of the people of color among us? is indeed a great question. We give no countenance to any theory which goes to deprive the black man of his full share in our common humanity, but hail him as a man and a brother in accordance with that grand affirmation of the Bible, which must forever settle the unity of the human race, that God "hath made of one blood all nations of men for to dwell on all the face of the earth." Hence, we cordially concede our obligation to do good to the colored race according to our ability and their necessity, as members of the wide-spread family of man. Here, then, is an extensive field open for benevolent enterprise, where a part of the large donations of the rich and the smaller contributions of those of less ability may advantageously mingle together; and where the

38 *Minutes of the Cincinnati Annual Conference* (September 1854), 34–36.

patriot, the statesman, and the philanthropist of every description may unite in the accomplishment of a noble work of charity and labor of love.[39]

The committee's and conference's vision moved beyond colonization and ending slavery to, at least, formational beginnings, albeit segregated and far from "separate but equal." Noting that "School-houses are almost unknown among the colored people of our country," it called for "separate schools for colored children." Furthering that cause, the committee recalled Methodism's early divisions over race, notably that led by Richard Allen, but now sought "a more confidential fraternization and closer communion of our Church with the African Methodist Episcopal Church than has heretofore existed, that we may unite our wisdom in devising and our influence in executing the best means for the intellectual and moral improvement of the colored race." It spelled out that second vision as well:

We might perhaps include some of their destitute neighborhoods in our domestic missions, or we might sustain with funds trustworthy colored preachers, to carry to such destitute settlements the Gospel of Christ, and labor for their salvation. We recommend that our ministers avail themselves of all opportunities which may be presented of preaching to them, and in every possible way encourage their ministry and membership to build up a holy people, who may exert great moral power over the colored race, and be the means of rescuing many of them from sin and ignorance in this life, and of securing their happy destiny in eternity.[40]

Heading where the Sunday School Union had feared to tread, the committee urged the conference to encourage formation of Sunday schools. In furthering the third initiative, the "colored people in our midst" ought "to be advised, and if possible influenced to organize Sunday Schools wherever ten of their children can be collected together, and teachers procured; and if need be, let white persons volunteer to become teachers."[41]

A fourth initiative also called for the shaping and forming of the state's and nation's black people at higher, albeit also segregated, levels.

39 *Minutes of the Cincinnati Annual Conference* (September 1854), 29.
40 *Minutes of the Cincinnati Annual Conference* (September 1854), 31–32.
41 *Minutes of the Cincinnati Annual Conference* (September 1854), 32.

> Your Committee recommend the establishment of one literary
> institution of a high order in the west for the more effectual train-
> ing of colored men for distinguished usefulness, but especially to
> prepare a sufficient number of teachers, male and female, to supply
> their schools with competent and well-trained instructors wher-
> ever colored teachers may be needed. There is a great lack of well-
> qualified ministers and teachers among the colored people; and
> we can think of no better plan than this to supply the lamentable
> deficiency. It is probable the number of colored people in our midst
> will greatly increase; hence the greater necessity of increasing the
> number of intelligent and pious ministers and teachers, to educate
> and train the race in a proper manner.[42]

The report did go on into outreach terrain, imagining that some of the
ministers and teachers might go "back to the father-land, to strengthen
the young republic and co-operate with our successful mission conference in Liberia" or help in leading "emigration to another country" should
that also beckon as a homeland.[43] Two years later, what the committee
had imagined resulted in the conference's launching Wilberforce University; and roughly a decade later, the "comity" with the AME church would
result in its being transferred into that denomination's "membership."[44]

The committee recommended that its four formational recommendations be furthered by appointment of an agent for that cause.
Duly assigned that responsibility was its chairman, J. F. Wright. The Ohio
Conference had, as well, a committee assigned the responsibility of
"Education of Free People of Color." In its very succinct report relative to
"documents, forwarded to this conference by a committee of the Cincinnati conference, relative to the education of the free people of color,"
it called for cooperation in the cause and for appointment of a general
agent. The two conferences ought, it judged, "to co-operate in the very
worthy object of elevating both intellectually and morally, the free people of color in the west."[45]

The next year (1855), the Cincinnati Conference made clearer its
commitment to formation for Ohio's "colored population" from Sunday
schools through to colleges:

---

42 *Minutes of the Cincinnati Annual Conference* (September 1854), 32.

43 *Minutes of the Cincinnati Annual Conference* (September 1854), 32–33.

44 On the AMEC and Wilberforce University, see Dennis C. Dickerson, *The African Methodist Episcopal Church: A History* (Cambridge: Cambridge University Press, 2020).

45 *Minutes of the Ohio Annual Conference of the Methodist Episcopal Church* (1854), 15.

1. Resolved, That we recommend the appointment of Rev. John F. Wright as general agent for this conference, to take the incipient steps for a college for the colored people in this state.
2. Resolved, That our delegates be, and are hereby instructed, to bring this subject before the next General conference for their sanction and assistance.
3. Resolved, That we make an effort to establish Sabbath and day schools among the colored people.
4. Resolved, That it be the duty of our general agent to co-operate with the African Methodist Episcopal Churches, in promoting Sabbath schools, and other educational interests of the colored people.
5. Resolved, That it be made the duty of the general agent to prepare and circulate a petition, to be presented at the opening of the next session of Ohio Legislature, praying for a grant toward the founding and endowment of a college for the colored population.
6. Resolved, That we can see no good reason why the prayer of the petitioners of the New-Street Colored Church, of Cincinnati, should not be granted; and if the present or any future work among the colored people, within the bounds of our conference, can be better supplied by colored than by white ministers, and suitable men be recommended to the conference, we can see no good reason why they should not be admitted.[46]

Notable in the above recommendations was encouragement of collaboration with the AMEs.

More remarkable was the last resolution, which broke new ground in proposing to bring black men into the ministry and into some form of conference membership. Unclear is whether the Cincinnati Conference proposed that "colored" preachers be fully ordained and admissible to conference membership. Perhaps conference members imagined ordaining black men as local preachers and, therefore, not sitting with them shoulder-to-shoulder in conference sessions. Even imagining elevating

46 *Minutes of the Cincinnati Annual Conference of the Methodist Episcopal Church, For the Year 1855* (Cincinnati: Printed at the Methodist Book Concern. R. P. Thompson, printer. 1855), 115–16.

blacks into the ministry (in whatever capacity) is remarkable. It took a decade for the MEC, as a denomination, to create black annual conferences, so restructuring the church, formally authorizing black ministry for black people, and establishing segregation as ecclesial policy. Thereby the Cincinnati brethren had anticipated what would be denominational policy and practice for over a century: segregation.

Also remarkable is that the move came despite the very, very small black membership in the Cincinnati Conference. For 1854, the "colored" membership in the whole conference was 132, having shrunk by 24 from 1853. And of that number, 113 belonged to the black church, New Street.[47] Two years later, New Street's numbers had declined further to 87, and the total to 98.[48]

The Northern church had not, like Southern Methodism, limited its formational agenda for black people to the catechism. And by the 1850s, the MEC had begun to imagine resourcing black neighbors and its few black members with portions of the educational apparatus with which it served its white men, women, and children. Notable among the for-blacks-only institutions was the move toward creating a college (Wilberforce, see below). The General Conference authorized such in 1856:

> On motion of Cyrus Brooks, the order of the day was suspended to receive a report from a special committee. Cyrus Brooks, Chairman of the Committee on the Education of Colored Youth, presented a report, which was read, and, on motion of J. Dodge, was adopted, and ordered to be printed. The report, as adopted, contained the following resolutions:
>
> 1.   Resolved, That, in the judgment of this General Conference, the religious education of the people of color in our land will tend most effectually and speedily, under God, to their elevation in this country, and to prepare the way for the restoration of the benighted millions of down-trodden Africa to all the blessings of civilization, science, and religion.
> 2.   Resolved, That we look upon the proposed plan for the education of the colored youth of our land, as of God, and as promising great good to the people of color among us, and untold blessings to the land of their ancestors; and we do most

---

47   *Minutes of the Cincinnati Annual Conference* (1854), 12, 9.
48   *Minutes of the Cincinnati Annual Conference* (1856), 13, 16.

earnestly recommend this noble work to the sympathy, the prayers, and the generous benefactions of all who desire the elevation of the entire family of man.

3. Resolved, That we bespeak for the agents of this enterprise a cordial reception on the part of all Christians and philanthropists, hoping that they may be successful, not only in awakening sympathy and enlisting prayers, but also in gathering funds to pay for the property purchased, and to afford a liberal endowment of the institution, so as to place it on an equal footing with the best institutions of learning in our country.[49]

The same General Conference moved to address the concerns that the Cincinnati and other conferences had sought, namely, to make provision for credentialing and gathering "colored" preachers. The following motions, duly inserted in the *Discipline*, established "separate and unequal" preaching rights and resourcing, but nevertheless moved toward recognizing black talents:

Chapter VIII.—Of the Rights and Privileges of Our Colored Members.

1. Our colored preachers and official members shall have all the privileges which are usual to others in quarterly conferences, where the usages of the country do not forbid it. And the presiding elder may hold for them a separate quarterly conference, when in his judgment it shall be expedient.

2. The bishop or presiding elder may employ colored preachers to travel and preach, when their services are judged necessary. Provided, that no one shall be so employed without having been recommended by a quarterly conference.

3. The Bishops may call a conference once in each year of our colored local preachers, within the bounds of any one or more of our districts, for the purpose of conferring with them with respect to the wants of the work among our colored people, and the best means to be employed in promoting its prosperity; at which conference, the presiding elder within whose district, and under whose care, the colored churches and congregations are, shall be present. Provided, that the holding of said conference or conferences shall be recommended by an

---

49 *Journal of the General Conference of the Methodist Episcopal Church* (1856), 104.

annual conference, and the Bishops, upon due inquiry, shall deem it practicable and expedient.[50]

So the Northern church charted a way forward on formation of black leadership.

Formation of German Methodism

By 1856, the Cincinnati Conference had moved to name its new institution "for the education of colored youth" Wilberforce University, approved purchase of "the grounds and buildings of the Tawawa Springs," and identified those to constitute its Board of Trustees. Among that body was William (Wilhelm) Nast. Nast, by that point, had emerged as the "Apostle Paul/Martin Luther/John Wesley/Francis Asbury" for German Methodism. Symbolic of his multi-agency and many roles were the Course of Study readings and examiners for the Cincinnati Conference.

COMMITTEES OF EXAMINATION FOR 1855 GERMAN

First Year. Bible—Doctrines: F. Schimmelpfenning. Wesley's Sermons, No. 1 to 15, G. Nachtrieb. Watson's Apology, C Bier. Discipline, H. Henke. Grammar, G. A. Reuter. Wesley's Life, to be read.

Second Year. Sacraments and the Distinctive Doctrines of the Methodist Episcopal Church, J. Rothweiler. Grammar, J. Rothweiler. Wesley's Sermons, No. 16 to 30, and Bogue's Divine Authority of the New Testament, C. Gahn. Wesley's Christian Perfection, N. Nuhfer. Discipline, P. Brodbeck.

Third Year. Fletcher's Appeal, John Hoppen. Church History, Christian Wydtenbach. Nelson's Causes of Infidelity, P. Schneider. Discipline, B. Browmiller. Grammar, **W. Nast.**

Fourth Year. Mental and Moral Philosophy, **W. Nast.** Grammar, **W. Nast**. Haldane's Authenticity and Inspiration of the Bible, P. Wilkins. Biblical History and Chronology, W. Ahrens. Church History, G. Danker. Methodist Economy, J. A. Klein.

On Composition, for the Four Classes, **Wm. Nast.**[51]

---

50 *Journal of the General Conference of the Methodist Episcopal Church* (1856), 183. *The Doctrines and Discipline of the Methodist Episcopal Church, 1856* (New York: Carlton & Porter, 1856), 86–87.

51 *Minutes of the Cincinnati Annual Conference* (1855), 56–57.

Not included in the array of texts were several that Nast himself had already written. Nor mentioned was the Luther-like theological/formative/practical/everyday guidance that he provided German Methodism through *Der Christliche Apologete*, which he had launched fifteen years earlier and edited for over half a century. By the late 1850s, it had a circulation of 8,900.[52]

He also produced a series of catechisms, hymn and prayer books, a biography of John Wesley, the German language versions of Wesley's sermons, and later, his own commentary on the Gospels. Also, after our time frame here, he aided in the founding of and served as first president of Baldwin-Wallace College, then a German American institution.

Nast's oversight of formation for children included publications by others: books, pamphlets, spiritual resources, and materials for the German children. The list of items in figure 11 were, as indicated, issued by the Cincinnati-based Western Book Concern in 1857:[53]

In his "apostolic" office, Nast had spread Methodism over the Midwestern world—as promoter, as author, as activitist, as founder. He began in the late 1830s, as missionary to Cincinnati's German community, gradually extended his Pauline service from Ohio into neighboring states, and eventually traveled to Europe to plant Methodism and save Germans from Catholic and Protestant heresies. Before the Cincinnati Conference launched in 1852, Nast had been party to establishing a German Missionary Conference.[54] Nast had carried the German districts across the Ohio "ocean" into the Cincinnati Conference. By 1856, and Asbury-like, his plantings had yielded four German districts: Cincinnati, Ohio, North Ohio, and Michigan. The appointments for the year listed "Wm. Nast, Editor of Christian Apologist, and member of Buck-eye Street Church quarterly conference."[55] The heroic metaphors used here for Nast may be overreaching or excessively cute but perhaps do serve to underscore the formative roles he played in the formation of German Methodism.

---

52 *Annual Report of the Sunday School Union of the Methodist Episcopal Church* (1859), 55.
53 *Annual Report of the Sunday School Union of the Methodist Episcopal Church* (1859), 55.
54 *Minutes of the Ohio Annual Conference of the Methodist Episcopal Church (1851)*, 211–218 and Reports.
55 *Minutes of the Cincinnati Annual Conference, at Cincinnati (1856)*, 39–40.

The following are the German Sunday-school books issued at the Western Book Concern during the year :

Blooming Hopes and Withered Joys. 18mo	$0 25
The Little Watercress-sellers. 18mo	0 15
The Lost Key. 18mo	0 20
The Great Journey. 18mo	0 20
Mary Oakland. 18mo	0 25
Poor Mary. 18mo	0 25
Six Steps to Honor. 16mo	0 40
Armor of Light. 16mo	0 40
Harry Budd. 16mo	0 40
Waltersdorf's Letter to the Youths. 16mo	0 35
The Star of Bethlehem, (Sunday Pictorial.) 4to	0 25
The Good Shepherd. 4to	0 25
Sisterly Stories. 48mo	0 02
Pious Negroes. 18mo	3 and 6
Good Children. 18mo	3 and 6
Blessings of the Bible. 18mo	3 and 6
Blessings of Tracts. 18mo	3 and 6
Help in Need. 18mo	3 and 6
Beware of Sin. 18mo	3 and 6
The Hottentots. 18mo	4 and 7
Triumph of Truth. 18mo	0 20
The Problem of the Christian Church in the 19th Century. 18mo	0 20
The Successful Merchant. 18mo	0 45
Hare on Justification. 18mo	0 30
Haldane's Genuineness and Divine Inspiration of the Bible. 18mo	0 35
Zeller's Psychology. 18mo	0 30
Alphabetical Cards for Children, twenty in one package	0 15
Reward Cards for Children, sixteen in one package	0 10

Figure 11

Education as Methodism's Business

Nast's *Der Christliche Apologete*—in its beckoning to, gathering in of, and orientation of German Americans to matters Methodist—functioned as Cincinnati's publishing outreach/connection/formation across language lines. [The Outreach chapter treats the *Ladies' Repository* and, passingly, the *Methodist Quarterly Review* and their Southern counterparts.] Following the example of the Wesleys, American Methodism printed, in various formats, to evangelize, connect, and shape its prospects and members. Each of the sections of this study, then, look to the notice and the page for explanation and illustration. Here, the use of papers, magazines, reviews, and books in the church's various formative activities for adults must be noted.

Perhaps their regular use and subscriptions owed much to the church's increased attention—year-by-year and decade-by-decade—to its educational enterprises, and especially to the effort to create, fund, and sustain colleges. The 1856 Cincinnati Conference instructed its members, in a "Report on Education," with updates on its own schools: Hillsboro Female College, Ohio Wesleyan University, Xenia Female College, Wesleyan Female College, Springfield Female College and High School, and its new venture, Wilberforce University. (Baldwin-Wallace as a school for German Americans—and for Nast as president—would come the next decade). Of the six schools, four served women and one served blacks; all were headed by white men. The gender disparity also existed at the national level for the Northern church. Of its one hundred three institutions, twenty-five were colleges and universities, mostly all male. The rest, the MEC listed under the *other* label, "Female Colleges, Academies, and Seminaries." Interestingly, the latter category applied to women's secondary schools; and the two very last institutions identified were Methodist General Biblical Institute and Garrett Biblical Institute, today's Boston University School of Theology and Garrett-Evangelical Theological Seminary.[56]

The detail on each school varied year-to-year depending on what the conference's visiting committee found and returned to recommend. The longest report in 1856 was for Wesleyan Female College. It began with accolades:

> The Wesleyan Female College continues to maintain a high rank among the literary institutions of this country. Its success, the past year, has fully met the expectations of its friends and patrons, and its deservedly high reputation has remained undiminished and unimpaired. Four hundred and one pupils have been enrolled during the year, and twenty-eight of that number, having completed the course of study, received the honors of the institution.

The committee detailed the college's financial condition, need for new buildings, costs, and scholarships for students, and recommendation that money for the latter be gathered by selling them. Then followed five resolutions attending to the school's needs, fundraising measures, appointment of trustees, and the reappointment of Rev. P. B. Wilber as principal.[57]

On Ohio Wesleyan, the first resolution recalled collaborative efforts between Kentucky and Ohio conferences to sustain Augusta College and

---

56 *Journal of the General Conference of the Methodist Episcopal Church, 1860* (New York: Carton & Porter, 1860), 458–63.
57 *Minutes of the Cincinnati Annual Conference* (1856), 32–33.

authorized their dedication to Ohio Wesleyan. The report attended pri-marily to finances:[58]

Ohio Wesleyan University

This, the great and central institution of learning for our Church in Ohio, your Committee are happy to report in a most healthy and prosperous condition. For its financial condition, we refer to the report of its Auditor, which shows its whole amount of assets over its indebtedness to be $182,203.15.

FINANCIAL CONDITION OF OHIO WESLEYAN UNIVERSITY, JUNE 10, 1856.

I. Assets—

University ground and buildings			$60,000.00
Apparatus and cabinets			2,000.00
Library			10,000.00
Permanent Fund—			
Loaned by Fund Commissioners	$66,233.07		
M'Kendree Professorship	10,000.00		
Biblical Professorship notes	7,600.00		
Scholarship notes; estimated value	1,500.00		
Notes for Allen Farm	18,000.00		
Notes due Library building, transferred to Permanent Fund	2,887.08		
Notes due Chapel Fund, $1,596; estimated value.	1,100.00		
Loans to Trustees, (old account) $3,000; on buildings, $2,781.31	5,781.31	$113,091.46	
Interest due on endowment and scholarship notes	1,283.00		
Interest due on M'Kendree Fund	1,750.00	3,033.00	
Notes and subscriptions to Library building*	2,090.00		
		$190,214.46	

II. Indebtedness—

To Permanent Fund	5,511.31	
To architect on Library building	2,500.00	8,011.31

58   *Minutes of the Cincinnati Annual Conference* (1856), 30–31.

III. Amount of Assets over Indebtedness $182,203.15

                                                    Wm. G. Williams.

[From the Auditor's report.]

*Of which, Cincinnati conference subscription unpaid $75.00

   " " " pledge by resolution, unpaid   <u>180.00</u>

                                                            $255.00

Your Committee recommend the appointment of brother Fee and brother E. G. Nicholson as the Visiting and Examining Committee for the ensuing conference year.

Visiting and examining committees constituted but one of the diverse ways in which conference engaged college and college engaged conference. Names served to identify the college with the church and its heritage: Wesley, Coke, Asbury, and M'Kendree. Names also claimed a town for Methodism, hence, Hillsboro, Xenia, and Springfield. Presidents, deans, principals, and faculty had "jumped" or "were jumped" from regular appointments into special roles. For instance, of the twenty-two preachers serving on the East Cincinnati District, six had administrative, faculty, or other non-pastoral assignments:

- Western Book Concern, L. Swormstedt, Agent, and member of Wesley Chapel quarterly conference.
- Ohio University, J. M. Leavitt, Professor, and member of Mt. Auburn quarterly conference.
- Floating Bethel, S. D. Clayton, and member of East Pearl-Street quarterly conference.
- Wilberforce University, J. F. Wright, Agent, M. French, Assistant Agent, both members of Mt. Auburn quarterly conference.
- Wesleyan Female College, P. B. Wilber, President, member of Wesley Chapel quarterly conference.[59]

Note especially the two white preachers assigned to boost Wilberforce, one more indication of Methodism's struggle with race.

Of the seven English-speaking districts, one had no school-related appointments, one had just one, and the other four had two. So the Urbana District boasted:

---

59 *Minutes of the Cincinnati Annual Conference* (1856), 36.

- Springfield Female College, J. W. Weakley, President, and member of High-Street quarterly conference.
- Ohio Wesleyan University, L. D. M'Cabe, Professor, and member of Columbia-Street quarterly conference.

On the four German American districts, only one enjoyed an appointment beyond the local church: "Wm. Nast, Editor of Christian Apologist, and member of Buckeye-Street Church quarterly conference."[60]

Led, staffed, and supported by Methodists—men as far as the conference *Minutes* indicate—the schools typically would have accepted other Protestants. But the church established them, in Ohio and across the country, to save "real Christians" (that is Methodists) from Presbyterian and Congregational hegemony over ostensibly state colleges and from those that bore those denominational names.[61] As one of Methodism's educational leaders, Stephen Olin, president of Wesleyan University, observed in 1844, in a talk entitled, "Christian Education":

> [N]o Christian denomination can safely trust to others for the training of its sons . . . history has too clearly demonstrated that, without colleges of our own, few of our sons are likely to be educated, and that only a small portion of that few are likely to be retained in our communion.

Estimating that three-quarters of those who had enrolled in schools of other churches, he complained, "Many of them have gone to other denominations, many more have gone to the world. All were the legitimate children of the Church. They were her hope, and they should have become the crown of her rejoicing."[62] Ohio Methodists had taken Olin's warnings to heart and founded schools of their own.

Schools—by design, purpose, resources, and environment—the Ohioans knew, would shape the church's new leadership, equipping their young women and men to bring Methodists of all ages into the world

---

60 *Minutes of the Cincinnati Annual Conference* (1856), 37, 38.

61 For Methodism's early contention with other denominations over their control of educational institutions and leaders of Wesleyan University (Stephen Olin and Willbur Fisk) see early chapters of my fraternity brother's (David B. Potts) *Wesleyan University, 1831–1910: Collegiate Enterprise in New England* (New Haven: Yale University Press, 1992).

62 *The Works of Stephen Olin, D. D., LL.D., Late President of the Wesleyan University* (New York: Harper & Brothers, Publishers, 1852), II: 249, 251.

of books, journals, papers, and Sunday-school materials. Teachers guided reading of the latter. Other publications were shared within the family and beyond. Of course, then the books, journals, and *Sunday School Advocates* had to be printed and distributed. Methodism's publishing enterprise had been "called" and "appointed' to serve its reading church folk and sustain the Wesleyan legacy.

Methodist Angels: Book Agents as God's Heavenly Servants

The editors in the Northern church, as in the Southern, served at the pleasure of General Conference. They, as we note in several places, had an across-the-church voice that bishops, individually and collectively, simply did not. Like bishops, editors were elected by general conferences. However, unlike bishops, who remained in office till death or they chose to retire, book agents served at the church's pleasure. General Conference could assess performance and retire the book agents who did not effectively, consistently, fully, and faithfully serve their readers. The 1860 General Conference so acted:

> The tellers for the ballot for Editor of the Central Christian Advocate reported that the whole number of votes cast was 217. Necessary to a choice 109. Charles Elliott received 131; Joseph Brooks received 83; scattering 3. Charles Elliott, having received a majority of all the votes cast, was declared duly elected editor of the Central Christian Advocate. . . .
>
> Thomas Carlton was elected Book Agent at New York by a hand vote, there being no other nominee. James Porter was elected Assistant Book Agent at New York by a hand vote, there being no other nominee. Adam Poe was elected Book Agent at Cincinnati by a hand vote, there being no other nominee.[63]

In 1860, Thomas Carlton and James Porter gave the Report of the Book Agents at New York to the General Conference of 1860. One important page of their 18-page report covered the books published and distributed for 1859 and three prior years. Note the three categories that commanded attention:

---

63 *Journal of the General Conference of the Methodist Episcopal Church* (1860), 242.

NEW ISSUES[64]

During the last four years ending Jan. 1, 1860, we have published new books as follows:

On General Catalogue	40
Sunday School	196
Tract Book	2
Tracts, 12mo	85
Total	323

To these may be added a considerable number of Sunday School Tracts, cards, and other small works.

Many of these books have sold very largely, amounting in some cases to thirty or forty thousand copies. Of the above bound books, we have printed 640,250 copies, making an average of 2,690 copies of each, and have but few of any one kind on hand. Yet the sale of them has hardly commenced. Few can fail to pay expenses, and many will pay the Concern large profits.

The editors' year-to-year comparisons covered circulation as well. And again, a single copy of a book or *Sunday School Advocate* might be studied by more than one child.

BOOKS AND TRACTS PRINTED

It may be interesting to you and the friends and patrons of the Book Concern to have more particular knowledge in relation to the circulation of our books. We have therefore made up the following schedule:

Bound volumes printed in 1856.

General Catalogue	233,000	
Sunday School	535,500	
Tract Book	52,500	
		821,000
1857		
General Catalogue	226,000	
Sunday School	572,000	
Tract Book	10,000	
		808,000

---

64 *Journal of the General Conference of the Methodist Episcopal Church* (1860), 334.

1858
  General Catalogue   243,000
  Sunday School   568,000
  Tract Book   6,500
                                                        817,500
1859
  General Catalogue   261,000
  Sunday School   1,088,750
  Tract Book   4,250
                                                      1,354,000
  Total for the four years   3,800,500

"General Catalogue" gives us some idea of what went to the church's adults. The tracts—produced for various reading levels—members could use to bring wandering sheep into the fold as well as to read themselves as they wanted or needed reminders of how to stay awake. Tracts aimed at adults and the youth, then, served teaching (Formational) as well as missional (Outreach) purposes. For children, the church produced twice as much for Sunday schools in 1856, 1857, and 1858 as it did in its various materials for adults. And in 1859, it was almost four times as much.

How many of the *Ladies' Repository* or *Quarterly Reviews*, of books, of tracts, and of Sunday-school materials reached Ohio readers, of course, the New York report does not indicate. However, some gauge of readership doubtless owed to efforts in the Midwest and by Midwesterners to reach the faithful. The book agents at Cincinnati-based Western Book Concern, L. Swormstedt and Adam Poe, belonged to the Cincinnati and North Ohio conferences. Both had moved their membership when those conferences were constituted and had earlier been colleagues in the Ohio Conference. Their report showed what Midwestern Methodists spent on publications and what they read.[65]

Report of the Book Agents at Cincinnati

TOTAL BOOK SALES FOR FOUR YEARS ENDING JANUARY 31, 1860.
  At Cincinnati $334,518 07
  At Chicago   211,935 98
                                       $546,454 05

---

65 *Journal of the General Conference of the Methodist Episcopal Church* (1860), 350. The Report extended from 350 to 359.

TOTAL PERIODICAL SALES.

At Cincinnati	$427,364 30
At Chicago	154,032 65
	581,396 95
	$1,127,851 00

Total sales at Cincinnati for four years ending	
March 31, 1856	$649,840 73
At Chicago for three years and five months to	
March 31, 1856	227,373 95
	877,214 68
Increase	$250,636 32

CIRCULATION OF PERIODICALS AT THE CLOSE OF 1859.

		Gain
At Cincinnati—Western Christian Advocate	31,000	2,282
Ladies' Repository	33,400	3,820
Sunday School Advocate	80,509	49,317
Missionary Advocate	6,000	945
Good News	6,500	. . .
Quarterly Review	625	183
Christian Apologist	9,166	2,199
Sunday School Bell	12,000	. . .
At St. Louis—Central Christian Advocate	8,016	. . .
At Chicago—Northwestern Christian Advocate	13,300	3,267
Ladies' Repository	8,200	1,000
Sunday School Advocate	36,500	23,200
Quarterly Review	510	292
Missionary Advocate	6,700	3,700
Good News	6,500	. . .

Writers and editors for the quarterly, monthly, and weekly publications reached out to and reached Methodists, their families, and friends. As a co-editor of the twenty-first-century *Methodist Review*, I envy the midwestern readership that the *Quarterly Review* reached in 1859. Our online scholarly endeavor reaches subscribers across the English-reading world and roughly equals what the book agents reported for the *Quarterly Review*. Nationally, the latter reported subscription of over four thousand.[66] Circulation of the other serials was also remarkable, especially that of the Cincinnati-based *Ladies' Repository.*

Churching the Little Children

Even more remarkable was the circulation of the Sunday-school materials. Readership for the *Sunday School Advocate* exceeded that for all the other Chicago-circulated serials and roughly equaled that of those that Cincinnati claimed (80,509 vs. 86,691). And if subscribers to the *Sunday School Bell* are added, Sunday school triumphed. Nationally as well as regionally, the Northern church recognized that formation starts in the family at the parent's knees and is regularized and sustained around the Sunday-school teacher. From "her" lap and the children's hands, eyes tracked the lessons of and appreciated the pictures in the *Sunday School Advocate.* Members of the 1860 General Conference heard that in statistical Methodist-speak:

> **The Sunday School Advocate.** The last General Conference recommended a change in the size and form of this sheet, which was carried into effect at the close of the then present volume. . . . The result has been very gratifying. The aggregate circulation before the change, as reported at the last General Conference, was 83,500. It has since reached 129,000 at New York, and 81,000 at Cincinnati, making an aggregate of 208,000 copies. We are now aiming to increase the circulation to 300,000 and have good hope that we shall succeed. The work has fully paid its expenses.[67]

Southern Methodism at its General Conference two years earlier had also championed the Sunday school formation. This chapter can end where it began:

> What are our Sunday-schools? Are they not the nurseries of the Church? And are we not to look to them for the best materials for

---

66 *Journal of the General Conference of the Methodist Episcopal Church* (1860), 341. The Report indicated: "The Quarterly Review. This long-cherished periodical has run a race of distinguished honor and success. Its subscription list has gone up from 2,750 to 4,250 copies, which is its present circulation."

67 *Journal of the General Conference of the Methodist Episcopal Church* (1860), 342.

supplying the ranks of our membership? We say the best materials, because those who enter the Church from the Sunday-school, have been already trained from early childhood in the knowledge of the Holy Scripture.[68]

68   MECS, *General Conference Journal* (1858), 571.

CHAPTER 4

Connection

*From Ground-Up, Conference-Out, Connectionally
Resourced to Churching from the Center-Down*

Being entirely restored to health, I went to conference, and was sent on the Zanesville district. Here, after many years, I returned to the same place from whence I started as from a point to travel round my first circuit. Old brother Spangler, whose hospitalities I first, and often subsequently, enjoyed, has long since left us, and I trust is now in heaven. Some of his family remain. David Spangler, Esq., a talented lawyer, resides in Coshocton. He was always a stanch friend of his father's people; and the same may be said of Isaac Spangler, a distinguished physician of Zanesville. Several of the daughters were Methodists, and perhaps are living still. Then Methodism was small and feeble, but Jacob has arisen and become strong. This city has some of the firmest Methodists: Moorehead, and Millis, and Howard, and the Coxes, Brush, and others, are an honor to any Church. Long may they live to honor God and Methodism!

I remained on the Zanesville district two years, and, at the request of the directors of the Ohio penitentiary, was appointed chaplain to that institution, where I remained three years and a half. A full account of my labors in that institution the reader will find in "Prison Life." In 1850, my health being feeble, I took a superannuated relation, in hopes that rest would prepare me again for active service.

The next year I was made effective, and appointed to Yellow Springs. Again I took rest for another year, and now, in the 72d year of my age, I have charge of Clinton-street Church, Cincinnati.

In the year 1845 the Wyandott nation, whom I adopted as my people, and who constituted me a chief of one of their tribes, were removed to the Indian territory beyond the Mississippi. It is a melancholy reflection, that all those powerful tribes which once inhabited these plains, roaming at freedom where we now reside, and who sped with their light canoes over the surface of our rivers, the monarchs of all they surveyed, have now no claim whatever even to the graves of their fathers. A dark and dismal fate rests upon them, and in their native land they are rapidly fading away beneath the gaze of the pale face.[1]

James B. Finley: Connectional Agent

In the final chapters of his *Autobiography,* James B. Finley concluded a narrative that, by and large, had covered other Methodist luminaries, beginning with bishops Asbury and M'Kendree. (On Finley's career and tributes paid to him by the Cincinnati Annual Conference at his death, we conclude this chapter.) Finley embodied and modeled what Methodism had become by the 1850s and what the title of this chapter should convey.

The churches, North and South, at all levels, were being continuously renewed and taking on new challenges. How? Regular resourcing came from popularly financed and membership-resourced connectional societies (often termed voluntary societies); need was conveyed to the people through conference outreach agents, societies, and mechanisms; and resources were claimed, used, and locally guided by the free people and their preachers in circuit or station. We return to this connectional fabric later in this chapter. Here, perhaps it might suffice to call attention again to the Missionary Society Reports in chapter 2 and their "command" of the conference *Minutes* for both Ohio and Cincinnati conferences. What did the huge portion of the *Minutes*—devoted to missions, the listing of donors by name, and the indication of money given, down to 50c.—convey? Mission, as described above and embodied by Finley, was embraced, supported, and often undertaken on the ground (with people and preachers); was orchestrated by the conferences; and depended upon voluntary agencies, like the missionary societies, for resourcing. Sunday-school outreach, formation, and connection looked similar. And these and other voluntary efforts depended upon the connectional publishing enterprises for the books and pamphlets, which

---

1   *Autobiography of Rev. James B. Finley, or Pioneer Life in the West,* W. P. Strickland, ed. (Cincinnati: The Methodist Book Concern, 1856), 378–79. Used as hardcopy but also accessed at HathiTrust Digital Library Rights Public Domain, Google-digitized. Permanent URL: https://hdl.handle.net/2027/nyp.33433082405915.

were conveyed through conference societies to the children and parents on circuits and in stations.

A Church Transformed

National turmoil, increased sectional tensions, race riots, Supreme Court decisions, and Mason vs. Dixon posturing laid the groundwork for the Civil War and necessitated Reconstruction endeavors that transformed the MEC and MECS. Exploration of that turmoil lies beyond this study. However, changes to which we turn our attention below resulted in a fundamentally different connectional order. The Northern church in 1872, and the Southern gradually thereafter, altered Methodism from ground-up, conference-out, connectionally resourced denominations into churches run from the top down, the modern bureaucratic scheme. The legislation of the 1872 MEC General Conference points to those changes.

The Report of the Special Committee on the Relation of Benevolent Institutions of the Church to the General Conference was then read and adopted, as follows:

REPORT OF COMMITTEE ON
BENEVOLENT SOCIETIES.

The special Committee appointed to consider and report concerning the relations of our various benevolent societies to the authorities of the Church, and whether any action is necessary, and if so what, to place them under the full control of the General Conference, has considered the subject stated, and now

REPORT

that there are five benevolent societies which have received the sanction of the General Conference, and with which it is more or less remotely connected, to wit:

1. The Missionary Society of the Methodist Episcopal Church, incorporated by the Legislature of New York;
2. The Church Extension Society of the Methodist Episcopal Church, incorporated by the Legislature of Pennsylvania;

3. The Board of Education of the Methodist Episcopal Church, incorporated by the Legislature of New York;

4. The Sunday-School Union of the Methodist Episcopal Church, incorporated by the Legislature of New York; and,

5. The Tract Society of the Methodist Episcopal Church, incorporated by the legislature of New York.[2]

The changes from voluntary society to manager-led bureaucratic governance occurred only gradually.[3] Many Methodists became aware of the full dimensions of the 1872 organizational revolution only a century later when caucuses emerged whose primary business was trashing boards and agencies. Had the caucuses—especially Black Methodists for Church Renewal—known of their origin in anti-slavery *and* slavery impulses, they might have directed attacks elsewhere.

Quest. What shall be done for the extirpation of the evil of slavery?

Answ. We declare that we are as much as ever convinced of the great evil of Slavery. We believe that the buying, selling, or holding of human beings, to be used as chattels, is contrary to the laws of God and nature, and inconsistent with the Golden Rule and with that Rule in our Discipline which requires all who desire to continue among us to "do no harm," and to "avoid evil of every kind." We therefore affectionately admonish all our Preachers and People to keep themselves pure from this great evil, and to seek its extirpation by all lawful and Christian means.[4]

---

2   *Methodist Experience in America: A Sourcebook,* 370–73, an extract from the 1872 *Journal of General Conference Held in Brooklyn, N.Y. 1872* (New York: Nelson & Phillips, 1872), 295–98.

3   Denominationalism has been a scholarly hobby from early in my career. A recent discussion is "Denomination," in the online *Oxford Encyclopedia of Religion in America.* My books on the topic are *Denominationalism,* editor and co-author (Nashville: Abingdon Press, 1977; WIPF & Stock, 2010); *Reimagining Denominationalism,* co-editor and co-author with R. Bruce Mullin (New York: Oxford University Press, 1994; paper edition 2010); and *Denominationalism Illustrated and Explained* (Eugene, OR: Cascade Books, Wipf & Stock, 2013).

4   *The Doctrines and Discipline of the Methodist Episcopal Church, 1860,* with an appendix (Cincinnati: Poe & Hitchcock, 1860), Part VI, Chapter 1, 266. From a personally owned copy. See also HathiTrust Digital Library Rights, Public Domain, Google-digitized. Permanent URL: https://hdl.handle.net/2027/nnc1.50192327. At the 1860 General Conference, a Majority Report on Slavery (404–09), ended with the motion putting the revision of the *Discipline* before the annual conferences with this resolution:

So, on the eve of the Civil War, the 1860 General Conference judged that the Methodist Episcopal Church should condemn slavery, do so resolutely, rebuke its own slaveholding members, and yield no longer to slavery-permitting laws and comparable practices within its fold.[5] The prior *Discipline* (1856) had echoed the compromise with slavery-within-the fold with which it had lived for half a century: "We declare that we are as much as ever convinced of the great evil of slavery: therefore no slaveholder shall be eligible to any official station in our Church hereafter, where the laws of the State in which he lives will admit of emancipation and permit the liberated slave to enjoy freedom."[6] The MEC earlier had conceded to slave-holders within. No more.

The 1860 General Conference, in revising the statement on slavery, took a forceful, clear, and unambiguous stance. (See appendix for the "Majority and Minority Reports on Slavery: 1860 General Conference of the Methodist Episcopal Church.") However, the new policy did not really

---

"Resolved, 3. By the delegates of the several Annual Conferences in General Conference assembled, that the following be and hereby is substituted in the place of the seventh chapter on slavery: Question. What shall be done for the extirpation of the evil of slavery? Answer. We declare that we are as much as ever convinced of the great evil of slavery. We believe that the buying, selling, or holding of human beings as chattels is contrary to the laws of God and nature, inconsistent with the Golden Rule, and with that rule in our Discipline which requires all who desire to remain among us to "do no harm, and to avoid evil of every kind." We, therefore, affectionately admonish all our preachers and people to keep themselves pure from this great evil, and to seek its extirpation by all lawful and Christian means."

A Minority Report followed at that general conference. It objected to stirring up the church and concluded "that great moderation should be observed in the public discussion of this subject, constantly maintaining the true antislavery position of the Church." *Journals of the General Conference of the Methodist Episcopal Church, v. 4, 1860* (New York: Carlton & Porter, [1855–1900]), 404–09; 410–22. HathiTrust Digital Library Rights. Public Domain, Google-digitized. Permanent URL: https://hdl.handle.net/2027/wu.89077109460. (*N.B.* Here and hereinafter items from the HathiTrust Digital Library are used according to its protocols and therefore with permission.)

Compare both the 1860 statements (majority and minority), here included in the appendix, with the vigorous and detailed anti-slavery account in the first *Discipline* (see the introduction) and with that issued by the bishops of the MECS in 1858 (see the Outreach chapter).

5 On Methodist postures on slavery, See David Sherman, *History of the Revisions of the Discipline of the Methodist Episcopal Church* (New York: Nelson & Phillips, 1874), 115–20; "Slavery" in EWM 2:2167–70; "General Conference" and "General Conferences of the Methodist Episcopal Church, 1792-1936," EWM 1:909–29 and "General Conferences of the Methodist Episcopal Church, South, 1846-1938," EWM 1:929–35.

6 *The Doctrines and Discipline of the Methodist Episcopal Church, 1856* (New-York: Carlton & Porter, 1856), 212–13.

address the realities of racial divisions, racist practices, and some slave-holding—even within the MEC—in border states. On those fronts, the Civil War moved the church forward, but regrettably, only partially and temporarily. That sad retreat from even the quasi-integrated patterns the MEC set up in former MECS states will have to wait for another study. Here, we note that the Southern church's General Conference also revised the little "On Slavery" chapter long positioned at the end of its *Discipline*.

By contrast to the MEC's action and just two years earlier, the Southern church had elected excision rather than revision. Its General Conference passed and sent to the annual conferences for ratification the report of a committee chaired by Thos. O. Summers. Its substantive action read:

> Whereas, The rule in the General Rules of the Methodist Episcopal Church, South, forbidding "the buying and selling of men, women, and children, with an intention to enslave them," is ambiguous in its phraseology, and liable to be construed as antagonistic to the institution of slavery, in regard to which the Church has no right to meddle, except in enforcing the duties of masters and servants, as set forth in the Holy Scriptures; and whereas, a strong desire for the expunction of said rule has been expressed in nearly all parts of our ecclesiastical connection; therefore,
>
> Resolved, 1. By the delegates of the Annual Conferences of the Methodist Episcopal Church, South, in General Conference assembled, that the rule forbidding "the buying and selling of men, women, and children, with an intention to enslave them," be expunged from the General Rules of the Methodist Episcopal Church, South.
>
> Resolved, 2. That, in adopting the foregoing resolution, this Conference expresses no opinion in regard to the African slave-trade, to which the rule in question has been "understood" to refer.

Bishop George Pierce followed with remarks intended to "allay the feelings" of those who might be troubled by the action or misunderstand the church's "views and motives." He noted:

> The Methodist Church divided on this question of slavery. The Southern Church has avowed as her settled belief and sentiment that slavery is not a subject of ecclesiastical legislation. It is not the province of the Church to deal with civil institutions in her legislative capacity. This is our position. We have avowed it. The primary,

single object, therefore, was and is to conform the Discipline to that profession.[7]

The Southern church decided finally to align its *Discipline* with operative policy and practice. In 1860, the Northern church, by contrast, elected to reshape its posture on slavery to frame its hopes and—for portions of its faithful—its beliefs and practice. After all, slaveholding remained legal and active in several border states, and slaveholding members continued within the Methodist fold.

The racial turmoil of the 1850s had induced both churches to revise their *Discipline* on slavery. Each did so in a fashion guaranteed to acerbate tension, even conflict, between the two communions. Southern and Northern Methodism declared war before the nation did.

Connection and Division: An American Methodist Drama

Despite its half-century of evasive language and efforts at compromise on slavery, the Methodist Episcopal Church had divided again and again, slavery often figuring in. Dis-connection had been a Methodist signature, really on both sides of the Atlantic, indeed, across the world. One schism followed the 1860 General Conference and its failure to address concerns that reformer B. T. Roberts[8] had voiced on a cluster of freedoms, one for slaves. Later that year, Roberts led the launch of the Free Methodists. Division, with very few exceptions, had occurred and continued to occur every decade, breaking the connection. In quite a few of the splits, racial policy and practices constituted the cause or occasion. A quick reminder of the divisions in American Methodism should help as we turn to the 1850s and that slavery barrier, the Ohio River. Methodism's decade-by-decade divisions:

- the Fluvanna schism of 1779–81 that divided the Methodist movement North and South;

7   *Journal of the General Conference of the Methodist Episcopal Church, South*, volume 4, 1858 (Nashville: Methodist Episcopal Church, South, 1858), HathiTrust Digital Library, Permanent URL: https://hdl.handle.net/2027/osu.32435053208484, 459–61.

8   On B. T. Roberts, the issues of connection and division, and the strains in mid–nineteenth-century Methodism, see Kevin M. Watson, *Old or New School Methodism? The Fragmentation of a Theological Tradition* (New York: Oxford University Press, 2019), and Howard A. Snyder, *Populist Saints: B. T. and Ellen Roberts and the First Free Methodists* (Grand Rapids, MI: William B. Eerdmans, 2006).

- the founding of the MEC, thereby separating Methodists in 1784 from the Church of England, from their once American Anglican compatriots, and from Wesley and British Methodism; action there elaborated detailed and rigorous rules for ending slaveholding by members of the new church;
- separate "prejudicial" organization also from 1780s of African Methodists upon whom were imposed: segregated class, chapel, and quarterly meeting seating arrangements; substandard congregational prerogatives; and limited ministerial status (AMEs traditionally date such from 1787);
- the 1792 walk-out of James O'Kelly and supporters to form the "Republican Methodists" in commitment to various freedoms and critiquing the MEC's early compromises on slavery;
- the coalescence of a Primitive Methodist movement around William Hammett in Charleston the same year;
- the United Brethren and Evangelical Association that took important steps toward denominational identity in the first decade of the nineteenth century;
- the New England–based Reformed Methodists launched by Pliny Brett in 1814;
- the formal organization of AMEs as a church in 1816;
- the Stillwellite and AME Zion movements of the 1820s, both launched in New York City;
- the Methodist Protestants whose reform efforts traumatized successive general conferences in the 1820s and divided Methodism at its heart, in the border states (1830);
- the exiting of abolitionists to form the Wesleyan Methodist Church in 1842;
- the split of the Methodist Episcopals in 1844, North and South, largely over race;
- the emergence of the Free Methodists in the late 1850s (formally organizing in 1860);
- the founding in 1864 of the Churches of Christ in Christian Union by MEC Southern sympathizers, a church that later would emphasize its holiness, not its Confederacy commitments;

- the extrusion of African Americans from the MECS in 1870 to constitute the Colored (now Christian) Methodist Episcopal Church; and
- the founding of the Church of the Nazarene in the 1890s.

Denominational division or dis-connection became an American pastime and a Methodist way of life. To those on both sides of a schism, the causes for which to stand overruled the central unitive commandments of the Christian faith. For Methodists, the compelling cause often involved evangelism and the why, how, when, for whom, and by whom thereof. But strangely, each division created two new connections, two new ecclesial realities, two new churches.

Here, we need to underscore what the series of denominational divisions indicate, namely that holding connectional policy and practice together proved challenging.

American Methodists had, at least implicitly, recognized and claimed John Wesley's renewal within-and-without the church but simplified and radically altered it. Almost from the beginning and across colony then state lines, the preachers recognized there was no viable "within"—no Church of England ruling cradle-to-grave, over all the people, across the entire seaboard, and overseen by crown and cross. The Americans had transformed Wesley's purpose statement into an evangelistic credo. Wesley had urged Methodists to "Reform the Nation, particularly the Church." His American followers determined that, instead, they must "reform the Continent, and spread scripture Holiness over these lands."[9] In 1787, the *Discipline* was altered, bringing what Wesley had buried in the "Large Minutes" upfront as rationale for the new church.[10]

Just divide, break the ecclesial bonds, connect to/with brothers and sisters in the cause; division became an American connectional practice. Denominational division is a logical, grammatical, conceptual violation of the Christian church's central affirmation as: one, holy, catholic, and apostolic. Although a creedal violation and theological impossibility, schisms became a Methodist way of being church.

Division and dis-connection worked well, worked evangelistic miracles. Connect into classes divided by gender, race, language, and

9   *Minutes of Several Conversations between the Rev. Thomas Coke, LL. D., the Rev. Francis Asbury and Others... Composing a Form of Discipline* (Philadelphia, 1785), Q. 4. A.

10 *A Form of Discipline for the Ministers, Preachers, and Members of the Methodist Episcopal Church in America... Arranged under proper Heads and METHODIZED in a more acceptable and easy Manner* (New York, 1787), 4.

ethnicity. Connect in two-day quarterly meetings housed in camp meetings in warm weather, divided both socially and by office: class leader, exhorter, local preacher, preacher, presiding elder, even bishop. Connect in conferences, for white men in full connection and then divide the conferences for outreach purposes. Connect in general conferences to write sometimes unitive, sometimes divisive policy. Division happened to and in Methodisms that sought to connect.[11]

Connection or connectionalism within Methodism and denominationalism there and more generally have been "Richey" topics, perhaps since birth, certainly since college (for that pattern, see the postscript). An array of articles and books have appeared addressing connectionalism centrally.[12] Other writings have done so implicitly. To division, particularly denominational division, I have returned again and again.

---

11   The topic of division has been treated in our overview volumes: *American Methodism: A Compact History,* Richey, Kenneth E. Rowe, and Jean Miller Schmidt (Nashville: Abingdon, 2012), and *The Methodist Experience in America,* Richey, Rowe, and Schmidt, 2 vols. (Nashville: Abingdon, 2000, 2010), vol 1. Footnotes in the latter point to the various studies on which the arguments contained herein rest. Specific chapters in my *Methodist Connectionalism: Historical Perspectives* (Nashville: General Board of Higher Education and Ministry, 2010) and *Doctrine in Experience: A Methodist Theology of Church and Ministry* (Nashville: Kingswood Books/Abingdon, 2009) treat the topic or unity and division. See in the latter, for instance, "Methodist Culture Wars" and in the former "Methodism as Machine." Division has been really a career-long interest as indicated in an array of articles and in three books: *Denominationalism Illustrated and Explained* (Eugene, OR: Cascade Books, Wipf & Stock, 2013), *Reimagining Denominationalism,* co-editor and co-author with R. Bruce Mullin (New York: Oxford University Press, 1994; paper edition 2010), and *Denominationalism,* editor and co-author (Nashville: Abingdon Press, 1977; Wipf & Stock, 2010). A number of my articles treat the topic, as for instance, "United Methodism: Its Identity as Denomination" in *Denomination: Assessing An Ecclesiological Category,* Paul Collins and Barry Ensign-George, eds. (London & New York: T & T Clark, 2011), 67–85, and the forthcoming "Denomination" in the *Oxford Encyclopedia of Religion in America.*

12   Russell E. Richey, *Methodist Connectionalism: Historical Perspectives* (Nashville: General Board of Higher Education and Ministry, 2010); *Doctrine in Experience: A Methodist Theology of Church and Ministry* (Nashville: Kingswood Books/Abingdon, 2009); *Connectionalism: Ecclesiology, Mission, and Identity,* primary co-editor with Dennis M. Campbell and William B. Lawrence, United Methodism and American Culture, I (Nashville: Abingdon, 1997); "Today's Untied Methodism: Living with/into its Two Centuries of Regular Division" in *The Unity of the Church and Human Sexuality: Toward a Faithful United Methodist Witness* (Nashville: GBHEM, 2018); "Connection and Connectionalism," in *Oxford Handbook of Methodist Studies,* James E. Kirby and William J. Abraham, eds. (Oxford & New York: OUP, 2009), 211–28; "The United Methodist Church at 40: Where Have We Come From?" *Methodist Review: A Journal of Wesleyan and Methodist Studies,* 1 (2009): 27–56.

Connectionalism: Multivalent and Numbered

Connection had been and ostensibly remained Methodism's creed, commitment, concern, campaign, and conviction. From 1773 until 1784 and the launch of the new church, the preachers recorded their commitments in "Minutes of Some Conversations Between the Preachers in Connection with The Rev. Mr. John Wesley."[13] In 1784, with American independence determined, Wesley finally recognized that he could not sustain his connectional authority/governance/oversight of the Americans. That year, he conveyed the several documents that would achieve that independence and transform a movement into a church. In the organizing Christmas Conference, the preachers recognized that they needed a different term to identify themselves and had to organize formally as a religious body. They, therefore, employed the word *church* in their name, so claiming and exhibiting their new ecclesial status.

The new Methodist Episcopal Church, however, continued to employ *connection* to identify how it hung together, who led it, and what it was. Up until 1816, formal documents (e.g., *Disciplines* and General Conference *Journals*) routinely used *connection* to refer to Methodism as church. The term continued to serve as the ecclesial reference on a popular level, in discourse, in minutes, and in autobiographies and journals. And to this day, preachers who receive ordination as elders and full members of conference continue to be identified by the Question (then in the *Minutes*, now in conference *Journals*): "Who are admitted into full connection?"

Connectionalism has been a Wesleyan precept but a multivalent one: a command, an ecclesial vision, a missional principle, a covenantal commitment, an ethic of equity and proportionality, a tactical stratagem, an elastic and evolving standard, a theology in praxis. John Wesley blessed the Americans with connection as the way of being church. As a Wesleyan precept, connection constituted an array of ways of being together. It served as a first-order affirmation, an identifying statement, a recognition of Wesley's authority and hence of those who have succeeded to his apostolic superintendency. To be Methodist has meant locating ourselves within a system that mandated claiming and living with the gifts from both John and Charles Wesley. To be Methodist has meant singing our hymns, accepting our doctrines, reading our literature, knowing our

---

13 See *Minutes of the Annual Conferences of the Methodist Episcopal Church, for the Years 1773–1828*, vol. 1 (New York: T. Mason and G. Lane, 1840), 5–21. Earlier versions of the *Minutes* had been published in 1794 and 1813.

story, recognizing the Methodist way as a full and adequate expression of the gospel witness, and accepting our place within a set of gracious relations. The latter—the acceptance of our acceptance into class, society, conference—gave connection its form by tying those fleeing the wrath to come in bond with one another and with Mr. Wesley. Americans first named themselves *Methodist* by precept, "Preachers in connexion with the Rev. Mr. Wesley."[14] Connectionalism makes a statement, a statement about authority, a statement about identity. Such multivalent patterns of connecting the prior chapters are documented again for Ohio and Kentucky gatherings. Conferences did everything Methodist and radiated their involvements and concerns over to national and regional societies and out to local preachers and their circuits and stations.

American Methodism also inherited from Mr. Wesley an obsession with numbers. As noted in chapter 1, gatherings at all levels counted. The very first gathering of preachers in 1773 identified the ten preachers in Quest. 1. Question 2 indicated "What numbers are there in the Society? Counts followed for New-York, Philadelphia, New-Jersey, Maryland, Virginia, and a total."[15] That simple pattern prevailed at least until 1850, when the *Minutes* still numbered white and "colored" members (see General Recapitulation in the Outreach chapter). The comparable conference-by-conference counting in 1854 no longer reported black membership but added the amounts "For Missions" and "Av. in cts. ea. mem." The comparable General Recapitulation for the MECS (also in the Outreach chapter) continued the counts by ethnicity, listing "Colored" and "Indian" members. Kentucky and Ohio conferences proved quite as number conscious for both activities or concerns requested by connectional societies and their own reasons.

What the *Minutes* did not capture numerically, other reports by the working societies of the two churches did. *The Annual Report of the Sunday-School Union of the Methodist Episcopal Church* listed—conference by conference—the counts (No. or No. of) for Sunday Schools, Officers and Teachers, S. Scholars, Volumes in Library, Bible Classes, Scholars in Infant Classes, Expenses of Schools, Amount raised for the S. S. Union, Sunday School Advocates taken, and Conversions. Totals for the entire Northern church for

---

14 Reflected in title of the minutes of the first conference: "Minutes of Some Conversations between the Preachers in Connexion with The Reverend Mr. John Wesley. Philadelphia, June 1773," *Minutes of the Methodist Conferences, Annually Held in America; From 1773 to 1813, Inclusive* (New York: Daniel Hitt and Thomas Ware for the Methodist Connexion in the United States, 1813), 5–6.

15 *Minutes of the Annual Conferences of the Methodist Episcopal Church… 1773–1828*, vol. I, 5.

the reported and prior years charted progress connectionally (see chart in Formation chapter). Individual annual conferences included comparable countings in their *Minutes*, as the "Recapitulation" for the Cincinnati Conference indicates (also in the Formation chapter). The Formation chapter also provides what the Kentucky Conference (MECS) provided itself, a large array of statistics: Whites; Colored; Sabbath Schools; Superintendents; Teachers, Sunday Schools; Volumes in Library; Sunday School Money; Missionary Money; Bible Money; Churches; Parsonages; and Local Preachers.

The other chapters in this book also capture numbers for various denominational activities, resources, institutions, or media that the two Methodist churches, their publishing outfits, and their respective conferences thought needed to be published and shared with members and the general public. The lists of colleges, journals and magazines, agencies within church or conference, and book structures point to the resources, organizations, and individuals then binding the church together. But how best to convey how the lists connected and churched the members? Binding together, or bonds, points to the unitive effect of these resources, activities, and societies. *Fabric*, to change the metaphor, would get at what their reports convey—the connective, wearable, interlaced results. *Tissue* or *muscle* would point to how the various activities constituted the living reality of Methodism. *Connection*—though then posited primarily for what preachers were or did—perhaps calls attention to what brains do and how the colleges, magazines, Sunday-school societies, and other organizations bonded the Methodist people; interlaced their activities; and muscled them toward their purposes.

The reports, as for instance of the Sunday-School Union, can only hint at their ongoing, involving, dynamic, enabling, formative, and changing effect on Methodists of all ages (albeit compromised by race and ethnicity in both Northern and Southern churches).[16] The *Annual Reports* get at the intent of the organization. However, the impact on local or conference levels has been harder to discern. Similarly, we discover the circulation for the Southern church's *The Home Circle* and *Sunday-School Visitor*: how such resourcing engaged women and children, what they absorbed. Whether it altered their self-understanding, relations with others, hopes for the future, we can only guess. The transformative effects of

16 Robert W. Lynn and Elliott Wright, *The Big Little School: Sunday Child of American Protestantism* (New York: Harper & Row, 1971); Anne M. Boylan, *Sunday School: The Formation of An American Institution, 1790–1880* (New Haven and London: Yale University Press, 1988).

the colleges on Methodist women and men are difficult to discern from reports to the conferences by the visiting committees. Note, for instance, in the Formation chapter, the detail given to the schools' administrative and fiscal issues but the difficulty in deriving much of a sense of what the experiences were like for the students.

Connectional Operations: America's Mid-century John Wesleys

Like John Wesley, mid-century American Methodists recognized current needs of the people; borrowed and adapted media by which to reach them; experimented with fresh ways of resourcing those reached; generated new patterns of leadership; but honored, if they partially sidelined, those officers and organizations nominally in charge. Bishops, presiding elders, and conferences—general, annual, and quarterly—continued to operate as they had for half a century in both Southern and Northern Methodism. Episcopal Methodism operated from the top down. Doubtless it so appeared to casual viewers of denominational gatherings, the laity within the fold, and perhaps to those holding these official posts. On paper as well as functionally, bishops ruled and delegated authority and power down the leadership and structural ladders.

However, over the course of the century and especially after "Pope" Francis Asbury died in 1816, American Methodism generated office-after-office, role-after-role, and organization-after-organization to care for a growing, more diverse, increasingly societally and politically savvy, continent-conquering people. Who and for what? Editors and book agents for the *Methodist Quarterly Review, Christian Advocate*(s), and numerous tracts, weeklies, and books! Corresponding secretaries and editors for the Sunday-School Union! Corresponding secretaries for the Mission Society! Counterparts in the Southern church also headed and ran its connectional apparatus. In both churches, the holders of these connectional, informational, and resourcing operations were elected by the general conferences. They assumed or resumed exercise of the several resourcing offices as balloting or standing affirmations by General Conference members determined.[17] (For the counterparts on conference levels, see figures 12 and 13.)

These Wesley-like men, qualified and credentialed for leadership, continued to operate faithfully and—to appearances—within the fold,

---

17   See references to balloting in the Formation chapter.

but in roles, with new impulses, and through organizations outside those formally recognized by those officially in charge. Bishops sat on the platform, convened the gatherings, presided over all sessions, and made many of the appointments to committees. General Conference journals, however, show the editors, corresponding secretaries, and the ministers deeply invested in their operations to be running the church's business.

The Board of Officers and Managers of the Sunday-School Union illustrate both the appearance of top-down authority and the reality of hands-on functioning, when roles and offices are recognized.[18]

BOARD OF OFFICERS AND MANAGERS.

OFFICERS.
President and Vice-Presidents.

EX-OFFICIO.

REV. BISHOP WAUGH, PRESIDENT.
BISHOP MORRIS,
BISHOP JANES,
BISHOP SCOTT,
BISHOP SIMPSON,
BISHOP BAKER,
BISHOP AMES.

Conference Vice-Presidents.

J. A. GERE,	Baltimore.	C. S. COIT,	New-Jersey.
B. I. DIEFENDORF,	Black River.	L. LANDON,	N. York East.
T. B. HUDSON,	East Genesee.	V. M. BEAMER,	N. Indiana.
W. H. PILLSBURY,	East Maine.	JAS. M'MAHAN,	North Ohio.
G. B. HAWKINS,	Erie.	F. TAYLOR,	N. W.Indiana.
PARKER JAQUES,	Maine.	FITCH REED,	Oneida.
Z. A. MUDGE,	N. England.	R. HOPKINS,	Pittsburgh.
JUSTIN SPAULDING,	N. Hampshire.		

REV. P. RICE, D. D.,
" JAMES FLOY, D. D., } VICE-PRESIDENTS ELECT.
D. P. KIDDER, D. D., CORRESPONDING SECRETARY.
WILLIAM TRUSLOW, RECORDING SECRETARY.
S. J. GOODENOUGH, TREASURER.

Figure 12

18 *Annual Report of the Sunday-School Union of the Methodist Episcopal Church, 1856* (New York: Printed for the Union, 1856), 5–6.

6 BOARD OF OFFICERS AND MANAGERS.

MANAGERS.

James Davis,	Asa Child,	T. Nicholson,
S. A. Purdy, M. D.,	Oliver Hoyt,	E. S. Johnston,
J. Longking,	Wm. Morgan,	Stephen Barker,
Walter Keeler,	M. F. Odell,	W. L. Christian,
Peter Badeau,	T. Macfarlan,	A. T. Serrall,
E. H. Brown,	J. P. Early,	J. O. Fowler,
Joel Sammis,	S. Booth,	C. C. North,
John Cook,	J. W. Corson, M. D.,	G. J. Hamilton,
John Pullman,	E. S. Halsted,	Henry B. Keen,
David Terry,	G. S. Boyce,	James Magee,
C. R. Disosway,	G. W. Collord,	John W. Griffith,
Ira Perego, Jr.,	J. B. Crawford,	R. Loomis.

COMMITTEES.

Committees of the Board at New-York.

Applications for Aid.	*Finance.*	*Publications.*
Rev. D. P. Kidder,	S. J. Goodenough.	Rev. J. Floy,
Rev. Z. Phillips,	Joel Sammis,	James Davis,
S. J. Goodenough,	E. H. Brown,	S. A. Purdy, M. D.,
John Cook,	W. Keeler,	C. R. Disosway,
David Terry.	M. F. Odell.	J. W. Corson, M. D.

Committees on Finance and Applications for Aid.

At Cincinnati.	*At Boston.*
Rev. D. W. Clark,	Rev. Daniel Wise,
William Wood,	Franklin Rand,
R. P. Thompson,	Jacob Sleeper,
J. P. Kilbreth,	B. H. Barnes,
J. M. Phillips,	James P. Magee,
Sec. and Treas.	*Sec. and Treas.*
At Chicago.	*At Pittsburgh.*
Rev. J. V. Watson,	Rev. W. A. Davidson,
Henry Whitehead,	Rev. I. C. Pershing,
Grant Goodrich,	Alexander Bradley,
J. K. Botsford,	W. H. Kincaid,
W. M. Doughty,	Rev. J. L. Read,
Sec. and Treas.	*Sec. and Treas.*

Figure 13

Reading from the top down on both lists, bishops and eminent ministers from the several conferences appear to be in charge. Only at the bottom of the first page (figure 12) does the name of the real operator, Daniel Kidder, appear. Corresponding secretary since 1844, organizer of national Sunday-School Union conventions and annual meetings, and editor of hundreds of Sunday-school books, he would, soon after this meeting, head onto the faculty of Garrett Biblical Institute and from there to Drew Theological Seminary (where I taught for seventeen years).

The Managers—named on the second page (figure 13) and selected for their prominence and influence—played consulting roles in the Union's operations. So did the working Committees of the Board and Committees on Finance and Applications for Aid. In the latter committees, the last name for each city's operations was designated "Sec. and Treas." They oversaw the Methodist Book Depository for their respective city's publishing, financial, and disbursement operations.

While the organization presented itself on paper and in the activities of its annual national gatherings (see the Formation chapter on that) as top down, on the working level it was professionally led. Further, the Sunday-School Union connected the Methodist people in various of its operations, as the chapters on Formation and Outreach demonstrate. Especially significant was the volume and diversity of its publications. That and the intended readership indicate the connectional purposes that the Sunday schools were to serve. Here, for instance, are the publications as listed for 1856:[19]

THE SUNDAY-SCHOOL PUBLICATIONS

I. SUNDAY-SCHOOL REQUISITES.
BOOKS OF REGISTRY
SPELLING AND READING BOOKS
CATECHISMS
QUESTION BOOKS
NOTES AND COMMENTARIES
LESSON BOOKS, MANUALS, ETC.
DICTIONARIES
HYMNS AND MUSIC
SCRIPTURES AND MAPS
CARDS, CERTIFICATES, TICKETS, ETC., in great variety

II. SUNDAY-SCHOOL REWARDS
ALPHABETICAL AND PICTORIAL CARDS
ALPHABETICAL TRACTS FOR CHILDREN, 100 VARIETIES
MISSIONARY TRACTS FOR CHILDREN, 54 VARIETIES

---

19 *Annual Report of the Sunday-School Union of the Methodist Episcopal Church* (1856), 178–79.

MISSIONARY STORIES FOR CHILDREN, 25 VARIETIES

SMALL BOOKS IN PAPER COVERS, 48mo., 200 VARIETIES {Sold in

Do.   Do.   Do.   18mo.: 150   Do.   packages

200 BOUND GIFT-BOOKS, ranging in price from 10 to 50 cents.

III. SUNDAY-SCHOOL LIBRARY BOOKS

1. CHILDREN'S LIBRARY. SERIES A. 219 Vols. Price $15.65

Do.   Do.   SERIES B. 214 Do. Price $17.12

The above libraries are neatly and uniformly bound in red, so as to form elegant as well as useful collections for young children.

2. YOUTH'S LIBRARY. 604 Volumes, averaging in price about 21 cents per volume.

This collection contains brief, but valuable works on BIOGRAPHY, MISSIONS, HISTORY, VOYAGES, NATURAL HISTORY, TRAVELS, ETC., and embraces numerous narratives and miscellaneous books, all bearing more or less directly on the subject of religion.

3. THE ADULT LIBRARY, containing books suitable for senior scholars, teachers, and families.

29 volumes, 12mo, have been printed expressly for this library, and more are in preparation. The publishers are also enabled to furnish, additionally, more than 100 well-selected and valuable works on CHRISTIAN EXPERIENCE AND DUTIES, THE DOCTRINES OF CHRISTI-ANITY, EXPOSITION OF THE SCRIPTURES, BIBLICAL AND ECCLESIAS-TICAL HISTORY, GENERAL READING.

IV. SUNDAY-SCHOOL SERIES OF TRACTS

Treating on the:

NATURE AND IMPORTANCE OF SUNDAY SCHOOLS

MOTIVES FOR BECOMING TEACHERS; EXCUSES, ETC.

DUTIES OF PARENTS

DUTIES OF SUPERINTENDENTS

QUALIFICATIONS AND DUTIES OF TEACHERS

MODES OF TEACHING, GOVERNING, ETC.

MISCELLANEOUS

NEW ISSUE

The diverse connectional purposes served by the Sunday-School Union come through best in this listing at the end of the 180-page report. "The Adult Library" explicitly catered to the country or small-town women doing the actual teaching. But implicitly, the entire report laid out the connectional, formational, and outreaching functions of the

Sunday schools. The lay leaders and preachers operating the classes or schools selected the "Books of Registry" and "Spelling and Reading Books." They chose which of the "Rewards" best served their children and young people. They determined whether their little church or their circuit could cough up the $15.65 for "Children's Library Series A" or how much for the six hundred four items in the "Youth's Library." "The 29-Volume Adult Library" mapped out the "Christian Experience" and the various formational dimensions thereof. But perhaps the publications designated "Tracts" most directly served the Sunday school's connectional purposes. These how-to pamphlets charted duties, expectations, roles, and structure for churching people open to living into the Wesleyan way.

Bishops had their names upfront in the Annual Report and doubtless convened the working sessions of the meetings. But effective leadership through the working of the Sunday-School Union came from its corresponding secretary and staff at its four operation centers. From such centers, Sunday schools connected Methodists with tremendous materials. And with those publications in homes and simple chapels, lay women and men connected Methodists in bedside reading and Sunday-school gatherings. Sunday schools bonded people regularly, daily, weekly— bottom-up connectionalism. These formational and outreach, on-the-ground activities and resources depended on the corporation-like staff who gathered, edited, promoted, sold, and distributed the huge array of Sunday School materials. Bishops might be depicted and certainly presided, but Sunday School editors, producers, and distributors connected Methodists from the several production centers.

Connection and Dis-Connection in Missions and Publications

Graphics, tables, illustrations, and explanations like the above, on both missions and publications, are exhibited in the chapters on Outreach and Formation. As with regard to Sunday schools, the treatments of missions and publications in those two chapters emphasizes the purposes, functions, operations, and mechanisms of the Missionary Society, the conference, local missionary efforts, and the various publications and publishing organizations. Here, the bottom-up and society-out connective force of the conference committees and national gatherings needs comment. For instance, the 1854 Cincinnati and Ohio *Minutes* reported on the activities for missions during the annual conference meeting. As indicated above for the Sunday-School Union, the bishops chaired and often spoke. The *Minutes* reported on the operation of the conference societies. What emerged as most striking were the name-by-name and dollar-and-cents accounting of the donations in the "Detailed Report" of the conference's Missionary Society. Women and men connected to the evangelistic cause with money from their pockets. And doubtless those commitments and collections came—not from today's annual church pledges and budgets—but from local meetings explaining and exhorting the mission's cause.

Similarly, the Southern church's bishops instructed readers of the 1858 *Journal of the General Conference* on the rationale for missions to the slaves (see the Outreach chapter). The *Journal* reported on missions to the various peoples within and beyond the country and the "national" and conference societies through which to order and carry out that outreach. The "General Recapitulation" captured the numbers for "colored," white, and Indian members. The Kentucky Conference's Committee on Missions detailed what that outreach looked like on the ground. Reports to the 1852 and 1853 conferences noted some of the on-the-ground challenges faced in reaching both whites and blacks. The Southern church's journals and minutes demonstrate the racial dis-connection and document the efforts made at all levels to make slavery divide religious life (as well as economic, political, and social life generally). The Northern church instead had, by the 1850s, elected to hide its racial dis-connections. It eliminated black-white counts from its reporting and, apparently, from both program and statistics for Sunday school and missionary outreach.

Much the same might be posited for the vitally important, connective, informative, and formative publishing enterprises of the two churches. The women's periodicals (also treated in the Outreach chapter) of the two churches, *The Home Circle* and *Ladies' Repository,* gave passing attention to race, the latter more and more consistently than the former (see appendix for "Poetry on Race—*The Ladies' Repository*—1858"). Both, however, reached into homes and offered church women's views of the world and their church's engagement with it, so circumventing the men's-only connectional conference life, and mapping a religious world no longer confined to home and Sunday-school. If women's magazines edged, if just slightly, toward opening vistas for women, they also freed male editors and the publishing businesses of the two churches to produce *Quarterly Reviews* and the incredible output of books for male readers. *The Home Circle* and *Ladies' Repository* connected in the homes but sustained gender and racial dis-connections.

Several sections in the Formation chapter illustrate and document how the MECS lived into the Wesleyan legacy. Through the *Quarterly Review* (QR), *Christian Advocate*, regional *Advocates* and *Catalogue of Southern Methodist Books*, the Southern church offered ample provisions for its reading membership. The catechisms—save for those for the slaves—began the educational process. The *Advocates* and diverse selection of books and tracts catered to all who could read. The *Quarterly Review* addressed the serious readers. Although it contained reportorial and updating columns on publications by the MECS and from across the English-reading world, the QR also offered remarkably serious scholarship.[20]

The Northern church's publishing empire served its diverse and multi-leveled readership similarly (see Formation chapter on this). The 1860 General Conference moved finally to think seriously about its black membership and of ways to support their educational needs, both programmatically and through publications. It continued the regular reporting by the book agents and offered publishing comparisons for the years 1856 to 1859: for the latter year, over a million items for Sunday-schools and a quarter of a million books in its General Catalogue. Particularly striking was the subscription number of 33,400 for the *Ladies' Repository*.

Both churches, then, resourced leadership from the bottom-up, supplying materials suited to all reading levels, made available at reasonable costs, and delivered to homes, circuits, or stations. The editors and corresponding secretaries—H. N. M'Tyeire, D. D., and Thomas O. Summers, D.D., for the Southern church; and the diverse array for the Northern church of Nathan Bangs, Abel Stevens, John M'Clintock, Daniel Wise, J. B. Wakely, James Porter, and J. P. Durbin—served at the pleasure of the respective general conferences. These men provided. The people subscribed. The bishops presided. Production, oversight, management, and delivery

---

20 As an aside, I would suggest that such essays would not be read by today's bishops and church leaders. I offer that as an editorial board member of the twentieth-century *Quarterly Review* and as co-editor of today's successor journal, the online *Methodist Review*. Modest subscriptions to both indicated and indicate that today's church leaders cannot stomach serious but quite accessible scholarship. Further, one of the UMC's Southeastern Jurisdiction bishops decided one year that his cabinet would subscribe to *Quarterly Review* and use its issues during cabinet retreats. After one year, the conference ended its cabinet subscriptions. The bishop explained that the articles—crafted for just such a readership—proved too taxing for his troops.

came from the mission societies, Sunday-school organizations, and book concerns. Bishops and presiding elders remained in charge. They served officially as connectional leadership and presided in conferences as well as at meetings governing missions, Sunday schools, and publications. The operators of Methodism's connective businesses, however, were the more modestly titled "corresponding secretaries" or "editors."

Methodism's Colleges—Female and Male[21]

Figure 14: Female Academy, Xenia, Ohio

Attendees at the 1858 Cincinnati Conference heard the Education Committee report on six collegiate institutions and on "German Education." With regard to the latter, the Committee noted that

> [T]he cause of education has begun to awaken a deep interest among the German ministry and membership of the Methodist Episcopal Church. The German preachers of the North Ohio, and Cincinnati, and South-Eastern Indiana conferences, having agreed to create an endowment fund for the support of a German Professor in the Baldwin University, at Berea, Ohio—of which endowment fund ten thousand dollars are subscribed, and partly secured—a

---

21   Image from the *Minutes of the Cincinnati Annual Conference of the Methodist Episcopal Church, The Year 1854,* 51.

German Professor, who promises great efficiency, has been elected, and the department is now in active operation, having already eleven students.[22]

Cincinnati's colleges by then consisted of Xenia Female Academy and Collegiate Institute (see figure 14), Springfield Female College, Hillsboro Female College, Wesleyan Female College, Wilberforce University, and Ohio Wesleyan University.[23] The report on the latter was much shorter than in other years (see the treatment in the Formation chapter) but with the typical enabling resolutions concerning visiting committee and trustees. The Visiting and Examining Committee for Wilberforce, the new black collegiate venture, judged that

[T]he Principal of this institution and his assistants have proved themselves well qualified for their difficult and responsible position. The examination showed conclusively that the minds of the present class of students are capable of a very high degree of cultivation. Some of them exhibited a proficiency in the higher branches of mathematics, which would be creditable to any institution in the country. The polite and genteel deportment of the students during examinations attracted particular notice. A large and intelligent audience were in attendance at the public exhibition at the close of the year. The music was excellent. The declamations and compositions made a deep impression upon the audience, and for hours they remained delighted spectators of the exercises. The pupils particularly excelled in declamation; a talent which must become an element of power of no mean importance in their future elevation.

The Board of Trustees unanimously voted to carry out the action of the conference at its last session in regard to the transfer of the University to the Cincinnati and Ohio conferences.

Your Committee find that the property is in a good condition, and with careful and prudent management believe it may be made to fully answer the expectations of its friends.[24]

A series of recommendations followed, calling for agents to raise money, for a visiting committee for the following year, and for procedures on

22 *Minutes of the Cincinnati Annual Conference of the Methodist Episcopal Church, For the Year 1858* (Cincinnati: Printed at the Methodist Book Concern, 1858), 11–15.
23 *Minutes of the Cincinnati Annual Conference* (1858), 14–15.
24 *Minutes of the Cincinnati Annual Conference* (1858), 13.

trustees and property to carry through the transfer of Wilberforce to the two conferences.

Two years later, the MEC General Conference heard a similar affirmation of Wilberforce from its Committee on Education:

> **Wilberforce University**. The Committee have had before them the memorial of Rev. John F. Wright in reference to the Wilberforce University, and, in view of its peculiar character and relation to the Church, we offer for adoption the following resolution: Resolved, That we heartily sympathize with the noble purpose contemplated in the establishing of the Wilberforce University, and we do hereby earnestly commend the institution to the prayers and liberal contributions of the friends of humanity.[25]

While the committee and General Conference celebrated the launch of this venture in black collegiate education, it also worried over the number, financing, leadership, and, therefore, stability of the one hundred three colleges and schools the church then needed to support.

Whole number of Institutions 103
Whole number of Teachers..633
Whole number of Students 21,616
Whole value of Institutions, buildings, and grounds........ $2,420.319
Whole value of Endowments and other property $2,058,325
Whole value of Apparatus and cabinets...................................... $89,433
Whole number of volumes in Libraries 110,281
Whole amount of indebtedness.. $487,612
Whole amount of property above indebtedness............$4,080,465[26]

To address such concerns, the committee recommended the establishing of an Educational Society for the church, with seven Educational Districts charged with advising and evaluating the existing colleges and determining whether a proposed "literary institution shall be recognized as under our denominational control or patronage." The legislation also called for "one traveling preacher and one layman" on the seven district boards, for a "Corresponding Secretary elected by the General Conference" and for "Auxiliary Educational Societies" within the annual conferences.[27]

---

25 *Journals of the General Conference of the Methodist Episcopal Church, v. 4, 1860,* 457.

26 MEC, *General Conference Journals* (1860), 463.

27 MEC, *General Conference Journals* (1860), 456.

Not clear in the report was how the church's two theological schools fit into the above regimen. Garrett Biblical Institute had been "inaugurated" five years earlier, and what would be Boston University School of Theology remained in Concord, New Hampshire, and was known as the Methodist General Biblical Institute.[28]

The Southern church, as noted in the Formation chapter, judged at its 1858 General Conference that a theological institution was not yet called for, indicating how its colleges would continue to care for that level of preparation for its ministry. That chapter, as well, illustrated the array of southern educational institutions across the connection and within the Kentucky conferences.

Connections at the Conference Level

By the 1850s, the various programmatic ventures of the two Methodisms garnered support at the annual conference level. With affiliate societies, committees, or set-apart times, the conferences undertook some of the business operations during their sessions or by deputizing members to carry out assignments. For other of the connective activities, the conference provided directives to the circuits and stations and to the preachers and lay leaders. Typically, the minutes show conferences being convened; led in Scripture readings, hymns, and prayers; and sometimes delivered exhortations by the bishop or bishops. Organizing motions and appointment or election of committees followed. In just such a fashion, the 1852 MECS Kentucky Conference proceeded. Bishops Joshua Soule and James O. Andrew shared episcopal duties. The committee ordering followed a template:

> A Board of Stewards was "moved and carried."
> "The Conference then proceeded to the appointment of the usual standing Committees, viz."
> Education (its members included H. H. Kavanaugh, elected bishop two years later)
> Books & Periodicals
> Bible Cause
> Sabbath Schools
> Necessitous Cases
> Memoirs

---

28   MEC, *General Conference Journals* (1860), 463.

Public Worship (three Presiding Elders)
Temperance.[29]

The Northern church had, by the 1850s, a more complex ordering. To indicate such, here are the opening pages for the 1854 Cincinnati conference:[30]

MINUTES OF THE CINCINNATI ANNUAL CONFERENCE
AT
CINCINNATI, OHIO, SEPTEMBER 23, 1854
BISHOP SCOTT, President.
JOHN T. MITCHELL, Secretary.

The Cincinnati conference held its third annual session in the Ninth-street church, Cincinnati, September 27, 1854.

At 9 o'clock, A. M., Bishop [Levi] Scott called the conference to order, and conducted the religious services, reading the holy Scriptures, singing, and prayer.

The Secretary of the last conference, at the request of the Bishop, called the roll. Of 157 members, only 95 were present the first morning of conference. Some were detained by affliction, and one—Rev. C. G. Meredith—had died during the year. Subsequently nearly all the members of conference were in attendance.

John T. Mitchell was elected Secretary, James F. Chalfant, Assistant, and Wm. P. Strickland, Official Reporter. Several reporters for the daily papers of the city were present during the session, and were invited to seats within the bar.

The conference met daily at 8 o'clock, A. M., and adjourned at 12, M.

The following committees were appointed:
Conference Stewards.—Brothers Field, Loyd, and Fyffe.
On Public Worship.—The pastors of the city churches.
Mission Committee.—The presiding elders.
On the Bible Cause.—Brothers Strickland, Brooks, and Finley.

29 *Manuscript Minutes of the Kentucky Conference*, MECS, 1852, Kentucky Wesleyan.
30 *Minutes of the Cincinnati Annual Conference of the Methodist Episcopal Church, the Year 1854* (Cincinnati: The Methodist Book Concern, 1854), 3–4.

On Sunday School Cause and Sunday School Statistics.—Brothers Cowden, Conrey, Fitzgerald, Harris, Hypes, Whitmer, Engel, Hoppen, and Rhem.

On Tract Cause.—Brothers Walker, Morrow, M. Smith, Warnock, Lawton, Murphy, Nast, Wydtenbach, and Rothweiler.

On Necessitous Cases.—Brothers Peregrine, Kauffman, Sargent, Kemper, J. B. Ellsworth, Bennett, Schimmelpfenning, Vogel, and Schneider.

On Education.—Brothers Crum, Crow, Sutherland, Dustin, Brooks, Fee, Nast, Danker, and Rothweiler.

On Post-Offices.—Brothers Glasscock and Klein.

On Temperance.—Brothers Rontidp, Thompson, Phillips, Spencer, Webster, Armstrong, Hencke, Hoppen, and Krehbiel.

On New York Accounts.—Brother James F. Chalfant.

On Memoirs.—Brothers W. I. Ellsworth, Gaddis, and Dr. Elliott.

On Colonization.—Brothers Lowrey, Young, and Harlan.

On Bethel Cause.—Brothers Langarl, W. Rowe, Lorrain, Finley, and Bontecou.

On Statistics.—Brothers Miller, Tibbits, Fitch, Harris, I. I. Beall, Shannon, Browmiller, Heitmeyer, and Nachtreib.

On the Sanctification of the Sabbath.—Brothers A. Brown, D. Reed, Gossard, Wheat, and Rothweiler.

On Ministerial Support.—Brothers Weakley, Spencer, and Lowrey.

To Publish Minutes of Conference.—John T. Mitchell, J. W. Fowble, and M. Dustin.

On Slavery.—Brothers Bontecou, Lowrey, Crow, W. Rowe, West, D. Reed, Dustin, Brooks, and Lawton.

The President was requested to appoint, at some time during the session, all the Committees of Examination for next year. . . .

Ordered, that Stevens's Church Polity, Peck on Rule of Faith, Hibbard on Baptism, and Tytler's Universal History be studied by the classes the next year.

. . .

The Reports of the Book Committees, and the Exhibits of the Book Concerns, east and west, were read, from which that important interest of the Church is shown to be in a highly-prosperous condition.

Note that the outreach and formational committees commanded nine members, as also the organizational one (Statistics) and the one that reached out to distressed members and their families (Necessitous Cases). Members for the committees on Sunday Schools, the Tract Cause, Education, Temperance, and Slavery were named. Of the outreach and formational committees, why were numbers and names not indicated for the Mission Committee? By its membership, identified as the presiding elders, its importance to the conference was validated and demonstrated. Representation for the East Cincinnati, West Cincinnati, Dayton, Urbana, Xenia, Hillsboro, Cincinnati German, Pittsburg, and North Ohio districts consisted of those in charge of the district. Implicitly, though not indicated in the *Minutes*, the other outreach and formational committees were represented by those named. Note that Colonization no longer commanded the backing it once enjoyed. Instead, the conference backed the Slavery Committee and anti-slavery cause. The prior year (1853) the Cincinnati Conference had taken a forceful stance against slavery (see the Outreach chapter).

By establishing committees on Mission, Sunday Schools, the Tract Cause, Education, Temperance, and Slavery, the Cincinnati Conference renewed its commitment to the connectional, outreach, and formational operations that the Northern church had put in place. The several committees provided oversight to ongoing efforts within the conference to further the several, discrete, and separately administered programs. Not listed among the committees, but perhaps even more transformative in connections, was the various and incredible output of Methodist publishing. Although it did not have operational authority over printing enterprises, the conference did rely for its programming on the books, magazines, papers, and materials that the Cincinnati enterprise produced. That dependence is reflected in the last sentence in the above quotation.

Equally connectional and also cited above, down to specific individuals, were the lines devoted to the Committees of Examination and the additions to the assigned reading for those in the ordination track. The Course of Study (see the Formation chapter) constituted—and to this day still constitutes—the route into ministry through multiple years of reading books deemed to orient candidates to the ways of the Methodists (my father oversaw Duke Divinity School's Course of Study for a number of years).

The committees and causes of the Cincinnati Annual Conference and the region-wide service of Cincinnati-based publishing connected white

Methodists on the North side of the Ohio River. The small black congregation and scattered "colored" Methodists in other churches seem to have been modestly served by the various connectional resourcing outfits.

The MECS Kentucky Conference's committees served comparable, if somewhat more modest programs and depended on Nashville-based publishing magnates for their reading material. That conference also collaborated with the Louisville and other conferences to augment the resourcing of its white membership.

The Kentucky Conference that aligned with the Northern church—its black members either slaves or surviving under the slavery regime—came to modify its pro-slavery stance on the eve of the Civil War. Connectional programming within the conference was modest as also its utilization of resources across the river.

On both sides of the river, however, various initiatives at the conference level—again at least for whites—connected Methodists in interesting and important ways. New programs—staffed mainly by men in new roles, new offices, and new societal/structural orders—beckoned the people into increasingly more ordered ways of life. The bishops, to be sure, still exercised their Wesley-like ceremonial presiding-at-the-gathering leadership. And their appointment power and ability to move men from one post to another gave them regal powers, as, theoretically, they possess to this day. Chairing and dominating annual and general conferences, the bishops officially ran formal, structural, ongoing, privileged, male-whites-only, by-the-*Discipline* Methodism. However, from the ground-up, from the conference-out, and from editors-and-book-agents-resourced publishing, American Methodism had charted new directions.

Ground-Up, Conference-Out, Much-Published Witness: James B. Finley, Connectional Agent

Whereas, the Discipline of our church forbids the doing anything calculated to destroy our itinerant general superintendency, and whereas Bishop Andrew has become connected with slavery by marriage and otherwise, and this act having drawn after it circumstances which in the estimation of the General Conference will greatly embarrass the exercise of his office as an itinerant general Superintendent, if not in some places entirely prevent it; therefore,

Resolved, That it is the sense of this General Conference that he desist from the exercise of this office so long as this impediment remains.

J. B. FINLEY,
J. M. TRIMBLE[31]

That motion—offered by Finley in 1844—passed. Dis-connecting Methodism, it effected the division of the church, North and South, creating Mason-Dixon Methodism. The action of the Southern delegates at that month-long General Conference, which set in motion the procedures and subsequent assemblages that would create the Methodist Episcopal Church, South, lie outside this study's orbit. Here, Finley's agency deserves comment, as he made nothing of it in his own autobiography.[32] Nor did he dwell on the other seven general conferences to which he was sent, or his appointment as presiding elder nine times.[33] Those around Finley, colleagues as well as bishops, recognized his giftedness, imagination, courage, and bravery in charting important new directions for Methodism. He led the church in outreach and shaped it formationally. However, his several books document—not his—but the roles of other actors in the ground-up ministry that he lived and to which he gave incredible leadership. The titles tell just a little of the connectional career:

- *History of the Wyandott Mission at Upper Sandusky, Ohio,* 1840[34]
- *Memorials of Prison Life,* 1850[35]
- *Autobiography of the Rev. James B. Finley: Or Pioneer Life in the West,* 1853

---

31 *Journal of the General Conference of the Methodist Episcopal Church, Held in the City of New York, 1844* (New York: G. Lane & C. B. Tippett, 1844), 65–66. See *Methodist Experience in America,* 2:268–269 for a prior motion calling for Bishop Andrew to resign. Finley's was offered as a substituted and passed.

32 *Autobiography of Rev. James B. Finley, or Pioneer Life in the West,* W. P. Strickland, ed. (Cincinnati: The Methodist Book Concern, 1856).

33 On Finley's role in the 1844 General Conference, his views on slavery and abolition, and his career over all, see Charles C. Cole Jr., *Lion of the Forest: James B. Finley Frontier Reformer* (Lexington: University Press of Kentucky, 1994).

34 James B. Finley, *History of the Wyandott Mission at Upper Sandusky, Ohio* (Cincinnati: Wright and Swormstedt, 1840).

35 James B. Finley, *Memorials of Prison Life,* Rev. B. F. Tefft, ed. (Cincinnati: Swormstedt and Power, 1850).

- *Sketches of Western Methodism: Biographical, Historical, and Miscellaneous, Illustrative of Pioneer Life*, 1854[36]
- *Life Among the Indians: Or, Personal Reminiscences and Historical Incidents Illustrative of Indian Life*, 1857[37]

The first and last of his books show his close, personal engagement with Native Americans as he led Methodism into at least recognizing that they too were God's children. His six-year tenure as missionary among the Wyandotts—life with them, accompanying a number on a reverse mission to the eastern US and to the church's seaboard leadership, and career-long advocacy for them—come through implicitly in his publications (but see his recollection in this chapter's epigraph). The second book relates his role as chaplain to convicts. All the books touch on aspects of his career but tend to dwell on what's happening around him and what others are doing. Even the *Autobiography* narrates Methodism's engagements. Note the topics he highlights as the "Contents":

CHAPTER XX. Personal narrative continued—Reappointed to the Ohio district—Wyandott Indians—Early modes of worship—Conference in Cincinnati—Bishops—Delegates to General conference—Appointed to Lebanon district—Local preacher—Camp meeting—Camp meeting at Mechanicsburg—Went to General conference—Discordant elements in the body—Proposal to make the office of presiding elder elective—Compromise—Rev. Joshua Soule's opposition—M'Kendree's request—Rule adopted to build churches with free seats—Declared to be advisory—Round of camp meetings—Solicited to send a minister to Detroit—Conference at Chilicothe—Returned to Lebanon district—First quarterly meeting at the Maumee Rapids—Dismal journey through the Black Swamp—Meeting with the Wyandotts at Big Spring—Religion of the natives—Adventurous trip to Detroit—Worship in the council-house—Governor Cass—Soldiers awakened under preaching—other appointments—Difficulty with an Indian—Indian reservation—Drew up petition for the Wyandott nation—Request

36 James B. Finley, *Sketches of Western Methodism: Biographical, Historical, and Miscellaneous, Illustrative of Pioneer Life*, W. P. Strickland, ed. (Cincinnati: Methodist Book Concern, 1854).

37 James B. Finley, *Life Among the Indians: Or, Personal Reminiscences and Historical Incidents Illustrative of Indian Life*, Rev. D. W. Clark, ed. (Cincinnati: Cranston and Stowe, 1857).

for my appointment at Detroit—Not granted—Appointed to the Wyandott mission—No missionary funds at that day—Mission family—Difficulties connected with the mission—Sister Harriet Stubbs—Progress of scholars in the mission school—Organization of a society—Religion takes hold of the mind of the nation[38]

His *Autobiography* first appeared in 1853. The next year he served on a committee at the Cincinnati Conference and was appointed to a committee and to a church. The following year, he was superannuated, one of several "retirements" because of health. In 1856, he was sent again to General Conference. At annual conference, the bishop made him the Conference Missionary. The following year, the conference passed the following:

Rev. James B. Finley

1. Resolved, That this conference has heard with profound emotion of the recent death of our beloved brother and father in the ministry, Rev. James B. Finley, one of the oldest and most respected members of the body.

2. Resolved, That while we deeply feel that we have lost a Christian brother and father in the Gospel, and the Church a faithful watchman from the walls of Zion, yet we would express our gratitude to the great Head of the Church that he was spared to us so long, and would bow with humble submission to the wisdom of that Providence which has removed from our midst, and gathered as a ripe shock of corn, another faithful laborer to the heavenly garner.

3. Resolved, That we highly appreciate the moral heroism, burning zeal, and indefatigable labors of our venerated father in the pioneer work of the Christian ministry; and that we will cherish an affectionate remembrance of his Christian and ministerial character—his many toils, privations, sufferings, and successes, during his long and useful life.

4. Resolved, That we respectfully request Dr. Clark, editor of the Ladies' Repository, to preach a funeral discourse on the death of our venerated father before this conference on next Tuesday, at half-past ten o'clock, A. M.

---

38 Finley, *Autobiography*, 9.

5. Resolved, That we, as a conference, deeply sympathize and
    condole with the friends of our deceased father, and especially
    his widow, in their recent and painful bereavement.
6. Resolved, That the Secretary of this conference is hereby
    requested to furnish the widow of our deceased brother with
    a copy of these resolutions.
7. Resolved, That Rev. Dr. Clark be requested to publish the funeral
    discourse preached by him before this body in memory of Rev.
    J. B. Finley, late senior member of this conference.[39]

Finley concluded his *Autobiography* briefly, as the header at the beginning of this chapter indicates, covering a broad expanse of his life and
highlighting the Wyandott (outreach), prison chaplaincy (formation), and
Zanesville (presiding elder, connection) that characterized his whole ministerial career.

In 1844, he had offered the motion that broke the Methodist Episcopal connection into two virulently opposed churches. The
Northern church reconceived its episcopacy and its connectional self-
understanding in terms of the argument it had presented for the removal
of Bishop Andrew. That presiding-officer role would thereafter make
space for just the local and regional connectional enterprises that typified Finley's career. The Southern church gave its bishops far more regal
dress. Its bishops and their administrative counterparts—M'Tyeire and
M'Ferrin—and their successors would exercise more power and authority. Slavery, the 1844 division, border conflict for a decade and a half, and
the Civil War pointed episcopal Methodism in two different directions.
Both would gradually experience the organizational transformation of
the 1870s; but the Northern church heeded democratizing beckoning,
while the Southern continued to honor its royal and princely leadership
(bishops and heads of agencies).

Conclusion

Finley lived into the new role that his motion triggered. He modeled a
ground-up, conference-out, adventuring, creating, and advocating connectional ministry. When quite young, Finley had witnessed his father lib-
erating his slaves. Mid-career, Finley replicated his father's commitment

---

39 *Minutes of the Cincinnati Annual Conference of the Methodist Episcopal Church, The Year
    1857* (Cincinnati: The Methodist Book Concern, 1858), 7.

on a grand, national scale. His 1844 motion recognized and derided Dixie slavery Methodism. His life showed denominational colleagues where they should head. James B. Finley epitomized and actualized Methodism's lived way of being church: its outreaching, formative, and connective commitment.

Conclusion

There is only one condition previously required of those who desire admission into these societies, a "desire to flee from the wrath to come, and to be saved from their sins." *But wherever this is really fixed in the soul, it will be shown by its fruits. It is therefore expected of all who continue therein, that they should continue to evidence their desire of salvation,*

First, By doing no harm, by avoiding evil of every kind, especially that which is most generally practiced: such as,

The taking of the name of God in vain.

The profaning the day of the Lord, either by doing ordinary work therein, or by buying or selling.

Drunkenness; or drinking spirituous liquors, unless in cases of necessity.

The buying and selling of men, women, and children, with an intention to enslave them.

Fighting, *quarreling, brawling, brother* going to law *with brother: returning evil for evil; or railing for railing: the* using many words *in buying or selling.*

The buying or selling goods that have not paid the duty.

The giving or taking things on usury, *i.e., unlawful interest.*

Uncharitable *or* unprofitable *conversation: particularly speaking evil of magistrates or of ministers.*

Doing to others as we would not they should do unto us. . . .[1]

---

1   *The Doctrines and Discipline of the Methodist Episcopal Church, South, 1855* (Nashville: E. Stevenson & F. A. Owen, Agents for the Methodist Episcopal Church, South, 1855),

The 1855 *Discipline* of the Methodist Episcopal Church, South carried the "General Rules" gifted by John Wesley to guide folks in leading the Christian life. As the MECS excerpt above should convey, Methodists had detailed, highly specific, and extensive commandments by which to live. The strictures instructed those forgiven for their sins and headed toward perfection—like those adhering to John Bunyan's *Pilgrim's Progress*—where to place each step. The Americans had, in 1789, added to Wesley's list of evils to avoid, this very significant prohibition:

> The buying and selling of men, women, and children, with an intention to enslave them.[2]

That specific mandate remained, even while successive Methodist *Disciplines* eroded the church's initial anti-slavery resolve.[3] Even the Southern church kept it through its 1854 General Conference. However, at its next gathering in 1858, the *Discipline* that resulted purged that little sentence from its General Rules. They forbade:

> Drunkenness; or drinking spirituous liquors, unless in cases of necessity.
>
> *Fighting*, quarrelling, brawling, brother *going to law* with brother; returning evil for evil, or railing for railing; the *using many words in* buying or selling.
>
> The *buying or selling goods that have not paid the duty*.[4]

29–31. HathiTrust Digital Library Rights, Public Domain, Google-digitized. Permanent URL: https://hdl.handle.net/2027/chi.18928153. Italics in the originals.

2   For an early version of the above, see Thomas Coke and Francis Asbury, *The Doctrines and Disciplines of the Methodist Episcopal Church, in America with Explanatory Notes by Thomas Coke and Francis Asbury* (Philadelphia: Henry Tuckniss, 1798), 133–34. For discussion from a Southern point of view, see Jno J. Tigert, *A Constitutional History of American Episcopal Methodism*, 3rd edition (Nashville: Publishing House of the Methodist Episcopal Church, South, 1908), 252. David Sherman, in *History of the Revisions of the Discipline of the Methodist Episcopal Church* (New York: Nelson & Phillips, 1874), carries the reader through the MEC's changes on slavery, 115–20. Donald G. Mathews, *Slavery and Methodism: A Chapter in American Morality, 1780–1845* (Princeton: Princeton University Press, 1965) remains the most valuable overview. For the significance of slavery in successive General Conferences, see *The General Conferences of the Methodist Episcopal Church from 1792 to 1896* by Lewis Curts and Western Methodist Book Concern Staff (Cincinnati: Curts & Jennings, 1900).

3   For this erosion, see our *Methodist Experience in America*, vols. 1 & 2; Mathews, *Slavery and Methodism*; *The General Conferences of the Methodist Episcopal Church from 1792 to 1896*; and virtually any monograph or history covering American Methodism.

4   *Journal of the General Conference of the Methodist Episcopal Church, South, v. 4, 1858* (Nashville: Southern Methodist Publishing House, 1859), 37. HathiTrust Digital

To be sure, successive *Disciplines* from 1792 on had chipped away at the anti-slavery commitments with which the Methodist Episcopal Church had been birthed (see appendix, "The First *Discipline* on Race Relations)." Still, even the Southern church had kept this stricture against slavery within its *Discipline,* at least through the 1854 General Conference. No more.

Unlike other Southern publications, the MECS *Discipline*—its official statement of principle and policy—had had little to say about slavery and its "colored" membership. The latter received mention four times in the whole *Discipline*, each time incidentally and in covering the various categories of people considered as within the fold. All but one of the references to slave or slavery occurred in section 2 of the first organizationally descriptive part of the *Discipline*.

CONTENTS

PART FIRST.

ORIGIN, ARTICLES OF RELIGION, GOVERNMENT, AND RITUAL.

CHAPTER I

SEC. 1. Of the Origin of the Methodist Episcopal Church,
and of the Methodist Episcopal Church, South
SEC. 2. Of the Organization of the Methodist Episcopal Church, South
SEC. 3. Articles of Religion
SEC. 4. The Nature, Design, and General Rules of our United Societies[5]

Why the importance of the attention to slavery in section 2? In the prefaces to the *Discipline*, the numerous American Methodist churches have declared their independence, charted their reasons for separating, and recalled the grievances that necessitated dis-union.[6] "Sec. 2"

Library Rights Public Domain, Google-digitized. Permanent URL: https://hdl.handle.net/2027/chi.18928211.

5 *The Doctrines and Discipline of the Methodist Episcopal Church, South,* Joshua Soule, ed. (Nashville: E. Stevenson & F. A. Owen for the Methodist Episcopal Church, South, 1856), iii, http://name.umdl.umich.edu/AJK2719.0001.001.

6 For examples, see our *Methodist Experience in America*, 1, and the italicized subsections, beginning with "Of the Origin of the United Brethren in Christ" and "Of the Rise of Methodism (so called) in Europe and America." See pp. 189–92 for the Southern

recounted the birthing of the MECS and referred to slavery six times as the presenting reason, typified by the strictly historical character of the first three mentions:

Of the Organization of the Methodist Episcopal Church, South

In the judgment of the delegates of the several Annual Conferences in the slaveholding States, the continued agitation of the subject of slavery and abolition in a portion of the Church, the frequent action on that subject in the General Conference, and especially the proceedings of the General Conference of the Methodist Episcopal Church of 1844, in the case of the Rev. James O. Andrew, D. D., one of the Bishops, who had become connected with slavery by marriage, produced a state of things in the South which rendered a continuance of the jurisdiction of that General Conference over the Conferences aforesaid, inconsistent with the success of the ministry in their proper calling.[7]

So the Southern church declared its (white) independence.

"Colored" Connection, Outreach, and Formation

The *Discipline* referenced slavery a seventh time and used the descriptive "colored" in sections that might be deemed as dealing with Connection, Outreach, and Formation. "Chapter II" dealt with general, annual, and quarterly conferences, episcopacy, and the levels and duties of preachers. Section 7 therein detailed the duties of preachers in charge of circuits, stations, or missions with sixteen directives. The specified recordkeeping and reporting in the excerpt below functioned connectionally. Promotion of books and periodicals and of the Sunday schools served to register formational activities. Documenting outreach were the array of office or status categories from baptism, through the ministerial levels to

---

statement, "Of the Organization of The Methodist Episcopal Church, South." For discussion of the historical preface as a Methodist distinctive, see my *Methodist Connectionalism: Historical Perspectives* (Nashville: General Board of Higher Education and Ministry, 2009), "Introduction: History, the Methodist Mode of Self-Identification," and "Chapter 1: The First Word about Methodism: History in the *Discipline*," 1–33.

7   *The Doctrines and Discipline of the Methodist Episcopal Church, South, 1856*, 9–10.

membership of white, "colored," and Native American persons and the support of missionary societies. The following excerpt, then, points to the Southern church's connectional, outreach, and formational accounting. Note that the numbers and names of "colored persons" were to be captured and reported.

> 9. To see that all the people within the bounds of his charge be duly supplied with our **books and periodicals. . . .**
>
> 12. To see that a permanent record be kept of all the **baptisms and marriages** within the bounds of his charge.
>
> 13. To see that a **register** be kept, in which shall be noted the names, with the time and manner of the reception and disposal of every person belonging to the Church in his station, circuit, or mission, **distinguishing between local elders, deacons, and preachers, members and probationers, white persons, colored persons, and Indians,** and report to the Annual Conference the number of each that may be under his charge at the time of its session.
>
> 14. To **promote** all the interests of the **Missionary, Sunday-school, and Tract Societies of our Church**, in such way as the Discipline or the Annual Conference may designate; and to report to the Conference the amount raised during the year within the bounds of his charge for these several societies.
>
> 15. To report at each session of the Quarterly Conference the number and state of the Sunday-schools; and annually to the Quarterly and Annual Conferences, for insertion in their respective journals, the number of Sunday-schools, scholars, teachers, superintendents, and Sunday-school library books in his circuit, station, or mission.[8]

Body counts and submission of other records have been signature denominational expectations. Such recordkeeping and reporting as specified above charted Methodism's commitments and the honoring thereof.

Similar specificity governed matters fiscal. "Part Second. Temporal Economy," treated the church's various financial concerns or obligations. Section 6, "Of the Support of the Ministry," required thirty-five points and

---

8   MECS, *General Conference Journal (1858)*, 68–70. Bolding added.

close to 20 pages. Here too, instructions covered the connection, outreach, and formation for/in the Southern church.

1. The allowance of the Bishops shall be estimated by the Committee on Episcopacy of the General Conference, and they shall divide the amount between the Annual Conferences and the Missionary Society, as herein provided. . . .

9. The claims of the Book Agent, Financial Secretary, and editors, at Nashville, shall be estimated by the Book Committee. . . .

11. The claims of missionaries laboring on **colored missions** shall be estimated by the stewards of the circuit or station within whose limits the largest portion of the mission may be located: in those cases where the mission is not within the bounds of any work, the allowance shall be estimated by the mission committee of the Annual Conference, as provided for by the Discipline. . . .

16. The missionaries to the **people of color**, in favor of whom no drafts are drawn, shall draw on any missionary money raised within the bounds of their missions—not otherwise directed by the donors—to the amount of their claims; and they shall report the amount of their receipts to the Annual Conference.[9]

Here, in dealing with monetary outlays, as in the previous sections, the *Discipline* attended to those involved in formation and outreach, not to the "people of color" over whom they had responsibility.

Such top-down guidance pertained to the chief connectional officer and authority, the bishop. Episcopal appointive powers ranged over the various connectional, formational, and outreach activities of the Southern church.

Quest. 3. What are the duties of a Bishop?

Ans. 1. To preside in the General and Annual Conferences.

2. To fix the appointments of the preachers in the Annual Conferences, provided he shall not allow any preacher to remain in the same circuit or station more than two years successively; except the presiding elders, the book agents and editors authorized by the General Conference, the corresponding secretary of the Missionary Society, the supernumerary and superannuated preachers, missionaries among the Indians, missionaries to our people of

---

9   MECS, *General Conference Journal (1858)*, 260, 263–64. Bolding added to call attention to the racial references.

color and on foreign stations, chaplains to state prisons and military posts, those preachers that may be appointed to labor for the special benefit of seamen, and for the American Bible Society, also the preacher or preachers that may be stationed in the city of New Orleans, and the presidents, principals, or teachers of seminaries of learning, which are or may be under our superintendence; and also, when requested by an Annual Conference, to appoint a preacher for a longer time than two years to any seminary of learning not under our care.[10]

[Seminaries of learning were not antecedents of today's post-collegiate divinity schools but pre-college or secondary schools.] Here, the array of ministerial offices, missions, and educational roles also point to the church's sense of its connectional, outreach, and formational commitments.

In section 7 of "Temporal Economy," the *Discipline* treated, as the rubric indicates, "the Support of Missions." A Constitution of the Missionary Society detailed officers in and the roles of the church-wide body, the duties and obligations of the conference societies, and procedures for appointing those to serve in missionary capacities (in the US and abroad). Ten Commandments detailed how money was to be expended and raised. Contributions and pledges constituted, as the Outreach chapter indicated, the act or commitment by and through which church members rallied to the missionary cause. Regrettably, the *Discipline* did not prescribe, and the General Conference journals and annual conference minutes did not report, what church members heard when making their commitments. Instead, what was detailed were the means for recording collections. Delineated as well were guidance for organizing slaves into missionary societies and attempting collections from them:

> 6. It shall be the duty of the preachers in charge of circuits and stations to appoint a suitable person in each class as a missionary collector, who shall keep a book, in which shall be enrolled the names of all the members of the class, and who shall collect from each member who may be disposed to contribute a cent or more a week, or fifty cents or more a year, and shall pay over the sums so collected to the preacher in charge, at or before the last quarterly meeting of the Conference year. And the preacher shall transmit the money thus paid over, together with such other sums as shall

10   MECS, *General Conference Journal (1858)*, 59–60.

have been collected from the congregations, or from branch societies, or otherwise, to the treasurer of the Conference Missionary
Society, to be duly reported.

    7. It shall be the duty of all our missionaries, except **those who
are appointed to labor for the benefit of the slaves**, to form
their circuits into auxiliary missionary societies, and to make regular quarterly and class collections wherever practicable, and report
the amount collected every three months, either by endorsing it
on their drafts, or by transmitting the money to the treasurer of the
parent Society.[11]

Laboring for the benefit of slaves might have prompted delegates to
MECS general conferences to lodge within the *Discipline* some guidance
on Sunday schools for slave children (see the appendix for "William Sasnett of MECS on Mission" and also "Address by the Confederate Clergy").
Of course, the Southern church did not; nor did the Northern church
(as the Formation chapter indicates) attend to education of its "colored"
membership. However, by 1856, the MEC had decided to enter into the
Discipline a chapter on "The Rights and Privileges of our Colored Members." And, in 1860, the MEC had radically reshaped what had long been
its last word of guidance to the faithful—"Of Slavery."

The Northern *Disciplines*

CHAPTER VII. OF SLAVERY.

Quest. What shall be done for the extirpation of the evil of slavery?

Answ. 1. We declare that we are as much as ever convinced of the
great evil of slavery: therefore no slaveholder shall be eligible to any
official station in our Church hereafter, where the laws of the State
in which he lives will admit of emancipation, and permit the liberated slave to enjoy freedom.

    2. When any travelling preacher becomes an owner of a slave
or slaves, by any means, he shall forfeit his ministerial character in
our Church, unless he execute, if it be practicable, a legal emancipation of such slaves, conformably to the laws of the State in which
he lives.

---

11   MECS, *General Conference Journal (1858)*, 289–91. Bolding added to call attention to
     the reference to slavery.

3. All our preachers shall prudently enforce upon our members the necessity of teaching their slaves to read the word of God; and to allow them time to attend upon the public worship of God on our regular days of divine service.

4. Our coloured preachers and official members shall have all the privileges which are usual to others in the district and Quarterly Conferences, where the usages of the country do not forbid it. And the Presiding Elder may hold for them a separate District Conference, where the number of coloured local preachers will justify it.

5. The Bishops may employ coloured preachers to travel and preach, when their services are judged necessary, provided that no one shall be so employed without having been recommended by a Quarterly Conference.[12]

So the Northern church addressed slavery as it had in the *Discipline* beginning in 1824. Prior to that—1820 and earlier—only the first two strictures appeared in the *Discipline*. Subsequent general conferences, after 1824, doctored the last two directives modestly. For instance, through 1844, the fifth permission concluded "provided that no one shall be so employed without having been recommended according to the form of discipline."[13]

The 1860 *Discipline* revised its antislavery commitment significantly, reducing the five-point belabored process to the simple, forceful call (quoted previously in the Connection chapter) for "our Preachers and People to keep themselves pure from this great evil, and to seek its extirpation by all lawful and Christian means."[14]

---

12 *The Doctrines and Discipline of the Methodist Episcopal Church, 1856*. (New York: Carlton & Porter), 212–13. Personal copy owned. Also used is *The Doctrines and Discipline of the Methodist Episcopal Church, 1856* (New York: J. Emory and B. Waugh, 1856), HathiTrust Digital Library Rights Public Domain, Google-digitized. Permanent URL: https://hdl.handle.net/2027/wu.89077101616.

13 *The Doctrines and Discipline of the Methodist Episcopal Church* (New York, G. Lane & C. B. Tippett, 1844), 202–03.

14 *The Doctrines and Discipline of the Methodist Episcopal Church, 1860*, with an Appendix (New York: Carlton & Porter), 266. From a personally owned copy. See also *The Doctrines and Discipline of the Methodist Episcopal Church, 1860*, with an Appendix (Cincinnati: Poe & Hitchcock, 1860), HathiTrust Digital Library Rights Public Domain, Google-digitized. Permanent URL: https://hdl.handle.net/2027/nnc1.50192327. At the 1860 General Conference, a "Majority Report on Slavery" (404–09), ended with the motion putting the revision of the *Division* before the annual conferences with a resolution (see it in the appendix).

With this forceful statement, delegates to the 1860 General Conference finally took an unqualified and clear stand against slavery.[15] As here, the church placed the slavery question where it had been for the nineteenth century at the end of the *Discipline*. But the 1860 declaration treated slavery and only slavery, not the limited prerogatives of black preachers and implicitly its black members.

That simplification and focus entirely upon slavery permitted the Northern church to treat its black members, rhetorically at least, as members, not as a horde cordoned off into slaves or freed slaves. Even through 1856, as indicated above, the Northern church had kept under "Slavery" its primary guidance to the faithful on white treatment of black members and their leaders. (See appendix, "Poetry on Race—*The Ladies Repository*—1858.") Indeed, in the 1856 "Address of the Bishops," that year's General Conference delegates heard their leaders plead for the status quo on slavery. That portion of their remarks, the last, followed mostly shorter guidance on what that gathering should treat. Prior topics—Changes of Discipline (the only one equal in length), Institutions of the Church, Education, Publishing Interest, The Tract Cause, Sunday Schools, Missions—preceded slavery.[16] The bishops urged the 1856 delegates not to alter the slavery statement in the *Discipline*. Their caution had in view the interests of the northern Kentucky Conference, as well as five others "wholly or in part in slave territory":

> In our administration in the territory where slavery exists, we have been careful not to transcend in any instance, or in any respect, what we understood to be the will and direction of the General Conference. That body having retained its jurisdiction over conferences previously existing in such territory, and having directed the organization of additional conferences, it became our duty to arrange the districts, circuits, and stations, and to superintend them as an integral part of the Church. As the result, we have six annual conferences which are wholly or in part in slave territory. These conferences have a white Church membership, including probationers, of more than one hundred and forty-three thousand, with the attendants upon our ministry making a probable population

---

15 See the appendix.

16 *Journals of the General Conference of the Methodist Episcopal Church*, v. 3, 1848–1856 (New York: Carlton & Porter, [1855–1900]), 191–201. HathiTrust Digital Library Rights Public Domain, Google-digitized. Permanent URL: https://hdl.handle.net/2027/wu .89077109437.

of between five and six hundred thousand. They have a colored Church membership, including probationers, of more than twenty-eight thousand, with the attendants upon our ministry making a probable population of upward of a hundred thousand. A portion of this population are slaves. The others are mostly poor. They are generally strongly attached to the Church of their choice, and look to it confidingly for ministerial services, religious sympathy, and all the offices of Christian kindness. The white membership in these conferences, in respect to intelligence, piety, and attachment to Methodist Discipline and economy, will compare favorably with other portions of the Church.

In our judgment, the existence of these conferences and Churches under their present circumstances, does not tend to extend or perpetuate slavery. . . .[17]

The 1856 General Conference heeded the bishops' counsel. Until 1860, consequently, the church had retained, with only minor changes, the five points about slavery that served as well to delineate its policy and standards for black membership and ministry.

The 1860 *Discipline* called for freeing black members to be members:

The enslavement from generation to generation of human beings guilty of no crime, is what no man has a right to desire for himself or his posterity, and what no man ever did or can desire. The constant liability of the forcible separation of husbands and wives, of parents and children, even in the mildest forms of slavery, is a state of things from which every enlightened mind desires to be free. The impediments which slavery interposes in the way of the observance of the

17 MEC, *General Conference Journals* (1848–1856), 199–200. That paragraph—cited in the 1860 *Journal* in opposition to changing the *Discipline* on slavery (and included here in the appendix)—continued: "They are known to be organized under a Discipline which characterizes slavery as a great evil; which makes the slaveholder ineligible to any official station in the Church, where the laws of the state in which he lives will admit of emancipation, and permit the liberated slave to enjoy freedom; which disfranchises a traveling minister who by any means becomes the owner of a slave or slaves, unless he executes, if it be practicable, a legal emancipation of such slaves, conformably to the laws of the state wherein he lives; which makes it the duty of all the ministers to enforce upon all the members the necessity of teaching their slaves to read the word of God, and allowing them time to attend upon the public worship of God on our regular days of Divine service; which prohibits the buying and selling of men, women, and children with an intention to enslave them, and inquires what shall be done for the extirpation of the evil of slavery."

conjugal and parental relations, depriving the parents from governing and educating their children, and the children from honoring and obeying their parents, as God has commanded, is a state
of things condemned alike by the Bible and all enlightened consciences, and from which the heart's holiest aspirations struggle to
be free. The sacredness and inviolability of the marriage covenant
.is one of the cornerstones of all Christian civilization. Slavery, as it
exists in the United States, is fundamentally at war with this most
ancient and sacred institution. What should we desire, and have a
right to desire, if we were in the place of the injured party? This is
the measure of our duty.[18]

The *Discipline* produced by General Conference in 1860 took other significant steps toward recognizing black membership, involvement, leadership, and ministry. Notably, it included within the *Discipline* a section on
"The Rights and Privileges of our Colored Members."

1. Our Colored Preachers and official members shall have all
the privileges which are usual to others in Quarterly Conferences,
where the usages of the country do not forbid it. And the Presiding
Elder may hold for them a separate Quarterly Conference, when in
his judgment it shall be expedient.

2. The Bishop or Presiding Elder may employ Colored Preachers to travel and preach, when their services are judged necessary.
Provided, that no one shall be so employed without having been
recommended by a Quarterly Conference.

3. The Bishops may call a Conference once in each year of our
Colored Local Preachers, within the bounds of any one or more of
our districts, for the purpose of conferring with them with respect
to the wants of the work among our colored people, and the best
means to be employed in promoting its prosperity; at which Conference, the Presiding Elder within whose district, and under whose
care, the colored Churches and congregations are, shall be present.
Provided, that the holding of said Conference or Conferences shall

18 *Journals of the General Conference of the Methodist Episcopal Church, v. 4, 1860* (New
York: Carlton & Porter, [1855–1900]), 404–05, HathiTrust Digital Library Rights Public Domain, Google-digitized. Permanent URL: https://hdl.handle.net/2027/wu
.89077109460.

be recommended by an Annual Conference, and the Bishops, upon due inquiry, shall deem it practicable and expedient.[19]

The prerogatives lodged here deal primarily and clearly with "our Colored Local Preachers," not the rights and privileges of black members generally. Further, the statements repeated and added to what had been conceded to its black membership in prior *Disciplines*. However, the 1860 General Conference positioned these statements to appear in a section specifically designated for its *"colored"* members, clearly declared them as "colored" *members*, and so appeared up front in the table of contents. Thereby the *Discipline* made provisions for African American people and for ministry to/for/with/by them. A fuller and clearer statement replaced what had been only partially affirmed and previously lodged at the end of the *Discipline* under "Slavery." Readers of the 1860 *Discipline*, especially black readers, must have appreciated not having these permissions treated under "Slavery."

Nevertheless, these prerogatives were segregated as a separate section in "Chapter VIII, Local Preachers." To be sure, being accorded a section in the *Discipline* represented a step forward by the Northern church for its black members. However, separate-but-not equal, they were not integrated into the overall treatment of local preachers or echoed in "Chapter X, The Membership for the Church." Further, the horizon for leadership in the black community and its leadership remained local and low. "Colored" leaders would not become traveling preachers, could continue becoming local preachers and might be ordained to that office. However, being accepted as traveling preachers and fully ordained awaited the creation of black (that is, segregated) annual conferences. Still, the Northern church had moved forward on race relations.

A *Partial* Northern Awakening

The MEC advanced the status of its black members as its sectional temperature boiled. That escalation can be seen in the journals of the prior general conferences. A quick check of references to "slave(ry)" in the 1848, 1852, and 1856 gatherings finds a total of four hundred ninety-three allusions. Roughly forty times the specific word and the implicit concern occur in the 1848 and 1852 journals, but four hundred eight times in

---

19 MEC, *General Conference Journals* (1860), 122–23.

1856.[20] The counts include those in the indexes and in multiple instances when slavery was the topic. The count in 1860? Over a thousand, specifically one thousand two hundred forty-one.[21] The Northern church's attention to slavery came as annual conferences presented petitions from its people calling for action (or inaction) on slavery. The Ohio Conference submitted quite a number of petitions, far fewer than most conferences, even others in Ohio. Two addressed slavery, as also other causes:

> Joseph M. Trimble presented a resolution of the twelve Quarterly Conferences of Chillicothe District against changing the Rule of Discipline touching the Presiding Elder's office and duties, and it was referred to the Committee on the Itinerancy; also, a resolution of the twelve Quarterly Conferences of Chillicothe District protesting against Lay Delegation, and it was referred to the Committee on Lay Delegation; also, the resolution of the twelve Quarterly Conferences of Chillicothe District against a change of the General Rule on Slavery, fourteen official members asking a change, and it was referred to the Committee on Slavery.

> Joseph M. Trimble presented a transcript from the Journal on a Law Question, and it was referred to the committee on that subject. Frederic Merrick presented a petition from Oak Grove for a change of the Rule on Slavery, signed by S. Rankin and twenty-two others, and it was referred to the Committee on Slavery.[22]

Similar complexity and divergence on the slavery question occurred in the numerous Cincinnati submissions:

> Granville Moody presented a petition from Piqua, signed by William Herr and twenty others, for the change of the Rule on Slavery, and it was referred to the Committee on that subject. He also presented two memorials on the subject of Boundaries: One from Greenville and Arcanum; and one from Arcanum, signed by Joseph

20 *Journals of the General Conference of the Methodist Episcopal Church*, v. 3, 1848–1856. New York: Carlton & Porter, [1855–1900]), HathiTrust Digital Library Rights Public Domain, Google-digitized. Permanent URL: https://hdl.handle.net/2027/wu.89077109437.

21 *Journals of the General Conference of the Methodist Episcopal Church*, v. 4, 1860 (New York: Carlton & Porter, [1855–1900]), HathiTrust Digital Library Rights Public Domain, Google-digitized. Permanent URL: https://hdl.handle.net/2027/wu.89077109460.

22 MEC, *General Conference Journals* (1860), 68, 104.

C. Shepherd and forty-seven others, and they were referred to the Committee on Boundaries.

Granville Moody presented a memorial from North Louisburgh in favor of a change of the Rule on Slavery, signed by Edmund Moore and forty-five others, and it was referred to the Committee on Slavery. . . . Michael Marlay presented a memorial from the Quarterly Conference of Baper Chapel, Dayton, against a change of the Rule on Slavery, and it was referred to the Committee on Slavery. He also presented a memorial from John F. Wright concerning the Wilberforce University, and it was referred to the Committee on Education; and it was also referred to the Editorial Committee to be printed, should they judge proper.[23]

In 1860, Ohio Methodists differed on the slavery question as they had for years.

Divergence on slavery was represented as well by the presence of delegates from the northern Kentucky Conference. Created only eight years prior by Methodists abandoning the Southern church, the conference was clearer on its dissent from the MECS than in commitment to changing the MEC's stance on slavery:

Kentucky Conference. William H. Black presented a petition from Orangeburgh Circuit against any change of the General Rule on Slavery, signed by C. B. Brewer and one hundred and three others, and it was referred to the Committee on Slavery.[24]

Kentucky Methodists would struggle over the war; that conference's members and leaders struggled thereafter with whether to remain in the Northern church.

The whole MEC struggled as well—as Methodists would through 1939, to 1968, and to today—over who its black members were, with whom they would congregate, under what constraints they might gather, and by whom they would be led. Just such confusion came to the floor in the report of a committee created for the 1860 General Conference:

[T]he Report of the Committee on Colored Membership was presented and adopted, as follows: The Committee on Colored Membership, to which was referred certain Memorials from Colored

---

23   MEC, *General Conference Journals* (1860), 122, 207.
24   MEC, *General Conference Journals* (1860), 60.

Local Preachers, respectfully represent, That, having examined said memorials, they find that they request this body,

1. To extend the bounds of the Conference of Colored Local Preachers called in accordance with the provisions introduced into the Discipline at the last General Conference.

2. To grant them power to try and expel their own members.

3. To confer upon the Conference of Colored Local Preachers power to elect to Deacons' and Elders' orders.

4. To invest said Conference with all the powers of a regular Annual Conference.

5. To admit Colored Preachers to membership in our Annual Conferences. Your Committee find that the first two objects prayed for, are in substance covered by provisions already existing in the Discipline, which appear to have been overlooked by the petitioners.

In regard to items three and four, referred to above, your Committee find that the prayer of the memorialists could not be granted without doing violence to our usages and disciplinary regulations. The fifth item, embraced in the memorials before us, was withdrawn by the representative of the petitioners, who appeared in person before the Committee.[25]

Unwilling to admit "colored preachers" to their (white) annual conferences or to establish black conferences, the 1860 MEC General Conference had awoken only partially to bringing its African American people into full Methodist membership. The Committee on Colored Membership reflected what Northern Methodism had shown in the period leading up to the Civil War. Black lives mattered only partially.

Your Conclusions?

If you have plowed through this treatise, what think ye of Southern and Northern Methodist policies and practices in the 1850s?

Mine: For the 1860 Southern church, black connection, formation, and outreach could occur under the oversight and often only in direct view of its white laity, preachers, and presiding elders. By 1860, the Northern church had come, gradually to be sure, to permit connection, formation,

---

25   MEC, *General Conference Journals* (1860), 308.

and outreach on black turf and terms. But the terms were those set by white Methodism, and the turf was fenced.

Today's United Methodists live with the connectional structures of Jurisdictions, gifted to us by slavery and then segregation. The lines drawn by slavery/segregation over the years separate Kentucky and Ohio in their respective policies, practices, and missions—or in their connective, formational, and outreach functioning.

A Long Personal Postscript

Race and the Renewal of the Church[1]

As the Ku Klux Klan "celebration" broke up, we raced to my car. Jumped in. Locked the doors. Before I could start the engine a dozen or more Klansmen circled us, glared in, and seemed ready to break the windows. I roared through them. Nobody passed the three of us from the Klan grounds outside Salisbury until we raced 150 miles and reached Durham. Dropping my two high school friends at their homes, I checked in at my folks. The next day I headed to the church in Rocky Mount, NC and my summer field work.[2]

A Klan Event

The "visit" to the KKK gathering took place in the summer of 1964. The United States was embroiled again in what may have been its greatest domestic challenge. Would it, could it, should it become a country

---

1 The title is borrowed from (and here acknowledged) Will D. Campbell, *Race and the Renewal of the Church* (Philadelphia: Westminster Press, 1962).

2 Excuse the first person in the above statement, in what follows, and variously within this book. The rationale for its use here as throughout this study should become apparent in what follows. I actually started drafting for the whole project in this postscript, initially designed as the introduction. Then, this postscript needed to explain why I would begin a study of nineteenth-century Mason-Dixon Methodism with a twentieth-century KKK experience. Hence the autobiographical nature of this postscript.

where all "men" are created equal and so treated?[3] Advocacy for and fervid opposition to that vision again dominated the nation's life, courts, legislatures.

Why, though, given such a national atmosphere, would three kids go to a Klan rally? And why the menacing crowd at the rally's end? I had taken a tape recorder to the gathering and was catching the rabid denunciations of Martin Luther King Jr., Bobby Kennedy, Civil Rights, and North Carolina progressive leadership. Midway in the ceremony, a Klan officer ordered me to stop recording and store the recorder. That I did, back in my car. The three of us then stayed by his side believing that his apparent authority and responsibility for order offered protection. During the rally it did. Afterward, we feared violence from the crowd around the car, who doubtless suspected that we belonged to some monitoring federal agency. Frightened and fearing they would harm us, we fled.

Why did I go to the Klan rally? Why drive halfway across North Carolina and take two Durhamite friends to such a despicable gathering? The three of us had graduated the prior year (1963) from Yale, Williams, and Wesleyan (Richey). One, working in communications in Chapel Hill at UNC, had for years been interested in various political events/causes/issues, an investment that has paid as a career in national political news commentary and counsel. The other, also in a Carolina program, shared common interests in the summer's racial and political turmoil. It was 1964!

I served that summer as an intern under the Student Interracial Ministry (SIM) venture.[4] It placed black seminarians in white churches in the North. White kids, like myself, went south to black churches, including King's in Atlanta. After a training session that summer (which included a presentation by Will D. Campbell, author of *Race and the Renewal of the Church*), I went to the Presbyterian church to which I had been assigned. Its pastor, James Costen, proved superb in guiding an impulsive but naïve

---

3   The full sentence in the Declaration of Independence: "We hold these truths to be self-evident, that all men are created equal, that they are endowed by their Creator with certain unalienable Rights, that among these are Life, Liberty and the pursuit of Happiness."

4   David P. Cline, *From Reconciliation to Revolution: How the Student Interracial Ministry Took Up the Cause of Civil Rights* (Chapel Hill: University of North Carolina Press, 2016). Cline's account gives attention to my placement in 1964 and the Klan event. It neglects, primarily because Cline did not arrange for a conversation with or seek submission of written testimony from me, the leadership role that I played as co-director for 1964–1965.

white southerner in learning ministry and stumbling around in the racially segregated community.

Costen—who would later move to a prominent black church in Atlanta, then assume leadership at Interdenominational Theological Center, eventually head it, be selected as presiding officer of the Presbyterian Church, help guide the reunion of that body with its Southern counterpart, and rise to presidency of the Association of Theological Schools—showed his early commitment to an inclusive church and inclusive society by ongoing participation in SIM. He did so in 1964 by inviting a Northern congregation to send a group of white kids to work with his congregation in repainting a country church. Located outside Elm City, and also pastored by Costen, the frame building claimed very few members. Costen knew that taking an interracial group to a small Southern town posed some risks. To head off trouble, he had gone to Elm City sometime in the spring; met with the mayor, chief of police, and council head; and explained what was forthcoming. How could he have known that, in those conversations, he chatted with the KKK?

Almost as soon as we had the kids out to Elm City, ladders up and scraping and prepping begun, the KKK arrived. So quickly as well did the state police and regional and national newspapers and TV networks. As I remember it, four rings joined in that "spiritual" occasion. Ours was the smallest, those of us immediately around the church, scraping. Next, encircling us, were the newsfolk, who did come and go. Then stood the grim-faced state troopers. And finally, the scowling white folk—Klansfolk and sympathizers.

After the day's drama, we returned to Rocky Mount, worrying that the Klan and fellow travelers might pose a night-time threat to all of us participating. Costen's parishioners organized patrols (via car) for the neighborhood. The black couple with whom I lived put a rifle by the front door. Our fears were not unwarranted. In a couple of days, the KKK held a rally in Rocky Mount. I went (as a white and unknown to the white community of Rocky Mount) to learn if any threats or invitations to violence would be issued. I taped that gathering. Soon thereafter, I undertook the later KKK jaunt with my two friends to learn if anything might be threatened by the state Klan. Thankfully, verbal abuse proved enough for the North Carolina white supremacists.

Others in SIM that year (some 30–40) and in subsequent summers suffered more directly than had I. I rehearsed my experience, as it constituted a pivotal point in my sense of my *whiteness* and of the importance of coming to understand America's racial challenges.[5] Back that fall at Union Theological Seminary, I would co-direct SIM for 1964–1965 and oversee the fundraising, recruitment, and placement of 1965's student ambassadors. We operated out of the National Council Building at 475 Riverside Drive, lent an office by the Presbyterians and guided by one of their black staff. SIM—the summer's experience and then staffing—helped orient me toward recognizing race relations as something of a calling, as I'll indicate further below.

Why Another Review of Religion and Race?
And from Richey?

Why do I write on race and racism? As a white North Carolinian I had virtually no relation with black kids in everyday play or regular schooling. Durham High School, from which I graduated in 1959, was completely white, except for the janitors and maids. So all my schooling had been. The next year (1959–1960), my dorm counselor and hallway companion at Wesleyan University and classmates were my first friendships across racial lines. Once through schooling and successively at Drew, Duke, and Emory, I would find black faculty to be among my closest colleagues.

Breaking segregation's tyranny, however, had been a family commitment, apparently, since my father's and mother's college and his seminary days. As an infant, I was taken from Cullowhee where Dad pastored to Nashville. There for a long weekend, white and black clergy and students labored together on painting the basement of a black church. Too young then to actually later recall the event, I was told about it years later.

My mother and father made a point of treating black folk as colleagues, co-workers, family members. My mother made a point of doing such with women who worked in our home and in the nursery schools she headed:

---

5   As this postscript addresses Richey and race, and the book addresses Methodism and race, I should acknowledge that I struggled as well with gender and homosexuality. I still recall an encounter, not in 1964 but a year or so after, with two of my closest Union Seminary friends. Visiting them as newlyweds in their apartment, I made some comment about "her" that—either with words or hurt facial expressions—they denounced as sexist. Later, while teaching at Drew (1969–1986) I may have been the last faculty member to recognize my three closest colleagues to be gay. Two of them had offices next to mine on either side. My wife and I were frequently in the home of one of them, and they (the two guys) in ours. With the third colleague, I co-authored and co-edited books. He and the second made a point, when I returned to Drew in the late 1990s, of obliging me to indicate verbally that I knew them to be gay.

Duke University Preschool (for six years) and Duke Memorial Church's (a similar period). Mom exercised an even more public and visible role in race relations as the Child Development Coordinator for Durham's daycare funding, oversight, training, and resourcing operation. For instance, Mom offered workshops to train workers, both the professional (directors and teachers) and non-professional (Youth Corps enrollees and other volunteers).

During my schooling in Durham in the 1950s, our family occasionally absented ourselves from our segregated downtown church to attend a start-up, house-based, interracial congregation frequented by Floyd McKissack and family. After joining the Duke Divinity faculty, my Dad occasionally preached at black churches and took his family with him. I recall several such trips. On one, I drove as he went back over notes for the sermon.

The Richeys stood for improvement of relations between the races and in all contexts. The church especially ought, my family believed and said, to live its creed and be welcoming of all. My Dad, I remember, spoke vigorously in the late 1950s for openness by/at our Trinity Church on seating those who sought to worship with us. One Saturday, my brother and I hid in the church and then lodged little slips in every hymnal at the page indicated for the first hymn. The slip invited the congregation to vote for or against racial segregation. Regrettably, an usher discovered that slap in the congregation's racial insensitivity and pulled the slips.

In various ways then, our family stood for improved race relations. When traveling, we would avoid or back out of a restaurant that displayed/advertised its segregation. I found a letter to the Durham newspaper by my Dad when I unearthed my copy of *Race and the Renewal of the Church*. Doubtless published in 1964; it begins:

> To the Editor:
>
> Have we recognized the honor done to us by the Negro and white student demonstrating for justice through the "sit-ins" and picketing.
>
> They have honored our community with their expectation that our principles might prevail over our prejudice and passion, our consciences over our color-consciousness, our intelligence over ignorance.

And concludes:

> Some of these students are now on trial; but the truth is, while they have honored us they have also put us on trial. Our courts,

our laws, our whole consenting, supporting community are on trial
before God and the World. How will our 'white justice' look to them.

McMurry S. Richey[6]

Nevertheless, living in the South, racism shaped our lives, despite the
family's clear and ongoing commitment to ending segregation. We lived
in a white world, had white friends, attended white schools, saw buses
with black kids headed to their schools, belonged to segregated churches
(including those that my Dad pastored in western North Carolina), and, in
the early 1950s, joined Trinity in Durham. Still our home-church and the
mother-church for Durham Methodists, its sanctuary hosted funerals for
our parents, our marriage, baptisms and marriages of our children, and
baptisms of grandchildren, Trinity charted the path from segregation to
welcome quite slowly.[7]

Journeying Out of a Racist World

In other Durham buildings, on its buses, indeed throughout its life, the
city structured life racially and did so despite being the Southern city
proportionally the most blessed with black leadership and with black
and black-led institutions serving the segregated South (bank, insurance

---

6   Three other and intervening paragraphs read as follows:
        "They have honored us with their trust that we shall voluntarily act for justice
     and right when present injustice is dramatically thrust on our attention, and that
     a responsible majority will restrain a wild minority of the violent and unprincipled.
        "They have honored our democratic heritage and our Judaic-Christian profes-
     sion with the hope that we shall be faithful, and that divine wisdom, power, and love
     will triumph over our resistance to evil and change us toward the community we are
     meant to be.
        "How shall we respond to such expectations, such trust and hope? In fury and
     resentment which betray our guilt, our selfish preference for evil and injustice? In uneasy
     but continued resistance to these challenges to our irresponsibility, apathy, and uncon-
     cern? Or in awakening concern, honest conviction, and wise, constructive action?"
7   Trinity's present policy, proclaimed in bulletins and online:
        "We believe that all persons are made in the image of God and that all persons
     are of sacred worth. We believe that God is diversity, and that by the power of the
     Holy Spirit through Jesus Christ, God calls us to love one another. We believe in liv-
     ing out that love through welcoming all persons into the fellowship of Christ's body
     here at Trinity.
        "We have differences in socioeconomic status, skin color, gender, age, sexual ori-
     entation, ethnicity, physical health, mental health, gifts and abilities, education, and
     in many other ways. We know that all of these differences bring richness to the Body
     of Christ. We give thanks for this richness, and we choose love and welcome for all."

company, college, hospital, array of business, churches, funeral homes, its own main street, and middle-class neighborhoods). Just such E. Franklin Frazier analyzed in his path-setting *Black Bourgeoisie*.[8] Of that I was unaware and discovered it only during seminary and graduate school and after leaving the South. As a youth, I lived in and therefore belonged in the racist world. My brothers and I went to movies that were segregated, with blacks in the balcony. And we lived in an apartment complex that was, as I recall, all white, and later in a new home in Duke Forest initially as segregated as the university. Racist epithets rang regularly to convey everyday disagreement and discord—in schoolyard and on the street.

A racist worldview came with growing up in the South. It was in the air, in the water, on the street, in the neighborhood, in the business world, *and* in libraries and children's books. I recall vividly, my mother— who worked hard to make black women who worked for us part of the family—reading to my brothers and me *Little Black Sambo*. Other children's books honored racism with pictures if not with text.

My own serious journey out of my whites-only world came gradually at Wesleyan (1959–1963). There, a black junior or senior served as counselor of the dozen or so freshmen on our dorm floor. My roommate for freshman and sophomore years had been raised in a similar sequestered environment, but as a Brooklyn Jew. I still vividly recall going to his Flatbush home over Thanksgiving and experiencing firsthand, if but briefly, a home where the grandfather observed strict Sabbath protocols (he turned on no switches at night). Playing intercollegiate basketball for four years and lacrosse for three (which I learned there), I experienced some, but surprisingly little, exposure to black athletes.

During the early 1960s, Wesleyan faculty (all white as I recall) became vocal about and committed to civil rights. Some went on the early Freedom Rides. The nation's struggles over racism became a Wesleyan project. Martin Luther King Jr. and Malcolm X both spoke in our chapel. The black pastor who had created Operation Crossroads Africa, James Robinson, came, spoke in chapel, and touted the importance of participating. I chose to do so and went with the interracial team for the summer of 1961 to the new nation of Ghana. Teamed with a like number of Ghanaian students, we worked together in adding a building to a small school. Our group also traveled north in Ghana. The little bus came to a stop behind a long line of trucks and cars, all waiting to travel across

---

8   E. Franklin Frazier, *Black Bourgeoisie* (Glencoe, Ill.: Free Press, 1957).

a river in a current-driven ferry. The northern Ghanaian Muslim peoples and quaint palm-covered homes exposed us to ways of life and religious cultures about which we had but glimmering knowledge. Similar discoveries occurred as we traveled through Togo and Dahomey (now Benin) to Nigeria. The experiences exposed me to the incredible range of African life. The summer jaunt manifested yet another way racism had shaped my life; one of the other students on our team, a black woman, I came to know only then and there, although we had both grown up in Durham and were being schooled in the North!

Back at Wesleyan, I wrote my senior honors thesis on West African tribalism, the Gold Coast-to-Ghana trajectory, new democratic leadership (Kwame Nkrumah) and the emergence of the nation states.[9] Other summer experiences (1962 and 1963) put me back home and in Duke University employment. One year I worked in the carpentry shop, the other in a back-office university secretarial operation. In the two, very different settings, I experienced firsthand and daily Duke's then segregationist employment patterns, overheard racist comments and jokes, and witnessed demeaning interactions between whites and blacks.

On graduating, I chose among three non-southern, non-segregationist options that had developed. My acceptance to the Peace Corps offered two possible assignments, either to the Middle East to work with Palestinian refugees from Israel or to Africa again but to Gambia. UCLA had admitted me to an M.A. and toward a Ph.D. program in African studies. Both options built on formative Wesleyan experiences. Yet Union Theological Seminary beckoned with exposure to a New York civilization I had experienced just passing through. That I chose.

---

9   "The Evolution of One-Party Rule in Ghana," a thesis submitted to the Faculty of Wesleyan University in partial fulfillment of the requirements for the Degree of Bachelor of Arts with Distinction in History. 216 pp. Among my observations in the introduction: the suggestion that Kwame Nkrumah is "the symbol of Ghana of the amalgamation taking place."

"If what is occurring here is the gradual destruction of African culture, a simple cultural clash in which Western values slowly come to have predominance over indigenous ones, perhaps the solution would be easy. However, that is not just what is happening; the blend is producing something *sui generis* and as yet indeterminate and indeterminable. For the sociologist and anthropologist, culture evolution is a productive enterprise, but can the historian also glean meaningful insights from study of it? What sense does it make to study Africa with the traditional Western rubrics which now constitute history?" (8–9).

Union Theological Seminary and the Student Interracial Ministry

My fourth-floor Hastings room looked out over 122nd Street. Our subway stop, 125th Street, took us onto main street Harlem. Harlem pizza and Chinese restaurants served Union, Teachers' College, Columbia, and Barnard residents. My first-year field education assignment? East Harlem Protestant Parish! Created and headed by George William "Bill" Webber, it included several congregations, was multiracially staffed, and deliberately modeled America's church-to-be. The congregation to which I was assigned was pastored by Letty Russell, who would later move to a faculty post at Yale Divinity School, where she championed various liberation causes. Visitors to the East Harlem church, typically white pastor groups, joined the mainly black congregation in singing "We Shall Overcome."

My duties, teaching black kids in Sunday school, visiting their families' apartments, and overseeing occasional field trips, exposed me to small glimpses of everyday black life. A field trip to the Bronx Zoo stands out in my memory. Why? Several kids would hop out of our subway car and into the next just to make me think they had fled. Week-by-week black America presented itself in the news but also in my travels to East Harlem. Sometimes, several Union seminarians bused to and from East Harlem. But often I (alone) walked crosstown, down Morningside Heights, through sometimes garbage-cluttered, sometimes tree-lined Harlem neighborhoods and into the open-gated, welcoming, and singing church. Early arrival permitted me and other field-work seminarians to join the weekly preliminary and preparatory staff worship.

Sunday evenings and for the rest of the week *Race and the Renewal of the Church* defined and filled Union Seminary life. Placards, daily sermons, campaigns, and Civil Rights events brought the several race issues to the fore. Segregation, freedom rides, South African atrocities, New York City racial patterns, and corporate/banking collusion in racist systems/ practices (South African especially) set Union agendas. With other Union students, I journeyed in pilgrimage to Washington's Lincoln Memorial for a sit-in against segregation. To protest corporate banking soiled by its South African ties, we opened accounts in a Harlem-based bank and moved a few coins there. To rid their stock holdings of companies doing substantial South African business, a Union classmate launched an investment advisory service that would show concerned folk alternate options.

After such a first year in seminary (1963–1964), going south with the Student Interracial Ministry seemed just the right way of taking Union's witness toward home. The KKK events, described above, might attest Richey's evolution out of his white-only world. However, day-to-day that summer, I learned how deeply racist patterns exist within the heart and instinctive behavior. I still recall eating watermelon on the church steps when Costen walked up. I employed the little word *my* to refer to something in that ministry or at that building. I do not remember to what the *my* applied, but I do remember that Costen joked about the adjective. His joking made me realize that claiming ownership, even in such a minor way, reflected a worldview, assumptions, notions about us-and-them. The joke made me aware—as I remain to this day—of how impulsively many of us live in an *us-them, me-you* world.

Another personal experience of racism working in an us-them world occurred earlier in June 1964. After the North Carolina Conference session in Burlington and my ordination as a deacon, I was to be picked up there by Costen. As he arrived, the Rev. William Quick, pastor of our Durham church and a close friend of the family, encountered us. Quick took a black person standing outside that white church obviously to be the custodian. He rather summarily directed Rev. Costen to go back into the church and turn out the lights. I introduced the two pastors and indicated to Quick that I was serving in Costen's church and under his direction. The memory of that ten-minute encounter is still haunting.

American racist patterns—overall and widely shared, if not always personal—surfaced in various ways in my three Union years. For two years, I participated in Columbia's International Fellows Program. Weekly seminars brought world-class scholars addressing current issues (South Africa) and national events (civil rights). A trip to Washington exposed us to the FBI, CIA, and VP Hubert Humphrey. The variety of social-political exposures doubtless induced me to select as a senior thesis project, engagement with the huge array of articles and books by the then recently retired faculty member, Reinhold Niebuhr.

Off-campus exposure continued after my first year at Union. The summer after my SIM experience (1965) I gained a job with a North Carolina venture committed to transforming the state in various progressive ways: the "North Carolina Fund." In this "statewide antipoverty program,"[10] my assignment was to pick up and drive three or four unem-

---

10   William S. Powell, ed., *Encyclopedia of North Carolina* (Chapel Hill: University of North Carolina Press, 2006), 815. Robert R. Korstad and James L. Leloudis, *To Right These Wrongs: The North Carolina Fund and the Battle to End Poverty and Inequality in 1962 America* (Chapel Hill: University of North Carolina Press, 2010). Korstad and Leloudis,

ployed black men from eastern North Carolina to job interviews in Piedmont towns within southern Virginia. Riding together for a number of hours, I heard their horrific stories of ill treatment by whites. I also learned afresh that textile and furniture factories, like much of Southern business, hired different races for different job sets or types: Loading and unloading trucks—for blacks. Shelving and other more responsible tasks—whites. Such sector racism—undertaken especially after more open hiring had been mandated—I had whispered to me by a high-school acquaintance overseeing staffing in a Raleigh company.

Another personal experience of prevalent racial patterns occurred later that summer when I happily and luckily was wed to Merle Bradley Umstead. The ceremonies at our church and everything associated with the marriage—aside from food preparation and delivery—followed prevalent and mandatory societal guidelines and was, of course, whites only. But to show how deeply such patterns were etched in my own psyche, it never occurred to me then that anything was amiss.

Race and the Renewal of the Church: Onto a Scholarly Plane

The next year at Union, my last, Robert Handy offered to a handful of us a reading course on Southern religion.[11] To this day, I urge Southern students to read books experienced in that seminar. W. J. Cash apparently committed suicide after publishing *The Mind of the South*.[12] Lillian Smith's *Killers of the Dream* and other books on Southern racism earned accolades and denunciation.[13] Thereafter, in graduate study in church history at Princeton University, in teaching at Drew, Duke, and Emory, and in various scholarly projects and events, I would be pulled again and again into reconsidering American Protestantism and race.

The doctoral program at Princeton put students through an array of disciplines. In addition to several broad-gauged church history courses were two on New Testament and two on Buddhism. My dissertation took

---

"Citizen Soldiers: The North Carolina Volunteers and the War on Poverty," *Law and Contemporary Problems*, 62, No. 4 (Autumn 1999): 177–97.

11   Robert Handy would later write *A History of Union Theological Seminary in New York* (New York: Columbia University Press, 1987). In passing he covers both East Harlem Protestant Parish and SIM.

12   W. J. Cash, *The Mind of the South* (Garden City: Doubleday & Company, 1954; initially published in 1941).

13   Lillian Smith, *Killers of the Dream*, revised and enlarged (Garden City: Doubleday & Company, 1963; initially published 1949).

me into eighteenth-century English religious squabbles among Protestant Dissenters that led to schisms and the emergence of Unitarianism.
The Princeton Ph.D. program then provided broad perspectives on religious commitments, conflicts, and divisions, aiming to prepare gradu-
ates to teach in several fields. The major exception to those wide-angled
and long-term exposures came my first semester in a seminar on early
nineteenth-century American history offered by Donald Mathews. His
Slavery and Methodism had just appeared.[14] That course and that book
oriented me to our denomination's long, long conflicts over race. So did
his several subsequent treatises on Southern religion and a presentation
for a major consultation, which I had a hand in putting together.

A comparable stimulus came from our family's next-door neighbor,
my dad's dissertation guide as also that for Mathews, and my instructor
as he weeded his yard, H. Shelton Smith. Several of his books had already
been important to me but his *In His Image, But... Racism in Southern Religion, 1780–1910*[15] would be the Old Testament as *Slavery and Methodism*
the New. These resources proved vital after I landed on the Theological
School faculty at Drew, launched American religion seminars, and took
advantage of the library's strong Methodist holdings. There I began my
own research and writing on our denomination's racial woes. Slavery and
segregation figured prominently in the survey courses I taught. And I
came to offer the school's first course specifically on black religion.

Reinforcing scholarly and drawing instructional attention to the
longer racial (also gender and, eventually, sexual orientation) strains in
Methodist life were major curricular, faculty, and program struggles then
ongoing at Drew. Oversight and small-group involvement were needed
for students whose field education and internship appointments were
in Harlem. The lot fell to me. For several years, I would drive over for the
regular, perhaps bi-weekly, seminar sessions, joining a black pastor who
would later be elected bishop (Herbert Skeete).

When the UMC launched and supported ethnic-studies centers at
several seminaries, Drew landed one that would be Multi-Ethnic (and
so titled) and serve Boston and Wesley as well. Initially led by Bobby
McClain, I served in some advisory or trustee capacity. About the same
time, I moved from a faculty role and office to become assistant to Drew's

---

14 Donald G. Mathews, *Slavery and Methodism: A Chapter in American Morality, 1780–1845*
    (Princeton: Princeton University Press, 1965).
15 H. Shelton Smith, *In His Image, But... Racism in Southern Religion, 1780–1910* (Durham:
    Duke University Press, 1972).

president, Paul Hardin. The move was, in part, to yield a faculty spot and permit a black appointment. Hardin, another Southerner and son of a bishop, added to my responsibilities and decided that I should serve as the university's Affirmative Action officer. That I did for four years and found myself thrust into a leadership post, as secretary of the New Jersey association dedicated to the cause. Serving Drew's Affirmative Action efforts came naturally, as almost instinctively, I appointed myself a mentor to the Theological School's newly appointed and young black faculty colleagues. One of them, now some years at Drew, recalled the supportive relationship when I was recently back there for research (summer 2019).

After Drew, I went to Duke and then to Candler in administrative roles. As both associate dean and dean I found the full array of racial, gender, sexual orientation, and nationality issues on my plate. These, large and small, do not lend themselves to quick description. An exception would be my relation with black faculty colleagues, most of whom struggled to balance their heavy, ongoing endeavors/duties/relationships in school, with administrators, with students, for colleagues, at church, with family, in research, and to academic societies. In various ways, they would express their appreciation for my efforts to navigate the seminary's policy and promotion and tenure labyrinths.

Conclusion

Life-long exposure to intimate, direct, daily, face-to-face *and* to huge, systemic, ongoing, and national dimensions of race relations has informed my life, as I've tried to indicate here. Yet in other ways, life was normal and typical at home, in school, throughout a teaching career, and in scholarship. In those more ordinary settings, observers and even friends might remain quite unaware of the influence of race on my life. This current exploration, I hope, suggests how sometimes such lack of awareness typified the everyday life and Methodist affairs of white Americans, male and female, at least in Kentucky and Ohio Methodism. At other points, slaveholders and Northern whites *and* their churches treated African Americans in beastly ways. Southerners made efforts to be pastoral across carefully delineated racial lines; Northerners, by contrast, showed indifference to their black members. Race and the renewal of the church was then, and often remains, a judgment on Methodism.

APPENDIX

Contents

The First *Discipline* on Race Relations

Minutes of Several Conversations Between the Rev. Thomas Coke, LL. D., the Rev. Francis Asbury and others, at a Conference, Begun in Baltimore, in the State of Maryland, on Monday, the 27th of December, in the Year 1784 (Philadelphia: Charles Cist, 1785)[1]

Q. 42. What Methods can we take to extirpate Slavery?

A. We are deeply conscious of the Impropriety of making new Terms of Communion for a religious Society already established, excepting on the most pressing Occasion: and such we esteem the Practice of holding our Fellow-Creatures in Slavery. We view it as contrary to the Golden Law of God on which hang all Law and the Prophets, and the unalienable Rights of Mankind, as well as every Principle of the Revolution, to hold in

---

1   Russell E. Richey, Kenneth E. Rowe, and Jean Miller Schmidt, *The Methodist Experience in America: A Sourcebook* (Nashville: Abingdon Press, 2000), 84–85.

the deepest Debasement, in a more abject Slavery than is perhaps to be found in any Part of the World except America, so many Souls that are all capable of the Image of God.

We therefore think it our most bounden Duty, to take immediately some effectual Method to extirpate this Abomination from among us: And for that Purpose we add the following to the Rules of our Society: viz.

1. Every Member of our Society who has Slaves in his Possession, shall within twelve Months after Notice given to him by the Assistant (which Notice the Assistants are required immediately and without any Delay to five in their respective Circuits) legally execute and record an Instrument, whereby he emancipates and sets free every Slave in his Possession who is between the Ages of Forty and Forty-five immediately, or at farthest when they arrive at the Age of Forty-five:

And every Slave who is between the Ages of Twenty-five and Forty immediately, or at farthest at the Expiration of five Years from the Date of the said Instrument:

And every Slave who is between the Ages of Twenty and Twenty-five immediately, or at farthest when they arrive at the Age of Thirty:

And every Slave under the Age of Twenty, as soon as they arrive at the Age of Twenty-five at farthest.

And every Infant born in Slavery after the above-mentioned Rules are complied with, immediately on birth.

2. Every Assistant shall keep a Journal, in which he shall regularly minute down the Names and Ages of all the Slaves belonging to all the Masters in his respective Circuit, and also the Dates of every Instrument executed and recorded for the Manumission of the Slaves, with the Name of the Court, Book and Folio, in which the said Instruments respectively shall have been recorded: Which Journal shall be handed down in each Circuit to the succeeding Assistants.

3. In Consideration that these Rules form a new Term of Communion, every Person concerned, who will not comply with them, shall have Liberty quietly to withdraw himself from our Society within the twelve Months succeeding the Notice given as aforesaid: Otherwise the Assistant shall exclude him in the Society.

4. No Person so *voluntarily withdrawn*, or so *excluded*, shall ever partake of the Supper of the Lord with the Methodists, till he complies with the above Requisitions.

5. No Person holding Slaves shall, in future, be admitted into Society or to the Lord's Supper, till he previously complies with these Rules concerning Slavery.

N. B. These Rules are to affect the Members of our Society no further than as they are consistent with the Laws of the States in which they reside.

And respecting our Brethren in *Virginia* that are concerned, and after due Consideration of their peculiar Circumstances, we allow them *two Years* from the Notice given, to consider the Expedience of Compliance or Non-Compliance with these Rules.

Q. 43. What shall be done with those who buy or sell Slaves, or give them away?

A. They are immediately to be expelled: unless they buy them on purpose to free them.

Poetry on Race—*The Ladies' Repository*—1858[2]

THE FUGITIVE'S HOME.

BY MRS. H. C. GARDNER.

HALF way up the mountain,
Hidden from the sight
By the hazel coppice
That adorns the hight,
Stands a rude log-cabin
In a covert warm,
Sheltered by the cliff-side
From the wind and storm.

Through the vernal net-work
Of the forest-trees,
Through the shrubs and brambles
Undergrowing these,
Comes a tinkling murmur
On the summer gale—
'Tis the Susquehanna
Sporting in the vale.

---

2   *The Ladies' Repository: A Monthly Journal,* Rev D. W. Clark, D. D., ed., v. 18 (Cincinnati: J.F. Wright and L. Swormstedt,1858), 528, 651. HathiTrust Digital Library, Permanent URL: https://hdl.handle.net/2027/nyp.33433104825652.

All the great world's sorrow
In the distance dies—
By that simple cabin
All its gossip flies;
None of all its changes
Or its noise comes nigh,
Save the fleet steam-carriage
Swiftly shooting by.

In the shaded doorway,
At the eventide,
Sits a manly negro—
Nestling to his side
Comes his little daughter,
And with childish care
Screens him from the current
Of the dewy air.

Where the southern rice-fields
Ripen in the sun,
Sleeps his wife—her mother,
Life's sad labor done.
Like a beast she perished,
Scourged and bruised, she died,
Trusting in the merits
Of the Crucified.

Then a sudden vigor
Seemed to nerve his frame;
Clasping to his bosom
Her who bore the name
Of his wife—now sainted—
Fast and far he fled,
Haunted by the mem'ry
Of the gentle dead.

Half way up the mountain
Has he reared his home,
Hiding, lest the slave fiend
To its shelter come.
Night and morn he bendeth

Low the suppliant knee,
Praying God, our Father,
To preserve him free.

THE DYING SLAVE-BOY TO HIS MOTHER

BY LINA LINWOOD

MOTHER, I am cold and weary;
Draw my head upon your breast;
All the darkened earth seems brighter,
Looked at from that place of rest;
Hold me where I'll feel the throbbing
Of the heart that beats for me;
Let me feel your hand upon my
Forehead pressed so tenderly;

For I'm dying—dying, mother—
Fold me closer to your breast,
And I'd die as oft I've slumbered,
With your arms around me pressed.
Let your face, that is the only
Thing of earth that's dear to me,
As my eyes shall close forever,
Be the last of earth they see.

Death is swiftly coming, mother,
And his breath is very chill,
But my panting heart is longing
For the welcome word,
"Be still!" For life is a heavy burden—
'T is a weary thing to bear,
And my heart is almost broken,
'Neath its weight of grief and care.

There is but one pang in dying—
It is that of leaving thee;
For I'm all of earth thou lovest—
Thou art all that's dear to me.
This is why my tears are falling—
Why I fain would linger here,

If it were our Father's pleasure,
Still thy dreary path to cheer.

Would that thou like me wert going!
Would that I could live for thee
Tho' a life of added darkness
Mine, bereft of thee, would be.
But I'd gladly bear the darkness,
Bear the stripes, the scorn, and pain;
Bear anew the life I'm living,
Rest and heaven for thee to gain.

Thou wilt weep when I am sleeping
Deep within the darksome grave,
But thou'st often wept, my mother,
That thy child was born a slave.
And when sorest is thy mourning,
Thou'st rejoice that I am free—
That the boon that man denieth,
God hath granted unto me.

Here we have no home, my mother,
But are captives and oppressed:
Living, but to labor—looking
Only to the grave for rest—
Sighing—longing—ever hoping
For the home beyond the grave,
For the land above whose green sward
Never trod the foot of slave!

But 't will soon be over, mother,
All these hopes and all these fears,
All this labor, spirit longing,
And these heart-corroding tears;
For the death will break these fetters
That consigns us to the tomb,
And the life be full of blessing
That shall call us from its gloom.

Then farewell—farewell, my mother,
It is only for a time!
We shall meet when o'er death's stillness

Heaven's morning bells shall chime,
In that land of chainless freedom,
Of the sinless and the blest—
Where the "wicked cease from troubling,
And the weary are at rest!"

William Sasnett of MECS on Missions, 1855

In his 1855 *Progress: Considered with Particular Reference to the Methodist Episcopal Church, South*,[3] The Rev. William J. Sasnett of Emory College outlined and recommended in some detail (320 pages) various forms of outreach for the MECS. His work, published by the Southern church's Vatican (Southern Methodist Publishing House), was edited by and carried with it the "papal" endorsement of T. O. Summers, an important indicator. Summers had carried articles by Sasnett in the *Quarterly Review of the Methodist Episcopal Church, South*.

Born in England, Summers had begun his American ministerial career in the MEC, accepted a missionary appointment in 1840 to Texas, and thereafter aligned with the MECS when the church divided. He served as secretary for the general organizing conference of 1845 at Louisville, KY, chaired the committee compiling a new hymnal, and joined the editorial staff of the *Southern Christian Advocate*. In 1846, Summers took on editing of the Southern church's Sunday-school publications, a role he exercised for the next twenty-four years. In 1850, he began a thirty-two-year role as secretary of general conferences for the MECS and as book editor of the church, turning out something like a hundred titles a year. Editor of the *Quarterly Review of the Methodist Episcopal Church, South*, 1858–1881, and of the *Christian Advocate Nashville*, 1868–1878, Summers, in endorsing and publishing Sasnett, gave the book his papal endorsement.[4]

3   William J. Sasnett, *Progress: Considered with Particular Reference to the Methodist Episcopal Church, South*, edited by T. O. Summers (Nashville: E. Stevenson & F. A. Owen, agents, Southern Methodist Publishing House, 1855), HathiTrust Digital Library: https://hdl.handle.net/2027/nyp.33433070782531.

4   Oscar P. Fitzgerald, *Dr. Summers, a Life-Study* (Nashville: Southern Methodist Publishing House, 1884); E. Brooks Holifield, *The Gentlemen Theologians* (Durham: Duke University Press, 1978) and *God's Ambassadors: A History of the Clergy in America* (Grand Rapids: William B. Eerdmans Publishing Co., 2007): James P. Pilkington, *The Methodist Publishing House, a History*, vol. 1 (Nashville: Abingdon, 1968); and James E. Kirby, Russell E. Richey, and Kenneth E. Rowe, *The Methodists*, Denominations in America (Westport & London: Greenwood Press, 1996). Among other "papal" pronouncements by

Sasnett sought to prescribe *outreach* for the Southern church in a series of descriptive and prescriptive chapters:

CONTENTS
I. More Complete Development of Church Functions Necessary
II. The Educational Function
III. The Literature Function
IV. The Eleemosynary Function
V. The Missionary Function
VI. The Ministerial Function
VII. The Spiritual Function
VIII. Additional Considerations in Favor of this Ampler and More Active Church System

In each, he would set the larger parameters of that portion of the church's calling, note (critically) how the Christian world had dealt with that function previously, describe the Southern church's practices, detail the problems exhaustively, and prescribe the remedies needed. All of the chapters pertain to *outreach,* but the fifth, "The Missionary Function," suffices to illustrate his judgments. Further and interestingly, only there did Sasnett deal with slavery and slaves. Excerpt after excerpt should illustrate:

> Whatever constitutes the subjective character of Christianity— faith, courage, love, hope, humility, patience, charity—these great elements of Christian experience all are kept in highest tension in the faithful discharge of missionary obligation. Indeed, missionary employment is but Christianity itself, in the full exercise of its own peculiar principles. The great field of missions, therefore, is the Christian's destined sphere for the maturity of all those qualities which make up the amplitude and symmetry of Christian character. In his own private sphere he may be restricted and confined, but the partial, unequal character, which he might accordingly assume, is rectified and perfected in this broader field of action. Indeed, so related are all the graces of the Christian to those exercises involved in doing good, in disseminating Christianity, that it may be well doubted whether they ever exist in a healthy, perfect condition, independently of them. . . .

Summers were works later than this book by Sasnett, namely *Biographical Sketches of Eminent Itinerant Ministers* (1858); *Catechisms of the Methodist Episcopal Church, South* (1860); and the two-volume *Systematic Theology, a Complete Body of Wesleyan Arminian Divinity* (1888).

In the cause of missions, all the resources of the Christian may find employment. Wealth, talents, position, personal exertion, however great or however small, each and all, may be usefully appropriated in this great field. All may be useful and all may employ all they have in the cause of God. However much, therefore, Christians may be restricted in all other departments in this great field, ample room is afforded for the practical manifestation of the highest zeal, and every evidence of devotion, to God. In every aspect in which it may be considered, the missionary field sustains a most important relation to the development and perfection of all those qualities which give symmetry and elevation to Christian character, and which secure the fullest preparation for heaven....

Though the achievements of missionary enterprise have been sufficient to excite our gratitude, and to evince in clearest light its obligations, yet to all who understand the potency of the gospel, as an aggressive agency, and the divine sanction of all legitimate means to advance it, the comparative inefficiency of missionary operations, both past and present, must be apparent. This fact, so lamentable and so pressing in its claims upon our attention, is attributable to several causes. 1. Missionary operations thus far have been a simple appendage—a mere incidental arrangement, as respects the whole Church, rather than the last, highest expression of all her principles in full proportion and activity....

2. Missionary enterprise has been greatly defeated by an unwise selection of some of the principal fields of its operation. The heathen and those of them most degraded, as being most helpless, have enjoyed the largest share of attention, while the more enlightened, though equally destitute, have been comparatively neglected. The darkest portions of Asia, of Africa, and America, have been the spots on which missionary labor has been, for the most part, expended, while the destitute portions of Europe, and many of the more civilized sections in America, except in a few isolated instances, have received but little attention....

3. The want of the requisite strength, at the various points at which missionary effort has been made, has contributed to limit the success of missions. The history of missionary operations, especially of those in foreign lands, shows the injurious effect upon their efficiency of a weakness of force—a weakness mainly consequent upon a multiplication of the fields of labor....

4. The concentration of the efforts of missionaries upon the adult classes, instead of a system of effort which looks to the ultimate evangelization of the people by the proper religious education and training of the young, has been another cause of the comparative failure of missions. Among a people so low as are the heathen, and as are even a large portion of our negroes, the adult classes are unsusceptible, in any permanent degree, of the transforming influences of the gospel; and if missionary effort is restricted to them, it must be a long time before they can assume the position of an evangelical people, if indeed they ever can. Their intellects are too contracted, and their existing ideas are too gross, to receive anything like, generally in any permanently impressible degree, the ideas of the gospel; and even if they could, the baser passions, by nature, have such ascendency, and are so much confirmed by cultivation and habit, as to overbear any degree of the feeble light which they are capable of receiving. Among them, there is too much ignorance to be overcome—too much error to be eliminated—too much of. natural opposition to be overborne—for the slight amount of truth which they are capable of receiving, to subject them to Christian dominion, and to mould them into the pure forms of a holy, life-giving Christianity. Restricted then as missionary effort has been mainly to them, it is not to be expected that much could be accomplished; and it is no reflection upon the capacity of missionary enterprise, that visible success has thus far been comparatively limited. . . .

5. Impatience—too great haste to realize results—has been an unvarying characteristic of missionary operations. So accustomed is the age to a system of pressure for compassing the fruits of enterprise—to the most rapid realization of schemes—to a constant succession of the most surprising changes, carrying forward individuals and communities with exciting, bewildering speed—that it is disqualified for any scheme that does not promise immediate reward. In all its operations, it is actuated by this same spirit. But the conversion of the world is a scheme of vast extent, and must require an indefinite time for its fulfillment. . . .

The missionary enterprise of the Methodist Episcopal Church, South, has, it is true, already directed itself into all those various fields which, if fully occupied, would cover the whole ground now claiming her attention. These are, first, the destitute sections embraced within the limits of our existing ecclesiastical organization; secondly, the foreign population in our midst; thirdly, the black population of the South; and fourthly, foreign lands. But we maintain that the proper development of the missionary function, requires that each of those fields be more fully and thoroughly occupied.[5]

To each of these, Sasnett devoted considerable attention, notably six pages of text. The following excerpts—each just a portion of a page with 330–345 words—serve well to indicate what outreach and mission to slaves actually meant.

> Thirdly: The slave population of the South. Slavery, both abstractly and concretely, is defensible on the ground of both philosophy and Scripture. But the slave has all the relations to God which his master sustains, and the slave state cannot be lawfully used, to shut out whatever is necessary to the fulfillment of the conditions which grow out of these relations. This would be to put that power between God and his creatures to the injury of the immortal interests of those creatures, and the defeat of his purposes in respect of them. Whatever other powers and relations the institution of slavery may of right subject to human control, that control has no right to touch those which connect the soul immediately with God and eternity. The institution of slavery, therefore, must not be allowed to work a forfeiture of religious privileges and opportunities. These constitute a sphere which it must not, because it cannot lawfully, restrain or appropriate. . . .
>
> Slavery is a patriarchal system, by which the master assumes the care of his slaves, as the parent does that of his children; and just as children must have, by the parents' act, the appliances of the gospel, so must slaves have provided for them all requisite facilities for their own personal salvation. They are in our hands, dependent as well for their eternal hopes as for their physical comfort upon us. It is with us to determine whether they shall live in heathenish degradation and perish in their sins, or whether, with such religious privileges as we enjoy, they shall rise from their moral debasement and live forever. . . .
>
> It was, doubtless, a prominent design of Providence, in recognizing the institution of slavery, that, by the relation in which it

---

5   Sasnett, *Progress*, 179–80, 181, 185–86, 188, 194, 195–96, 197–98.

placed the enlightened to this inferior race, it would, at the same time that it devolved upon the former the duty, would secure to them the required opportunities of affording to the latter those advantages, which alone could be successful in their moral elevation and final salvation. So inferior were this race naturally, in both intellectual and moral endowment, that it is probable that nothing short of constant contact with the ameliorating influences which this institution opens the way for, could be effectual for the realization in them of the contemplated objects of the gospel. . . . The very nature of the institution of slavery, therefore, and the relation which it sustains to God's own purposes, impose upon us, as a Church, the unavoidable duty to provide for the black population of the South the religious advantages they may need. These people have immortal souls, and they can be evangelized, only as the light of the gospel is diffused among them. . . .

The Methodist Episcopal Church, South, sustains a peculiar relation to this population. The very reason of her distinctive organization as a Church, grew out of her unwillingness to relinquish her privilege to serve the slaves of the South; and, coming into a separate existence upon this basis, she is committed before men and God to this praiseworthy work. The slave population, cut off from all relationship to all other churches, is dependent for the light that is to bless them upon those alone of the South; and to the Methodist Episcopal Church, South, more than all others, perhaps, this sacred trust is committed. Let us appreciate this high calling, and prove ourselves equal to the responsibility.[6]

Sasnett and the MECS grasped and were grasped by **outreach** and the missionary mandate. They understood it to claim their attention, effort, financial outlay, and "manpower" for the several worlds to be engaged: "first, the destitute sections embraced within the limits of our existing ecclesiastical organization; secondly, the foreign population in our midst; . . . and fourthly, foreign lands." Doubtless most of southern Methodism, including many in Kentucky, would have seen the world much as did Sasnett from Georgia (and my former employer, Emory). Outreach to "the black population of the South" required adherence to the "powers and relations the institution of slavery" that "of right" subjected slaves to human control. Beyond that control was the realms of the spirit "which connect the soul immediately with God and eternity. The institution of slavery, therefore, must not be allowed to work a forfeiture of religious privileges and opportunities." The whip and slave balcony defined **outreach**.

Majority and Minority Reports on Slavery: 1860 General Conference of the Methodist Episcopal Church

MAJORITY REPORT ON SLAVERY[7]

THE Committee on Slavery offer the following Report:

When He who spake as never man spake would comprehend the sum of all human duty as between man and man in one brief sentence, he embodied that sentence in the following memorable words: "All things whatsoever ye would that men should do unto you, do ye even so unto them; for this is the law and prophets." The same sublime epitome of human duty is expressed in the words, "Thou shalt love thy neighbor as thyself." These precepts form the moral mirror which God has hung up before all humanity. Into this mirror every man is bound to look and see his own conduct as others see it, and as he sees that of others. Or, to change the figure, these precepts form the moral scales in which every man is bound to weigh his own actions as he weighs the actions of other men. This Golden Law of God sheds its divine light upon all the relationships which subsist between man and his fellow; and that which we would have a right to desire from any human being with whom we have to do, if we were in his circumstances and he in ours, is the exact measure of our duty.

The enslavement from generation to generation of human beings guilty of no crime, is what no man has a right to desire for himself or his posterity, and what no man ever did or can desire. The constant liability of the forcible separation of husbands and wives, of parents and children, even in the mildest forms of slavery, is a state of things from which every enlightened mind desires to be free. The impediments which slavery interposes in the way of the observance of the conjugal and parental relations, depriving the parents from governing and educating their

---

7   *Journals of the General Conference of the Methodist Episcopal Church, v. 4, 1860* (New York: Carlton & Porter, [1855–1900]), 404–22, HathiTrust Digital Library, Rights Public Domain, Google-digitized. Permanent URL: https://hdl.handle.net/2027/wu.89077 109460.

children, and the children from honoring and obeying their parents, as God has commanded, is a state of things condemned alike by the Bible and all enlightened consciences, and from which the heart's holiest aspirations struggle to be free. The sacredness and inviolability of the marriage covenant is one of the corner-stones of all Christian civilization. Slavery, as it exists in the United States, is fundamentally at war with this most ancient and sacred institution. What should we desire, and have a right to desire, if we were in the place of the injured party? This is the measure of our duty.

A system which converts a human being into merchandise, which denies a man the rights of property, of family, of "liberty and the pursuits of happiness," and generally of the power to read the record which God has given for the regulation of all human conduct, is a state of things in which no intelligent and right-minded person ever did or can desire to be placed. In reference to all these, and to all other conditions of human wrong, the solemn mandate comes down from Heaven: "All things what-soever ye would that men should do unto you, do ye even so to them."

God has laid the foundation of religious education in the family rela-tionships. His claims upon us find their readiest response [when] the honor and obedience due to parents are properly inculcated. The obligation to love God, because he first loved us, finds its strongest response where the tenderness and affection breathed upon childhood, by its divinely constituted guardians prepare the young heart for this high duty. The strongest terms by which the indissoluble affection subsisting between God and his Church are expressed in Scripture, are taken from the paren-tal and conjugal relationship. The inimitable prayer commencing, "Our Father which art in heaven," is a further recognition of the same thing.

What then must be the religious effect of an institution which tram-ples these sacred relationships in the dust?

In short, there is not, in our judgment, one distinctive attribute of chattel slavery which is not incompatible with the Golden Rule.

The foregoing considerations, as it seems to us, are sufficient to justify the opposition which from the beginning we have manifested toward slavery; for, be it remembered, this opposition is no new thing among us, but is coeval with our very existence as a Christian organization.

The opinions of our revered founder need not be recounted here. Imbibing in larger measure than was common in his day the spirit of Him whose sympathies gush forth as an everlasting fountain toward the poor and the oppressed, Mr. Wesley uttered a testimony against slavery immortal as his own name.

His genuine sons in the Gospel have followed his example. The Conference of 1780 declared "slavery to be contrary to the laws of God, man, and nature, and hurtful to society; contrary to the dictates of conscience and pure religion, and doing that which we would not that others should do unto us."

The General Conference of 1784 declared the practice of slaveholding to be "contrary to the Golden Law of God, and contrary to the inalienable rights of mankind, as well as to every principle of the Revolution." The Conference say: "We think it our most bounden duty, therefore, to take immediately some effectual method to extirpate this abomination from among us, and for that purpose we add the follow[ing] to the rules of our society."

Then followed a plan of emancipation, specifying the age at which every person held in slavery should be free, and declaring that no person thereafter holding slaves should be admitted into the society or to the Lord's Supper till he had previously complied with these rules concerning slavery. A note followed these stringent measures, declaring that they were to affect the members no further than they were consistent with the laws of the states in which they resided; and also, in view of peculiar circumstances, giving the members in Virginia two years in which to comply with these regulations. As these measures were admitted to constitute a new term of membership, all persons were allowed to choose between voluntarily retiring and being expelled.

About six months after it was thought best to suspend, for the time, the execution of these rules, and give the members a longer time before the minute should be enforced. The suspension proved to be indefinite, but immediately following the suspension is the declaration: "We do hold in the deepest abhorrence the practice of slavery, and shall not cease to seek its destruction by all wise and prudent means." In 1789 the General Rule read: "The buying and selling the bodies and souls of men, women, or children, with an intention to enslave them." In 1792 it read: "The buying or selling of men, women, or children, with an intention to enslave them." From 1808 until now the rule has read as at present, no one knowing how the *or* came to be substituted by *and.*

For seventy-six years the question at the head of our present chapter on slavery has remained substantially what it now is: "What shall be done for the extirpation of the evil of slavery[?]" During all this period and more there has no day intervened in which our Church has not testified against slavery as a great evil, and one whose extirpation is to be sought by all lawful and Christian means. Nor has our acknowledged antislavery position been unproductive of good fruit. There is a power in the truth, when faithfully uttered, to influence the conscience of mankind. The testimony which our Church has borne has done much toward the formation of a correct public opinion. Under its influence many thousands of slaves have been set free; and many thousands who otherwise would have been slaveholders have refrained; and many thousands more who are still holding slaves are doing so with consciences ill at ease. But for this testimony a number of Western States, now free, and embracing a vast range of territory, would probably to-day be slave states.

These facts are our answer to the question: "What good has our Church action on the subject ever done. Is it a small thing that thousands of immortal beings have been delivered from bondage; that thousands more have been restrained from oppressing their fellow-men; and that regions of country by many times larger than some of the mightiest empires of the earth have been secured to freedom?

To the charge that we are violating the laws of the land, a brief answer must suffice. If we choose to keep as free as we can from the evils of slavery, how do we thus violate the laws of the land? Do the laws of the land require the members of the Methodist Episcopal Church to hold slaves? How do we then violate the law by declining to hold them? Must we practice every evil which the laws will permit, lest we be charged with violating them?

While we have no sympathy with, but on the other hand strongly condemn the mad projects of reckless and desperate men, who, in defiance of law, seek by violent means either to establish or destroy slavery, we earnestly pray that the time may soon come when, through the blessed principles of the Gospel of peace, slavery shall cease throughout the length and breadth of this fair land.

But why should we seek any change in our Discipline if it has worked so well?

We answer, 1. Much of our present Chapter on Slavery has become obsolete by the changed circumstances since its introduction, and the chapter is now in consequence no sufficient answer to the question with which it commences. Owing to the present laws of many of the slave states, the rule in the chapter can have no practical application where we have any considerable membership.

Again, the chapter, by making one rule for official and another for private members of the Church, fails, we think, to embody our real doctrine on the subject of which it treats. We do not see the propriety of having one rule for the class-leader and another for the members of his class; one rule for a trustee and another for the member sitting by his side; one rule for a steward and another for the person of whom he collects quarterage. Such discriminations, we presume, will be admitted to be without any sufficient foundation, and we believe they are practically disregarded.

2. Within a comparatively recent period differences of opinion have sprung up as to the bearing our present General Rule has on the subject of slaveholding. A few among us have contended that the rule condemns only the African slave-trade; others believe that it condemns both the foreign and domestic traffic; others, that while it condemns the traffic, it thereby legalizes the holding of slaves; others, and we think by far the larger portion, hold that while the rule in express terms condemns the traffic for a certain purpose, it also by fair implication condemns the holding for the same purpose.

To this last view we ask a somewhat more particular attention. What is the specific thing which the terms of the General Rule forbid? Not the buying or selling of a human being simply, but the buying or selling *with an intention to enslave*. The buying or selling with an intention to free is not forbidden. What, then, is the meaning of the qualifying phrase, *"with the intention to enslave them?"* This question can admit of but one answer. The person has already been reduced to slavery before he can be either bought or sold. Even in the foreign slave-trade the persons have been seized and reduced to slavery before they come into the hands of the trader; and in the domestic traffic the persons bought or sold are already in a state of slavery. What, then, we repeat, is the meaning of the phrase, *"with the intention to enslave them?"* The only answer that can be given is, it means with the intention to continue them in slavery, by continuing to hold and use them as slaves; or, as in the case of selling, putting it in the power of others to continue them in slavery.

What, then, is it which, in the eye of the rule, gives criminality to the act of buying or selling? The only answer is, *it is the intention to enslave them*; that is, the intention to *continue their enslavement*. This is what clothes the act of buying or selling with moral turpitude. It is the *enslaving*, therefore, by the continued holding and using as slaves which gives criminality to the buying and selling. The holding and using are the only stimulus to the guilty traffic. We conclude, therefore, that as the holding and using are the only stimulating causes for the traffic, and as the intention to continue their enslavement is the only sinful element, so far as the rule condemns it, the spirit of the rule must condemn the holding and the using, as well as the buying and selling. The intention which gives criminality to an act, and without which the act would not be criminal, must itself be criminal.

We do not affirm that the holding of a slave is, under all circumstances, sinful; nor is the buying or selling. Otherwise it would be wrong to purchase a slave, even to free him. And the moral right to purchase a slave to free him involves also the moral right to hold the legal relation of owner to that slave until the benevolent intention of freeing can be carried into execution. So when, owing to whatever circumstances, the immediate sundering of the legal relation would be manifestly a greater injury to the slave than its temporary continuance; and when the evident intention is to give freedom at the earliest practical moment, such an act of holding is not only not wrong, but it may be a duty. It is something necessary to be done in order to confer permanent freedom upon the person so held. In such a case the holder is not released from the obligation to give unto the servant "that which is just and equal," and to guard with the most religious care the sacred and divine rights of the conjugal and parental relations, and to see by all means that such legal provisions as are practicable shall be made to prevent such persons and their posterity from passing into perpetual slavery.

From the foregoing considerations it appears to us that the General Rule should in plain words embody the honest doctrine of the Church, as well on the subject of *slaveholding* as on that of the slave traffic. If the traffic for mercenary and selfish purposes should be condemned, so also should the holding. And if, as is almost universally admitted among us, the *spirit* of the rule condemns mercenary and selfish slaveholding, then why may we not clothe this *spirit* in a visible *body,* and insert the word *holding* in our present rule, subject to the same discriminating clause as the buying and selling? Such a rule would read: "The buying, selling, or holding of men, women, or children, with an intention to enslave them." This, we think, is only embodying in plain language the true doctrine of our Church on the subject.

So long ago as the year 1840 our bishops, in their Episcopal Address, in view of the different interpretations put upon the General Rule, desired the General Conference, then in session in Baltimore, to give an official exposition of it. The following is their language:

"We think it proper to invite your attention in particular to one point intimately connected with it, [the subject of slavery,] and, as we conceive, of primary importance. It is in regard to the true import and application of the General Rule on Slavery. The different constructions to which it has been subjected, and the variety of views which have been entertained upon it, together with the conflicting acts of some of the Annual Conferences, North and South, seem to require that a body having legitimate jurisdiction should express a clear and definite opinion, as a uniform guide to those to whom the administration of the Discipline is committed." This address is signed by R. R. Roberts, Joshua Soule, Elijah Hedding, James O. Andrew, Beverly Waugh, and T. A. Morris.

Without expressing an opinion here as to the constitutional right of the General Conference to place an official and legal exposition of the General Rule in the Discipline without the concurrence of the Annual Conferences, we judge it the more prudent course that the exposition should be embodied in the rule itself by a process which can leave no doubt as to its constitutionality. We therefore recommend for adoption the following resolutions:

Resolved, 1. By the delegates of the several Annual Conferences in General Conference assembled, that we recommend the amendment of the General Rule on Slavery, so that it shall read: "The buying, selling, or holding of men, women, or children, with an intention to enslave them.

[This resolution required a vote of two-thirds to carry it. There were 138 votes cast for it, and 74 against it, so it was lost. See Journal, pp. 244–246.—EDITOR.]

Resolved, 2. That we recommend the suspension of the 4th Restrictive Rule, for the purpose set forth in the foregoing resolution.

[This resolution was laid on the table, inasmuch as the first resolution failed. See Journal, page 262.—EDITOR.]

Resolved, 3. By the delegates of the several Annual Conferences in General Conference assembled, that the following be and hereby is substituted in the place of the seventh chapter on slavery:

Question. What shall be done for the extirpation of the evil of slavery?

Answer. We declare that we are as much as ever convinced of the great evil of slavery. We believe that the buying, selling, or holding of human beings as chattels is contrary to the laws of God and nature, inconsistent with the Golden Rule, and with that rule in our Discipline which requires all who desire to remain among us to "do no harm, and to avoid evil of every kind." We, therefore, affectionately admonish all our preachers and people to keep themselves pure from this great evil, and to seek its extirpation by all lawful and Christian means. B. F. CRARY, Secretary. C. KINGSLEY, Chairman.

[For the action of the Conference amending and adopting the third resolution, and adopting the report as a whole and as amended, see Journal, pages 259, 262.—EDITOR.][8]

MINORITY REPORT ON SLAVERY

The Minority of the Committee on Slavery appointed by this General Conference to take into consideration the interests of the Church in relation to this grave and perplexing subject, and also its duty in the premises, being unable to agree with the majority of the Committee, and believing that the present occasion demands at our hands a full exposition of our principles, submit the following report:

In order to present our position on this question with entire clearness, we ask attention to the following

FACTS OF HISTORY

Up to 1844 we remained an undivided Church, wonderfully owned of God, and eminently successful in spreading Scriptural holiness over these lands; our ministers went to and fro, and the knowledge of God was greatly increased; the people felt and acknowledged the power of our antislavery Gospel, and by thousands were converted and gathered into our Methodist fold. In no part of this country did our Church find more favor and meet with more success than in the slave-holding states. Firm in our convictions, and honest in our avowal of them, we placed our Discipline in the hands of the slaveholder, containing provisions which limited his authority over the slave, and made him in reality the slave's guardian, under the supervision of the Church. In short, we taught the converted slaveholder to look upon his slave as an immortal being, and to provide for his moral and religious cultivation, by "teaching him to read the word of God, and allowing him time to attend public worship on our regular days of divine service." Under this Scriptural Discipline we were instrumental in converting both masters and slaves, besides breaking the

---

8   The three bracketed statements appeared in the *Journal*; EDITOR refers to the *Journal*'s editor.

yoke from the neck of thousands even in those states where emancipation was not possible by law, except under great difficulties.

This was our condition as a Church when the General Conference of 1844 held its session. An episcopacy till then untarnished by connection with slavery had become implicated in the great evil, in the person of one of our bishops. Then came the trial of our antislavery principles, and the Border was true to its trust. The South contended that as the laws of the state in which the bishop lived would not permit emancipation, the General Conference should not interfere in the case. The majority of the delegates insisted that as a bishop was required "to travel through the connection at large," "any connection with slavery would embarrass both him and the Church in the performance of his duties," and declared their judgment to be that Bishop Andrew should cease from the exercise of episcopal functions until he could relieve himself of this impediment. Then followed that separation which has become one of the great facts of ecclesiastical history. In this contest for antislavery principles no portion of the Church was more inflexibly true to our Discipline than that which is now the Border.

Returning to their homes, the Border delegates discerned (what has since proved to be a well-grounded apprehension) a new source of danger in the preponderance given to the North by this separation. Already had the spirit of ultraism begun to agitate portions of the Church, and fears were entertained that innovations destructive to the peace of the Border conferences would be proposed and effected. These fears were to some extent quieted by the assurance that our northern Churches were true to the interests of the Border, and would faithfully resist all attempts to destroy its power or to change the Discipline. These assurances were corroborated by the sympathy expressed for the Border in the organs of the Church generally, and the decided action of at least one of the New England Conferences. The Christian Advocate and Journal asked about this very time the direct question: "Does New England propose to contend for a rule of Discipline which shall make the emancipation of slaves by those who hold them a condition of membership? Zion's Herald replied: "Deeming it both unjust and impolitic, it is her intention to abide by the Constitution of the Church *as it now is*, and to use her constitutional powers for the *extirpation* of slavery as prudence, the best interests of the whole Church, and the providence of God may demand."

New England sustained the Herald in this declaration, and the Providence Conference, to show its sincerity and to quiet the fears of the

Border brethren, at its session in 1847 passed the following by a rising vote of 54 to 4:

> "Resolved, That we are satisfied with the Discipline of the Church as it is on the subject of Slavery; and as we have never proposed any alteration in it, so neither do we now; and that in connection with our brethren of the other conferences, *we will ever abide by it.*"

This same conference, at a subsequent session, reaffirmed the pledge previously made, as follows: "We pledge ourselves to maintain the same conservative and true antislavery ground by which the Providence Conference has already become distinguished." The late President Olin about the same time addressed a letter to the East through its paper, Zion's Herald, declaring that as the Methodist Episcopal Church, *South,* was now gone, the internal controversy should now be considered as closed, and the church should turn its energies to its great interests, namely: Missions, revivals, education, etc. This was not only the sentiment of New England, but of the whole church, and was fully indorsed by its official action. In support of this, we call attention to the fact the General Conference of 1848 appointed no Committee on Slavery, and but one petition was presented on the subject. The same General Conference abolished the "plan of separation," and took under its care the scattered membership which had been cut off by that plan in Kentucky, Arkansas, and Missouri.

It created conferences there, and thousands have been converted and gathered into the church in those states. The sentiment of the church remained substantially the same during the four succeeding years.

At the General Conference of 1852 no committee was appointed on slavery, and only seventeen petitions were presented on the subject. These facts are not only significant, but they are conclusive. The General Conference was satisfied with the position of the Border Churches, and the membership North gave these suffering brethren their most hearty support.

During the eight years immediately succeeding "the separation" the church, in her official action and sympathy, was faithful to her pledge to abide by the Discipline as it is.

In 1850 the danger of future aggressions on the part of the North and East was distinctly foreshadowed; and between the sessions of the General Conference in 1852 and 1856 this agitation on the question of slavery in the church made its first real development. The papers in those portions of the church began to denounce their brethren on the Border, and this so far influenced the popular opinion in the North as to shake its confidence in the ministry of these conferences. *Here was the origin of the outside pressure, which the North note pleads as the only reason why the Discipline should be changed on the subject.*

In the General Conference of 1856, the first official effort to change the Discipline was made by the ministry of the North, without the support of the membership. Out of 790,000 not quite 5,000 petitioned for a change, and most of these were obtained by the personal efforts of preachers. That this first act of aggression was made by the ministry was admitted in 1856. The reason assigned was that twenty-nine annual conferences out of thirty-eight had asked the General Conference to make a change in our Discipline on the subject of slavery. In obedience to this demand the first Committee on Slavery for eight years was appointed, and a report presented in accordance with their views. That report presented two propositions: One for a general rule by the constitutional process to prohibit "the buying, selling, or holding of a human being as property;" the other for a new chapter making slaveholding *prima facie* evidence of guilt, and declaring the man charged with this offense to be guilty until he proved himself innocent. That chapter was laid on the table, and the new rule failed to receive the vote necessary to send it to the annual conferences. The failure of this first effort on the part of the ministry only redoubled their exertions. They have, during the four years past, employed both the pulpit and the press to the utmost extent in preparing the sentiment of the church for action at the present session. This controversy has been marked by most peculiar features and attended with the most deplorable results. Churches in the North have been torn and severed, new and independent societies have been organized, papers in opposition to official organs supported, the friendship of years destroyed, confidence and fraternal affection between the North and the Border lost, our preachers mobbed by lawless and pro-slavery men, and bitterness of feeling engendered, until it has become almost impossible for us to remain a united people.

There are now two parties in the church, the one contending for an alteration in our Discipline on the subject of slavery, and the other opposed. The question vital to the issue, therefore, is: Which one of these two parties has changed its position? We answer most emphatically: *The Border has not.* The Border was truly antislavery in 1844; it is as truly so now. It resisted the encroachments of the South then; it resists the encroachments of the South now. It has steadily resisted the South till this present moment, at fearful cost and constant conflict. It has resisted pro-slavery assaults in the pulpit, on the platform, and through the press. The Border has stood faithfully to the Discipline, under the charge of pro-slaveryism from the North and of abolitionism from the South. It has never denied being antislavery; it could not if it would and would not if it could. The Border stands now where it has ever stood, and though pressed sorely by the friends it has never forsaken, and by the foes it has always resisted, its representatives come to this General Conference, asking for no change in the Discipline, and willing to abide by it as it is. We have always taught, and still teach that slaveholding for mercenary and selfish purposes is wrong; but we have never held that the relation of master to slave, when either necessary or merciful, is sinful. On this principle we have received the slaveholder into the Church, and by it we have regulated our administration. If in any case the administration has been defective it has been the exception, and not the rule. While our brethren in the North and Northwest have yielded to the pressure of an ultraism, which by their own action they have largely contributed! to create, we still battle for old-fashioned antislavery Methodism. No human administration can be perfect, and our Border brethren do not claim that theirs is any exception to this rule; but they do claim that integrity of purpose has characterized their action. With the laws of the state against emancipation, so far as to prevent the liberated slave from enjoying freedom without the liability of being arrested and expatriated, they have, by their moral influence and discipline, lifted the yoke of bondage from the necks of thousands, who, with their children, are now contented and happy. Of late, owing to the agitated state of the country, their influence has been to some extent limited, but for this the Church of the Border is not responsible. This is the position claimed for itself by the Border, and the claim is sustained by the testimony of others.

The bishops, in their Address to the General Conference of 1856, gave the results of their observation in regard to the position and moral influence of our churches on the Border. In the Episcopal Address of the present session they reaffirm their statements and refer the General Conference to the language used by them in 1856.

The following is the passage referred to, namely:

"In our administration in the territory where slavery exists, we have been careful not to transcend in any instance, or in any respect, what we understood to be the will and direction of the General Conference. That body having retained its jurisdiction over Conferences previously existing in such territory, and having directed the organization of additional Conferences, it becomes our duty to arrange the districts, circuits, and stations, and to superintend them as an integral part of the church. As the result, we have six Annual Conferences which are wholly or in part slave territory. These Conferences have a white church membership, including probationers, of more than one hundred and thirty-six thousand, with the attendants upon our ministry, making a probable population of between five and six hundred thousand. They have a colored church membership, including probationers, of about twenty-seven thousand, with the attendants upon our ministry, making a probable population of upward of one hundred thousand. A portion of this population are slaves. The others are mostly poor. They are generally strongly attached to the church of their choice, and look to it confidingly for ministerial services, religious sympathy, and all the offices of Christian kindness. The white membership in these Conferences, in respect to intelligence, piety, and attachment to Methodist discipline and economy, will compare favorably with other portions of the church.

"In our judgment, the existence of these Conferences and Churches under their present circumstances does not tend to extend or perpetuate slavery. They are known to be organized under a Discipline which characterizes slavery as a great evil; which makes the slave-holder ineligible to any official station in the Church, where the laws of the State in which he lives will admit of emancipation, and permit the liberated slave to enjoy freedom; which disfranchises a traveling minister who by any means becomes the owner of a slave or slaves, unless he executes, if it be practicable, a legal emancipation of such slaves, conformably to the laws of the State wherein he lives; which makes it the duty of all the ministers to enforce upon all the members the necessity of teaching their slaves to read the word of God, and allowing them time to attend upon the public worship of God on our regular days of divine service; which prohibits the buying and selling of men, women, and children with an intention to enslave them, and inquires what shall be done for the extirpation of slavery.

"With this Discipline freely circulated among the people, or certainly within the reach of any who desire to examine it, and with other Churches existing in the same territory without these enactments, these societies and Conferences have, either by elective affinity, adhered to, or from preference associated with the Methodist Episcopal Church. In a few instances their Church relations have exposed them to some peril, and in numerous cases to sacrifice. But such have been their moral worth, and Christian excellence, and prudent conduct, that generally they have been permitted to enjoy their religious immunities and serve and worship God according to their consciences."

This testimony of the bishops in 1856 was corroborated by the delegates from the Border, and the Committee on Slavery appointed at that session confirmed its truth by the following language, which forms part of their report, namely:

"It is also affirmed and believed that the administrators of Discipline within the bounds of slave territory have faithfully done all that in their circumstances they have conscientiously judged to be in their power, to answer the ends of the Discipline in exterminating that great evil."

"Such is the position of the Church on the Border, and it is the position held by most of the members of this General Conference. Very few indeed of the members of this body believe or teach that slave-holding, except for mercenary or selfish purposes, ought to be made a test of membership. Our view of the subject is sustained by the Scriptures, and also by Mr. Wesley, who received slaveholders into his societies, and is in strict accordance with the instructions given by the Wesleyan Connection to their missionaries in Jamaica. These instructions are in the following words, namely:

"As in the colonies in which you are called to labor a great proportion of the inhabitants are in a state of slavery, the Committee must strongly call to your recollection what was so fully stated to you when you were accepted as missionaries to the West Indies, that your only business is to promote the moral and religious improvement of the slaves to whom you may have access, without, in the least degree, in public or private, interfering with their civil condition." Who then have changed position on this subject? *The Border preachers have NOT.* The change of ground is with those who ask for an altered Discipline, a new term of membership.

In conclusion, the minority respectfully submit, 1. That the action proposed in the report of the majority has been recommended without the proper consideration, in Committee, of the documents referred to them by the General Conference, which, in our judgment, the gravity and importance of the subject demand.

2. The minority further represent, that the desire of the Church at large for any important change in our rules on the subject of slavery is not sufficiently indicated in the petitions that have been referred to this Committee to demand such action as is set forth in the report of the majority. The whole number of petitioners is less than one in twenty of the entire membership, and in those Conferences that have spoken most largely, two thirds of the entire membership have remained silent.

3. The action of the Annual Conference, as expressed in their recorded votes, does not indicate such a desire for a constitutional change as to call on this General Conference to inaugurate an attempt to secure it by sending down a new rule for their action. This will be evident if we consider that, taking the highest vote obtained in the several Annual Conferences by any single measure, it falls short to the extent of over five hundred of the requisite number among those voting, and falls short more than three thousand of three fourths of the whole number of the traveling preachers in the Methodist Episcopal Church.

4. The change in the General Rule proposed in the report of the majority is still further objected to, in that the action they recommend approaches nearest in form to the one coming from the Providence Conference, and would be likely to be understood by our people as embodying the spirit of that most objectionable of all the changes which have been previously proposed.

5. The form of the chapter proposed in the report of the majority, the minority confidently believe will not be considered by the Church as embodying sufficient advantages over the present chapter to warrant the risk incurred in making any change. Though being intended only as a *declaration of sentiment*, as it is placed in what is regarded as a book of ecclesiastical law, it may become a source of embarrassment by being misunderstood by our people and misrepresented by our enemies.

6. The minority further represent, that the action proposed in the report of the majority will very greatly embarrass and cripple, if it does not altogether destroy our Church in the slaveholding States and along the border. It is especially calculated to do this in the present highly excited state of the public mind in that territory.

7. The minority still further believe that such a result would involve a loss of position and influence in slaveholding territory, by the most decidedly antislavery Church among the larger denominations of the land, which it might require many long years to regain. Such a surrender of

advantages now possessed must be deprecated by every one who sincerely asks, "What shall be done for the extirpation of the evil of slavery?"

8. It is further objected to the action proposed, that it would operate most disastrously upon the interests of the enslaved. It would not only deprive them of ministrations by which thousands of them have been blessed and saved, but from those by whom their emancipation can only be secured it would withdraw the influence of that Church, in regard to which the majority of the Committee on slavery in 1856 say: "It is affirmed and believed that it has done more to diffuse antislavery sentiments, to mitigate the evils of the system, and to abolish the institution from civil society, than any other organization, either political, social, or religious."

9. The members of the minority representing Conferences located in non-slaveholding territory also submit, that the action proposed in the report of the majority would in its results, as admitted by the majority (in committee) themselves, expose our ministerial brethren and their families, in the Border work, to privations and perils which, while they ought not to be shrunk from, if necessary to maintain uprightness and truth, yet if brought about without sufficient cause might properly be considered an unbrotherly recklessness as to their condition, specially calculated to alienate them from us in spirit and affection.

10. The testimony of the representatives of the work on the Pacific coast in this Committee, impresses us with the conviction that the results of the action proposed in the report of the majority would he highly disastrous in that quarter, destroying much of the fruit of their past labor, and greatly retarding the work for many years to come.

11. The minority are still further impressed with the conviction that among the results of the action proposed in the majority report, one painfully probable is the enfeebling of the prestige and moral power of the whole Church by the strifes and divisions that may ensue, which will greatly incapacitate her for the performance of that grand work, both at home and abroad, to which God in his providence is now so evidently calling her, in this the opening of the second century of her history, and in which, if her resources and influence are properly husbanded and guarded, she may achieve so eminent and glorious a success.

12. The minority are not insensible to the fact that an embarrassing pressure, produced by misrepresentations of our antislavery position, is felt in some portions of our work in non-slaveholding territory; but they believe that this may be relieved by a distinct and emphatic testimony on the subject, in a mode which would not involve the disasters

apprehended from the course to which they object. They therefore recommend the adoption of the following RESOLUTIONS:

Resolved, 1. That the Methodist Episcopal Church has in good faith, in all the periods of its history proposed to itself the question, "What shall be done for the extirpation of the evil of slavery?" and it has never ceased openly before the world to bear its testimony against the sin, and to exercise its disciplinary powers to the end that its members might be kept unspotted from criminal connection with the system, and that the evil itself be removed from among us.

Resolved, 2. That any change of our Discipline upon the subject of slavery in the present highly excited condition of the country would accomplish no good whatever, but, on the contrary, would seriously disturb the peace of our Church, and would be especially disastrous to our ministers and members in the slave states.

Resolved, 3. That the Committee on the Pastoral Address be instructed to state our position in relation to slavery, and to give such counsel to our Churches as may be suited to the necessities of the case. JOHN S. PORTER, Chairman. P. COOMBE, Secretary.

BUFFALO, May 16, 1860.

SUBSTITUTE FOR THE MAJORITY REPORT ON SLAVERY

1. We are in the presence of a very serious question, the settlement of which, in the public judgment, will exercise a great influence over our Church and over the community. The question itself, as we judge, considered apart from the temporary circumstances which surround and embarrass it, would not be of very difficult solution. But circumstances in the Church, and circumstances without the Church, some of a political, some of an ecclesiastical, some of a social, and some of a personal character, are exerting a subtle and powerful influence over our feelings, and are thus likely insensibly to affect our judgments and conduct in the adjustment of this grave matter.

2. In proof of what we have said, we need but to advert to the substantial agreement of the two great parties in the General Conference, on the subject of slavery and the Church, as set forth in the doctrinal and narrative portions of the reports of the majority and minority of the Committee on Slavery. With but slight shades of difference on unessential points, and in mere forms of expression, they agree, not only substantially,

but manifestly, on all the moral, religious, ecclesiastical, and historical relations of our Church to slavery. This is the view we hear expressed in conversation everywhere in regard to the essential parts of the reports. All other parts should be deemed and taken to be not essential to a right settlement of this great and pregnant question.

3. But while the two reports agree substantially in the main points as stated above, they part asunder when they come to advise what is best to be done, as may be seen in the resolutions appended to the reports respectively. And yet one great fundamental fact appears, as a common and foundation element in the resolutions, and this fact is, both claim to be within the true intent and meaning of the provisions in the Discipline, as they have been for many years on the subject of slavery, and to comprehend neither more or less than the letter and spirit of these provisions. This material fact reduces the difference between the reports to this, namely: In what manner shall the true intent and spirit of the provisions of the Discipline on the subject of slavery, as explained in the reports in question, be set forth to the Church under the authority of the General Conference, acting as a Supreme Court, from which there is no appeal; and thus settling, beyond doubt, the true sense of the provisions of the Discipline on the subject of slavery as connected with our Church? The majority wish the judgment of the General Conference to be embodied in statutory forms. The minority say that it is so embodied now in the Discipline, and all that is needed is the judicial decision of the General Conference, settling beyond a doubt the meaning of the existing statutes.

4. Upon a frank comparison of opinions and judgments, with a sufficient number of judicious brethren on both sides, we are satisfied that the report of the majority, as far as it relates to the moral, religious, and ecclesiastical relations of slavery and the Church, would clearly express the judgment of this General Conference in regard to the same; and that a resolution or resolutions following this declaration of principles, designed to insure their faithful application in the administration of discipline, should be appended to the said report containing said declaration of principles; and that such declaration of principles, and resolution directing their faithful application, contain the true and safe solution of the difficulty which now confronts us and indicates great and complicated troubles to our Church.

5. Hoping that this General Conference will see the grave matter contained in the majority and minority reports, from the Committee on Slavery, in the light set forth above, we offer as a substitute so much of the

report of the majority as relates to the moral, religious, and ecclesiastical aspects of Slavery in our Church, together with an additional paragraph, and two resolutions, as follows:

"The Committee on Slavery offer the following report:

"When He who spake as never man spake would comprehend the sum of all human duty, as between man and man, in one brief sentence, he embodied that sentence in the following memorable words: 'All things whatsoever ye would that men should do unto you, do ye even so to them; for this is the Law and the Prophets.' The same sublime epitome of human duty is expressed in the words, 'Thou shalt love thy neighbor as thyself.' These precepts form the moral mirror which God has hung up before all humanity. Into this mirror every man is bound to look, and see his own conduct as others see it, and as he sees that of others. Or, to change the figure, these precepts form the moral scales in which every man is bound to weigh his own actions as he weighs the actions of other men. This Golden Law of God sheds its divine light upon all the relationships which subsist between man and his fellow; and that which we would have a right to desire from any human being with whom we have to do, if we were in his circumstances and he in ours, is the exact measure of our duty.

"The enslavement from generation to generation of human beings guilty of no crime is what no man has a right to desire for himself or his posterity, and what no man ever did or can desire. The constant liability of the forcible separation of husbands and wives, of parents and children, even in the mildest forms of slavery, is a state of things from which every enlightened mind desires to be free. The impediments which slavery interposes in the way of the observance of the conjugal and parental relations, depriving the parents from governing and educating their children, and the children from honoring and obeying their parents, as God has commanded, is a state of things condemned alike by the Bible and all enlightened conscience, and from which the heart's holiest aspirations struggle to be free. The sacredness and inviolability of the marriage covenant is one of the cornerstones of all Christian civilization. Slavery as it exists in the United States is fundamentally at war with this most ancient and sacred institution. What should we desire, and have a right to desire, if we were in the place of the injured party? This is the measure of our duty.

"A system which converts a human being into merchandise, which denies a man the rights of property, of family, of 'liberty and the pursuit of happiness,' and generally of the power to read the record which God has given for the regulation of all human conduct, is a state of things in which no intelligent and right-minded person ever did or can desire to be placed.

"In reference to all these, as to all other conditions of human wrong, the solemn mandate comes down from Heaven: 'All things whatsoever ye would that men should do unto you, do ye even so to them.' God has laid the foundation of religious education in the family relationships. His claims upon us find their readiest response where the honor and obedience due to parents are properly inculcated. The obligation to love God because he first loved us, finds its strongest response where the tenderness and affection breathed upon childhood, by its divinely constituted guardians, prepare the young heart for this high duty. The strongest terms by which the indissoluble affection subsisting between God and his Church is expressed in Scripture, are taken from the parental and conjugal relationship. The inimitable prayer commencing: 'Our Father which art in heaven,' is a further recognition of the same thing.

"What then must be the religious effect of an institution which tramples these sacred relationships in the dust?

"In short there is not, in our judgment, one distinctive attribute of chattel slavery which is not incompatible with the Golden Rule.

"The foregoing considerations, as it seems to us, are sufficient to justify the opposition which from the beginning we have manifested toward slavery; for be it remembered this opposition is no new thing among us, but is coeval with our very existence as a Christian organization.

"The opinions of our revered founder need not be recounted here. Imbibing in larger measure than was common in his day the spirit of HIM whose sympathies gush forth as an everlasting fountain toward the poor and the oppressed, Mr. Wesley uttered a testimony against slavery immortal as his own name.

"His genuine sons in the Gospel have followed his example. The Conference of 1780 declared 'slavery to be contrary to the laws of God, man, and nature, and hurtful to society; contrary to the dictates of conscience and pure religion, and doing that which we would not that others should do unto us.'

"The General Conference of 1784 declared the practice of slaveholding to be 'contrary to the golden law of God and contrary to the inalienable rights of mankind, as well as to every principle of the Revolution.' The Conference say: 'We think it our most bounden duty, therefore, to take immediately some effectual method to extirpate this abomination from among us; and for that purpose we add the following to the rules of our society.'

Then followed a plan of emancipation, specifying the age at which every person held in slavery should be free; and declaring that no person thereafter holding slaves should be admitted into the society or to the Lord's Supper till he had previously complied with these rules concerning slavery. A note followed these stringent measures, declaring that these were to affect the members no further than they were consistent with the laws of the states in which they resided; and also, in view of peculiar circumstances, giving the members in Virginia two years in which to comply with these regulations. As these measures were admitted to constitute a new term of membership, all persons were allowed to choose between voluntarily retiring and being expelled.

"About six months after, it was thought best to suspend for the time the execution of these rules, and give the members a longer time before the minutes should be enforced. The suspension proved to be indefinite, but immediately following the suspension is the declaration: 'We do hold in the deepest abhorrence the practice of Slavery, and shall not cease to seek its destruction by all wise and prudent means.' In 1789 the General Rule read: 'The buying or selling the bodies and souls of men, women, or children, with an intention to enslave them.' In 1792 it read: 'The buying or selling of men, women or children with an intention to enslave them.' From 1808 until now the rule has read as at present, no one knowing how the *or* came to be substituted by *and*.

"For seventy-six years the question at the head of our present chapter on slavery has remained substantially what it now is: 'What shall be done for the extirpation of the evil of slavery?' During all this period, and more, there has no day intervened in which our Church has not testified against slavery as a great evil, and one whose extirpation is to be sought by all lawful and Christian means. Nor has our acknowledged antislavery position been unproductive of good fruits. There is a power in the truth, when faithfully uttered, to influence the conscience of mankind. The testimony which our Church has borne has done much toward the formation of a correct public opinion. Under its influence many thousands of slaves have been set free; and many thousands who otherwise would have been slaveholders, have refrained; and many thousands more, who are still holding slaves, are doing so with consciences ill at ease. But for this testimony, a number of Western States now free, and embracing a vast range of territory, would probably to-day be Slave States.

"These facts are our answer to the question, 'What good has our Church action on the subject ever done?' Is it a small thing that thousands of immortal beings have been delivered from bondage; that thousands more have been restrained from oppressing their fellow-men; and that regions of country by many times larger than some of the mightiest empires of the earth have been secured to freedom?

"To the charge that we are violating the laws of the land a brief answer must suffice. If we choose to keep as free as we can from the evils of slavery, how do we thus violate the laws of the land? Do the laws of the land require the members of the Methodist Episcopal Church to hold slaves? How do we thus violate the laws by declining to hold them? Must we practice every evil which the laws will permit, lest we be charged with violating them?

"While we have no sympathy with, but on the other hand strongly condemn the mad projects of reckless and desperate men who, in defiance of law, seek by violent means either to establish or destroy slavery, we earnestly pray that the time may soon come when, through the blessed principles of the Gospel of peace, slavery shall cease throughout the length and breadth of this fair land."

Seeing, then, that our uniform testimony, and our practice also, have been opposed to the traffic in slaves, and that the spirit of the provision in the Discipline is, and has been opposed to slaveholding for selfish or mercenary purposes, and that we have faithfully borne this testimony and applied these provisions in the administration of Discipline as far as a due regard to the laws of the several states have permitted in which the cases have arisen; therefore,

1. *Resolved,* That the administration of Discipline should be made faithfully to conform to the foregoing declaration of principles, so far as the laws of the several states will permit in which the cases may arise.

2. *Resolved,* That in view of the clear declaration of principles and advice in regard to the administration of Discipline, as set forth in the

preceding report and resolution, we judge that great moderation should be observed in the public discussion of this subject, constantly maintaining the true antislavery position of the Church.

HENRY W. REED, JOHN C. AYERS, PHILO E. BROWN, JOHN P. DURBIN.

Address by the Confederate Clergy, 1863

ADDRESS TO CHRISTIANS THROUGHOUT THE WORLD BY THE CLERGY OF THE CONFEDERATE STATES OF AMERICA.[9]

Christian Brethren,—In the name of our Holy Christianity, we address you in this form, respecting matters of great interest to us, which we believe deeply concern the cause of our Blessed Master, and to which we invoke your serious attention.

We speak not in the spirit of controversy, not by political inspiration, but as the servants of the Most High God, we speak the "truth in love," concerning things which make for peace.

In the midst of war—surrounded by scenes that pain the souls of all good men—deploring the evils which are inseparable from national contentions—we feel most deeply impressed by the conviction, that for our own sake, for the sake of our posterity, for the sake of humanity, for the sake of truth, and, above all, for the sake of our Redeemer's Kingdom, it behooves us to testify of certain things in our beloved land, which seem to be neither understood nor appreciated by our enemies, nor yet clearly appreciated by Christians of other nations.

We put forth this address after much prayer, solemnly invoking the blessing of Almighty God, and committing what we say to that Providence by which we trust we are directed, and by whose authority and power the governments of the earth stand or fall.

If we were moved to make this address by any fears of the final issue of the war in which our country is now engaged, by any inclination to meddle with political questions, by any desire to resume controversy in respect to matters which have been referred to the arbitration of the sword; if indeed anything that compromised the simplicity, dignity, and purity of Christian duty moved us to issue this address, we should deserve

9   Edward McPherson, "Address of the 'Confederate' Clergy, 1863," in *The Political History of the United States of America, During the Great Rebellion,* 2nd edition (Washington, D.C.: Philip and Solomons, 1865), 517–21. Excerpts.

to have it despised by you, and could hope for no blessing of God to rest upon it. But for all that we say in the following declarations, we are willing to be judged by succeeding generations, and to answer in that day when the secrets of all hearts shall be made known.

We do not propose to discuss the *causes* of the war. They are matters of recent history, easily known and read of all men. To discuss them would obviously involve much more than, as Christian ministers, we feel it our province to argue.

We submit for your consideration as the first point of our testimony and ground of protest,—

That the war waged against our people, in principle and in fact, proposes to achieve that which, in the nature of the case, it is impossible to accomplish by violence. The war proposes the restoration of the *Union.*

We can rationally suppose a war for conquest, or to expel an invader, or to compel respect for stipulations of peace and international intercourse which have been violated: but how measures of violence can reunite independent States, restore their broken fellowship, re-establish equality of representatives' rights, or coerce a people to brotherly kindness, unity, and devotion to each other, is utterly beyond our conception.

But if our enemies be disingenuous in their professions—if they fight not to *recover* seceded States, but to *subjugate* them, what promise do men find in the numbers, intelligence, courage, resource, and moral energies of the millions who inhabit the Confederate States, that such a people can ever become profitable or happy, as subordinate to mere military force? If subjugation, therefore, were possible, is it desirable? Would Christian civilization gain anything? . . .

Christian brethren, could the hand of violence win you to desire fellowship with a people while it destroyed your peace, polluted your sanctuaries, invaded the sacred precincts of your homes, robbed you of your property, slaughtered your noble sons, clothed your daughters in grief, filled your land with sorrow, and employed its utmost strength to reduce your country to the degradation of a subjugated province? Would it not rather animate you to prefer death—honorable death—the patriot's alternative, the Christian's martyrdom?

As an excuse for violence, our enemies charge that the Confederate States have attempted to overthrow the "*best Government on earth*;" and call us "traitors," "rebels." We deny the charge: . . . . .

It will appear singular when men reflect upon it, that so many intelligent and Christian people should desire to withdraw from the "*best*

Government on earth." And we need not discuss the kindness of those who so generously propose to confer on us by *force of arms "the best Government."*

No attempt has been made to overthrow the Government of the United States, unless by the fanatical party which now administers its affairs. The South never entertained such an idea. If that Government fall for lack of Southern support, let men discriminate between the downfall of an oppression when the oppressed have escaped, and a wanton effort to break up good government. So Pharaoh fell, but not by the hand of Israel. The dismemberment of the Union by secession was not a blow at the Government. It was for our own deliverance. It was an election of the people, only hastened and rendered in some cases imperative by the violent movements of the Executive of the United States. . . .

So far, therefore, from desiring to destroy the United States Government, the great object of those States which *first* seceded was to secure their own rights, and their tranquility; . . . .

The war is forced upon us. We have always desired peace. After a conflict of opinions between the North and the South in Church and State, of more than thirty years, growing more bitter and painful daily, we withdraw from them to secure peace—they send troops to compel us into re-union! Our proposition was peaceable separation, saying, "We are *actually* divided, our *nominal* union in only a platform of strife." The answer is a call for *seventy-five thousand* troops, to force submission to a Government whose character, in the judgment of the South, had been sacrificed to sectionalism. . . .

The second general point which we submit for your Christian consideration is,—

The separation of the Southern States is universally regarded by our people as final, and the formation of the Confederate States' Government as a fixed fact, promising in no respect, a restoration of the former Union.

Politically and ecclesiastically, the line has been drawn between North and South. It has been done distinctly, deliberately, finally, and in most solemn form. The Confederacy claims to possess all the conditions and essential characteristics of an independent Government. Our institutions, habits, tastes, pursuits, and religion, suggest no wish for the reconstruction of the Union. We regard the Confederacy, in the wise providence of the Almighty, as the result of causes which render its independent existence a moral and political necessity, and its final and future independence of the United States not a matter that admits of the slightest doubt.

Among all the indefensible acts growing out of the inexcusable war waged against us, we will refer to one especially, in regard to which, for obvious reasons, we would speak, and as becometh us, plainly and earnestly:— *The recent proclamation of the President of the United States, seeking the emancipation of the slaves of the South, is, in our judgment, a suitable occasion for solemn protest on the part of the people of God throughout the world.*

First, upon the hypothesis that the proclamation could be carried out in its design, we have no language to describe the bloody tragedy that would appal humanity. Christian sensibilities recoil from the vision of a struggle that would inevitably lead to the slaughter of tens of thousands of poor deluded insurrectionists! Suppose their owners suffered; in the nature of things the slaves would suffer infinitely more. Make it absolutely necessary for the public safety that the slaves be slaughtered, and he who should write the history of that event would record the darkest chapter of human woe yet written.

But, *secondly*, suppose the proclamation—as indeed we esteem it in the South—a mere political document, devised to win favor among the most fanatical of the Northern people, uttering nothing that has not already been attempted, practically, but in vain, by the United States; suppose it to be worth no more than the paper upon which its bold iniquity is traced, nevertheless it is the avowal of a principle, the declaration of a wish, the deliberate attempt of the chief magistrate of a nation to do that which, as a measure of war, must be repugnant to civilisation, and which *we* calmly denounce as worthy of universal reprobation, and against which Christians in the name of humanity and religion ought to protest.

What shall sound Christianity say to that one-idea of philanthropy which, in the name of an *imaginary* good, in blind fury rushed upon a thousand *unquestionable* evils?

If it were the time for such argument, we should not fear the issue of a full discussion of this whole question of Slavery. We fear no investigation— we decline no debate; but we would not, at an hour like this, and in an address which is chiefly a protest, invoke the spirit of controversy. We content ourselves with what we regard as infinitely more solemn; we stand before the world, while war silences the voices of disputants, and men in deadly contention wrestle on fields of blood, *protesting* against the crimes that in the name of liberty and philanthropy are attempted! Let it go forth from our lips while we live; let it be recorded of us when we are dead, that we—ministers of our Lord Jesus Christ, and members of His holy church, with our hands upon the Bible, at once the sacred charter of our liberties and the foundation of our faith—call heaven and earth to record, that in the name of Him whose we are, and whom we serve, *we protest!* No description we can give of this measure of the Executive of the United States, even though indignation alone inspired us to utter it, would exaggerate what we regard as an unholy infatuation, a ruthless persecution, a cruel and shameful device, adding severity and bitterness to a wicked and reckless war.

When it is remembered that, in the name of a *"military necessity"* this new measure was adopted, we may pass by the concession of weakness implied in this fact, and content ourselves with calling attention to the *immorality* of a necessity created by a needless war of invasion....

... we solemnly protest *because, under the dispute of philanthropy, and the pretext of doing good, he would seek the approbation of mankind upon a war that promises to humanity only evil, and that continually.*

Let philanthropists observe, even according to its own terms, this measure is in no proper sense an act of mercy to the slave, but of malice toward the master. It provides for freeing *only the slaves of those who fight* against the United States. The effort is not to relieve that Government of slavery, where the philanthropy has full opportunity for displaying its generosity, and the power to exercise it in respect to slavery, if it exists at all, can be indulged; but the effort is simply to invoke slavery as an agent against the South, reckless of the consequences to the slaves themselves. Shall a pretext at once so weak and so base mislead intelligent men, and make them imagine Abraham Lincoln is a philanthropist? His position ought to be offensive to every sincere abolitionist, as well as disgusting to every sincere friend of the slave, of every shade of opinion on the question of slavery....

We submit further: *That the war against the Confederate States has achieved no good result, and we find nothing in the present state of the struggle that gives promise of the United States accomplishing any good by its continuance.* Though hundreds of thousands of lives have been lost, and many millions of treasure spent; though a vast amount of valuable property has been destroyed, and numbers of once happy homes made desolate; though cities and towns have been temporarily captured, and aged men and helpless women and children have suffered such things as it were even a shame to speak of plainly; though sanctuaries have been desecrated, and ministers of God been dragged from the sacred altars to loathsome prisons; though slaves have been instigated to insurrection, and every measure has been adopted that the ingenuity of the enemy could devise, or his ample resources afford by sea and land; yet we aver, without fear of contradiction, that the only possession which the United States hold in the Confederate States is the ground on which the United States' troops pitch their tents; and that whenever those troops withdraw from a given locality in our territory, the people resident therein testify a warmer devotion to the Confederate cause than even before their soil was invaded. Nothing is therefore conquered—no part of the country is subdued; the civil jurisdiction of the United States, the real test of their success, *has not been established by any force of arms.* Where such civil jurisdiction exists at all along the border, it had existed all the while, was not obtained by force, and is not the fruit of conquest. The fact is admitted by our enemies themselves.

The only change of opinion among our people since the beginning of the war, that is of material importance to the final issue, has been the change from all lingering attachment to the former Union, to a more sacred and reliable devotion to the Confederate Government. The sentiments of the people are not alterable in any other respects by force of arms. If the whole country were occupied by United States' troops, it would merely exhibit a military despotism, against which the people would struggle in perpetual revolutionary effort, while any Southrons remained alive. Extermination of the inhabitants could alone realise the civil possession of their soil. Subjugation is, therefore, clearly impossible. Is extermination desired by Christians?

The moral and religious interests of the South ought to be appreciated by Christians of all nations.

These interests have realised certainly no benefit from the war. We are aware that, in respect to the moral aspects of the question of slavery, we differ from those who conceive of emancipation as measure of benevolence, and on that account we suffer much reproach which we are conscious of not deserving. With all the facts of the system of slavery in its practical operations before us, "as eyewitnesses and ministers of the Word, having had a perfect understanding in all things" on this subject of which we speak, we may surely claim respect for our opinions and statements. Most of us have grown up from childhood among slaves; all of us have preached to and taught them the word of life; have administered to them the ordinances of the Christian Church; sincerely love them as souls for whom Christ died; we go among them freely, and know them in health and sickness, in labor and rest, from infancy to old age. We are familiar with their physical and moral condition, and alive to all their interests; and we testify in the sight of God, that the relation of master and slave among us, however we may deplore abuses in this, as in other relations of mankind, is not incompatible with our holy Christianity, and that the presence of the Africans in our land is an occasion of gratitude on their behalf before God; seeing that thereby Divine Providence has brought them where missionaries of the Cross may freely proclaim to them the word of salvation, and the work is not interrupted by agitating fanaticism. The South has done more than any people on earth for the Christianization of the African race. The condition of slaves here is not wretched, as northern fictions would have men believe, but prosperous and happy, and would have been yet more so but for the mistaken zeal of the Abolitionists. Can emancipation obtain for them a better portion? The practicable plan for benefiting the African race must be the Providential plan—the Scriptural plan. We adopt that plan in the South; and while the State should seek by wholesome legislation to regard the interests of master and slave, we, as ministers, would preach the word to both as we are commanded of God. This war has not benefited the slaves. Those who have been encouraged or compelled to leave their master have gone, and we aver can go, to no state of society that offers them any better things than they have at home, either in respect to their temporal or eternal welfare. We regard Abolitionism as an interference with the plans of Divine Providence. It has not the signs of the Lord's blessing. It is a fanaticism which puts forth no good fruit; instead of blessing, it has brought forth cursing; instead of love, hatred; instead of life, death—bitterness, and sorrow, and pain; and infidelity and moral degeneracy follow its labors. We remember how the apostle has taught the minister of Jesus upon this subject: "Let as many servants as are under the yoke count their own masters worthy of all honor, that the name of God and His doctrine be not blasphemed. And they that have believing masters, let them not despise them because they are brethren; but rather do them service because they are faithful and beloved, partakers of the benefit. *These things teach and exhort.* If any man teach otherwise, and consent not to wholesome words, even the words of our Lord Jesus Christ, and to the doctrine which is according to godliness, he is proud, knowing nothing, but doting about questions and strifes of words, whereof cometh envy, strife, railings, evil surmisings, perverse disputings of men of corrupt mind, and destitute of the truth, supposing that gain is godliness; from such withdraw thyself."

This is what we teach, and, obedient to the last verse if the text, from men that "teach otherwise"—hoping for peace—we "withdraw" ourselves.

The Christians of the South, we claim, are pious, intelligent, and liberal. Their pastoral and missionary works have points of peculiar interest. These are hundreds of thousands here, both white and colored, who are not strangers to the blood that bought them. We rejoice that the great Head of the Church has not despised us. We desire as much as in us lieth to live peaceably with all men, and though reviled, to revile not again.

Much harm has been done to the religious enterprises of the Church by the war; we will not tire you by enumerating particulars. We thank God for the patient faith and fortitude of our people during these days of trial.

Our soldiers were before the war our fellow-citizens, and many of them are of the household of faith, who have carried to the camp so much of the leaven of Christianity, that, amid all the demoralizing influences of army life, the good work of salvation has gone forward there.

Our President, some of our most influential statesmen, our commanding general, and an unusual proportion of the principal generals, as well as scores of other officers, are prominent, and we believe consistent members of the Church. Thousands of our soldiers are men of prayer. We regard our success in the was as due to Divine mercy, and our Government and people have recognized the hand of God in the formal and humble celebration of His goodness. We have no fear in regard to the future. If the war continue for years, we believe God's grace sufficient for us.

In conclusion, we ask for ourselves, our churches, our country, the devout prayers of all God's people,—"the will of the Lord be done!"

Christian brethren, think of these things; and let your answer to our address be the voice of an enlightened Christian sentiment going forth from you against war, against persecution for conscience' sake, against the ravaging of the Church of God by fanatical invasion. But if we speak to you in vain, nevertheless we have not spoken in vain in the sight of God; for we have proclaimed the truth—we have testified in behalf of Christian civilization—we have invoked charity—we have filed our solemn protest against a cruel and useless war. And our children shall read it, and honor our spirit, though in much feebleness we may have borne our testimony.

"Charity beareth all things, believeth all things, hopeth all things, endureth all things." We desire to "follow after charity;" and "as many as walk according to this rule, peace be on them, and mercy, and upon the Israel of God."

Signatures to the Address.
BAPTIST CHURCH . . .
DISCIPLES . . .
METHODIST EPISCOPAL.

J. O. Andrew, D.D., Alabama, Bishop of Methodist Episcopal Church, South.

John Early, D.D., Virginia, Bishop of Methodist Episcopal Church, South.

G. F. Pierce, D.D., Georgia, Bishop of Methodist Episcopal Church, South.

A. M. Skipp, D.D., President of Wofford College, South Carolina.

Whiteford Smith, D.D., South Carolina.

J. T. Wightman, Charleston, South Carolina.

W. A. Gamewell, Marion, South Carolina.

Wm. A. Smith, D.D., President of Randolph Macon College, Virginia.

Leroy M. Lee, D.D., Virginia.

D. S. Doggett, Richmond, Virginia.

J. E. Edwards, Richmond, Virginia.

James A. Duncan, D.D., Editor "Richmond Christian Advocate," Virginia.

Braxton Craven, D.D., President of Trinity College, North Carolina.

Joseph Cross, D.D., Tennessee.

C. W. Chalton, Editor of "Holston Journal," Knoxville, Tennessee.

S. D. Huston, D.D., Editor of "Home Circle," Tennessee.

E. H. Myers, D.D., Editor of "Southern Christian Advocate."

METHODIST PROTESTANT.

W. A. Crocker, President of Virginia District.

R. B. Thompson, President of Lynchburg College, Virginia.

F. L. B. Shaver, President of Alabama District

PROTESTANT EPISCOPAL . . .
PRESBYTERIAN . . .
UNITED SYNOD . . .
ASSOCIATE REFORMED . . .
CUMBERLAND PRESBYTERIAN . . .
LUTHERAN . . .
GERMAN REFORMED . . .

NOTES

1. In publishing the foregoing Address, it is proper to declare explicitly, that its origin was from no political source whatever, but from a conference of ministers of the Gospel in the city of Richmond.

The signatures are confined to this class because it was believed that, on the points presented, the testimony of men holding this office might be received with less prejudice than that of any other. These signatures might have been indefinitely increased. Only a limited number of names—much less than at first intended—was solicited; and as they are still coming in, some will probably be received too late for insertion. Those appended represent more or less fully every accessible section of the Confederacy, and nearly every denomination of Christians. They are ample for the chief objects intended; namely, to bear witness to the Christian world that the representations here made concerning the public sentiment of the South are true, and to carry a solemn protest against the continuance of this fruitless and unrighteous war.

2. From the best sources of information it is ascertained that the whole number of communicants in the Christian churches in the Confederate States is about two millions and fifty thousand.

Of these the number of white communicants is about *one million five hundred and fifty thousand*. Supposing the total white population to be *eight millions*, and one-half that number to be over eighteen years of age, a little more than *one-third* of the adult population are members of the Church of Christ.

The number of *colored communicants* is about *five hundred thousand*. Assuming the colored population to be four millions, there would be, upon the same method of computation, *one-fourth* of the adult population in communion with the Church of Christ. Thus has God blessed us in gathering into His Church from the children of Africa more than twice as many as are reported from all the converts in the Protestant Missions throughout the heathen world.